KNOWLEDGE, EXPERIENCE, AND RULING RELATIONS: STUDIES IN THE SOCIAL ORGANIZATION OF KNOWLEDGE

Dorothy Smith is considered one of the most original sociologists and social theorists of our time, and her writings have attracted much attention in Europe and the U.S. as well as in Canada. This collection of original essays, written by scholars who worked or studied with Smith, exemplifies Smith's approach to social analysis.

Each author takes an empirical approach. Some analyse texts (the maps and documents of land use planning, photographs, an influential history of British India, reports of a task force on battered women); some draw on interviews (with clerical workers, with Japanese corporate wives), while others (an AIDS activist, a teacher of adult literacy, a social worker) reflect on personal experiences. In each case we are introduced to specific themes in Smith's approach. The essays put Smith's methodology to work in diverse ways and in the process offer intriguing insights into their topics.

This tribute to Smith's empowering contribution as a thinker and teacher reveals how empirical studies can illuminate concepts usually presented in the abstract. As the first compilation of applications of Smith's methodology, this is a landmark work in the developing field of the social organization of knowledge.

MARIE CAMPBELL is an associate professor in the Faculty of Human and Social Development, University of Victoria.
ANN MANICOM is an associate professor in the School of Education, Dalhousie University.

D0920996

EDITED BY MARIE CAMPBELL AND
ANN MANICOM

Knowledge, Experience, and Ruling Relations: Studies in the Social Organization of Knowledge

UNIVERSITY OF TORONTO PRESS
Toronto Buffalo London

© University of Toronto Press Incorporated 1995
Toronto Buffalo London
Printed in Canada

ISBN 0-8020-0720-1 (cloth)
ISBN 0-8020-7666-1 (paper)

Printed on acid-free paper

Canadian Cataloguing in Publication Data

Main entry under title:

Knowledge, experience and ruling relations : studies
in the social organization of knowledge

Includes bibliographical references and index.
ISBN 0-8020-0720-1 (bound)
ISBN 0-8020-7666-1 (pbk.)

1. Sociology – Methodology.   2. Knowledge, Sociology
of.   3. Feminist theory.   4. Smith, Dorothy E.,
1926–   .   I. Campbell, Marie L. (Marie Louise),
1936–   .   II. Manicom, Ann.

HM24.K56 1995   301'.01   C95-931552-7

University of Toronto Press acknowledges the financial assistance to its
publishing program of the Canada Council and the Ontario Arts Council.

This book has been published with the help of a grant from the Social Science
Federation of Canada, using funds provided by the Social Sciences and
Humanities Research Council of Canada.

This book is dedicated to Dorothy E. Smith with affection and appreciation for the ways she has nurtured the intellectual and political lives of countless students.

It also marks the loss of George W. Smith who was Dorothy's friend and research associate for many years and a valued colleague of all the contributors.

Contents

viii   Contents

Foreword

The essays collected here are a tribute to the power, influence, value, and wisdom of the work of Dorothy E. Smith: scholar, activist, friend, and guide.

When I arrived on the campus of the University of British Columbia in 1969 I heard from my fellow students that I ought to take at least one course from Dorothy Smith. I did. Three times. The course was titled 'Interpretive Procedures,' and it introduced us to Max Weber, Alfred Schutz, Harold Garfinkel, and Dorothy Smith. Some of us taped and transcribed seminars, relistened to the tapes, reread the transcripts, all with the (always vain) hope that just by listening and pondering the words we would understand their referents, that is, what Dorothy Smith was showing us. We came to earth from our flights of abstraction when we worked with texts or what we then called 'accounts.' Accounts of a person purportedly going mentally ill, rioting (police) in Berkeley, and political speeches, paintings, media reports, and research articles as 'accounts.' It was in working with these accounts that we were able to discover what we could say, and what it made sense to say, using (and finally comprehending) the terms we had been absorbing: social organization, interpretive procedures, null point, reflexivity, practical accomplishment, and so forth.

In these efforts Dorothy Smith was more like a senior colleague than an instructor. She was always ahead of us, like a magnetic force, pulling us, rather than pushing us, to grasp 'how things actually work.' This orientation to 'social things themselves' (to rework Husserl's line) was a key part of the frame one had to use to interpret, share, and further the project she was developing. It was never enough just to generate or interpret theory. Indeed, if one started or stayed in the realm of theory, making abstract connections between categories, one was guaranteed to go wrong, entangled in ideological practice. Dorothy Smith's pedagogy was invigorating as it brought us safely out of theory, and from the safety of theorizing, to how the everyday world worked, as a matter that any of us could investigate.

As I recall, by the third time I sat in on the Interpretive Procedures course, both Marxism and feminism were contributors to the project. Using Marx, but also George Herbert Mead, the notion of social relations was coming to have a place in our understanding of how everyday events, say in the rice fields and jungles of Vietnam, were shaped by decisions and actions elsewhere, in command posts and in Washington. Work on texts and the situations of their use put the spotlight on how texts enter into experience. The experience of women became a focal point as Dorothy Smith's project unfolded within the course and settings of her own life and work situation. Feminism now had a standpoint, in everyday/everynight life. That standpoint, as a matter for investigation, and as a starting point for investigation, was provided by what had by the early 1970s become the enterprise Dorothy Smith speaks of as 'the social organization of knowledge.' This is my recollection, my reconstruction, of some of the early days of Dorothy Smith's work.

This Foreword begins with my recollections because they bring out what may be missed by the many readers who have come to know Dorothy Smith as a feminist scholar. Both her 'standpoint of women' and her work on the social organization of knowledge are informed by early work on 'interpretive procedures.' These procedures for knowing, and the nature of things thereby known, mark a terrain crossed by Weber, Schutz, Garfinkel, Marx, and Mead, among others. I will not here map this terrain, address the work of these thinkers, nor attempt to trace connections between these thinkers and Dorothy Smith. I wish merely to set off Dorothy Smith's unique and brilliant accomplishment of a form of sociological inquiry having tremendous potential to transform our understanding of everyday/everynight life. To appreciate what Smith has done it is useful to compare, if only briefly, her sociology of knowledge with those of Marx, Mannheim, and Berger and Luckmann.

Consider this quote from Marx and Engels in *The German Ideology*, where they begin their discussion of the first premises of the materialist method: 'The premises from which we begin are not arbitrary ones, not dogmas, but real premises from which abstraction can only be made in imagination. They are the real individuals, their activity and the material conditions under which they live, both those which they find already existing and those produced by their activity' (1970: 42). There is much in these two sentences that resonates with Dorothy Smith's work, including the avoidance of ungrounded abstraction, the focus on real individuals, activity and material conditions, and an appreciation of the reflexive relation between activity and material conditions. Marx and Engels, though they write passionately about real individuals, activity, and conditions, do not begin inquiry from the standpoint of individuals so situated. Rather, their contribution is at the level of social relations of production and the work processes involved. Dorothy Smith extends the notion of work to unpaid labour, understood as activity – usually women's activity. Her sociology of knowledge takes up the organization of work processes, and their embeddedness in social relations, from the standpoint of persons engaged in those processes. This standpoint, as I read Dorothy Smith's work, was developed from phenomenology (Schutz and Merleau-Ponty) and is not to be found in Marx.

Marx's sociology of knowledge was formulated as a concern with ruling ideas, which were everywhere to be seen as the ideas of the ruling class. How these ideas ruled, through the work of the ruling class, was the Marxian problematic in what we have come to call the sociology of knowledge. While Marx's discussion of Hegel's 'three tricks' for proving the hegemony of spirit in history (Marx and Engels 1970: 67) is the acknowledged source for Dorothy Smith's formulation of ideological practice (Smith 1990a: 31–57), we do not find Marx retaining a focus on ideological practice. Marx's focus was on ideas, their generation, the interests they serve, and the distortions of reality thereby introduced. Dorothy Smith's vital contribution retains the focus on ideology-in/as-practice: how ideology operates and is used in particular settings, tied to local work processes, and anchored in definite social relations (for example, her treatment of 'suicide,' 1990a: 141–73).

Karl Mannheim, whose sociology of knowledge is considered to be the classic formulation, moved beyond Marx's conception and concern with ideology. Where Marx saw ideology as distortive, to be replaced by true knowledge, Mannheim distinguished between three conceptions of ideology. The 'particular' referred to only a segment of someone's thought. The 'total' conception of ideology referred to the whole of someone's thought. The 'general' conception of ideology referred to all thought, as being from a perspective. Mannheim held that the focus of the sociology of knowledge ought to be the total and general conceptions of ideology; but because ideology had a negative connotation, he preferred to speak of the 'perspective' of a speaker. All knowledge claims, not only the claims of 'the ruling class,' are from a perspective, are relational.

Mannheim understood himself as moving beyond Marx, but his sociology of knowledge retained the focus on ideas, now conceived as assertions, propositions, and thinking. For Mannheim, the sociology of knowledge was a 'theory of the social or existential determination of actual thinking' (Mannheim 1936: 267). His sociology of knowledge concerned 'when and where social structures come to express themselves in the structure of assertions, and in what sense the former concretely determine the latter' (ibid.: 266).

Mannheim's universe of inquiry seems a static one, where assertions can be plucked from the firmament, and analysed for their relation to earthly social structure. Dorothy Smith's universe is always in motion, moved by what people do to keep it alive and aloft. She sees claims as relational, always from a perspective, but for the perspective which most interests her, the standpoint of women, the issue is not how claims reflect social structure. The issue of import does not concern claims, but activities of knowing and doing. The issue is not how activities reflect social structure; rather, the issue is how activities are organized and shaped extra-locally, as work processes given form and purpose by social relations, relations felt but not seen.

Tying back to Marx, these social relations are typically relations of ruling: 'the complex of extra-local relations that provide in contemporary societies a specialization of organization, control, and initiative' (Smith 1990b: 6). While 'Marx's time lacked the developed social relations of reasoning and knowledge externalized as textually mediated forms of organization and discourse' (ibid.: 7), Mannheim's time saw the development of these relations. In fairness to Mannheim, while these textual relations begin with the stabilization of the text in the twelfth century (Morrison 1987), it is not until the middle of the twentieth century that textually mediated organization became dominant, with the advent of the managerial revolution and what Galbraith called the 'new industrial state.' Dorothy Smith's sociology of knowledge gives particular attention to texts and their uses as technologies that shape action and experience in local settings while linking the local to the extra-local, for example, a primary level classroom to a Ministry of Education via curriculum guidelines.

The attention which Dorothy Smith gives to local settings connects with the focus of Peter Berger and Thomas Luckmann in their treatise on the sociology of knowledge, *The Social Construction of Reality*. Berger and Luckmann set a new course for the sociology of knowledge in 1966 when they parted company with Marx and Mannheim, asserting that the proper topic for analysis is not the grand ideas and ideologies of an era. Instead, 'the sociology of knowledge must first of all concern itself with what people "know" in their everyday, non- or pre-theoretical lives. In other words, common sense 'knowledge' rather than 'ideas' must be the central focus for the sociology of knowledge' (1966: 15). Consistent with their roots in idealism, Berger and Luckmann equated what we know with what is real. This equation allowed them to proclaim: *'The sociology of knowledge is concerned with the social construction of reality'* (ibid.: 3).

Drawing on the work of their mentor, Alfred Schutz, Berger and Luckmann sought to reconcile and integrate the theoretical positions and enterprises of Max Weber and Emile Durkheim. They sought to answer the 'central question for sociological theory': 'How is it possible that subjective meanings *become* objective facticities?' (ibid.: 18). For them, this is a question of how reality is constructed. In answering this question they understand themselves to be addressing sociology's core problematic: How is social order possible? In telling us how reality is constructed they are telling us how order is possible: 'Social order exists *only* as a product of human activity' (ibid.: 52).

While Dorothy Smith's work shares with Berger and Luckmann a rootedness in Schutz's analyses of the organization of the life-world from the here-and-now standpoint of a person in a social world, Schutz's work is taken up for a different problematic. What drives Dorothy Smith's work is not a concern with the problem of social order. Indeed, it may be that pursuit of this problem offers no escape from the relations of ruling (Smith 1994: 5). Instead, Smith takes up a standpoint from within the life-world to address a different problematic, one concerned with the organization of experience: 'How does it happen to us as it does? How is this world in which we act and suffer put together?' (Smith 1987a: 154).

Dorothy Smith's interest is not at the same level as Berger and Luckmann's problematic. The latter seek a general, principled account of how 'subjective meanings *become* objective facticities.' This is a theorist's problem, which can be answered only 'in theory,' as there is no empirical way of answering such a question. Dorothy Smith's question, though, is always to be read (and used) as a question about particular persons, their experiences and circumstances. It is in this sense an empirical problematic. While the account of social organization of experience, in terms of work processes and social relations, is just as general and abstract as the objects of Berger and Luckmann's theorizing, the processes and social relations are empirical, or material. One could conceivably discover that some experiences which people share cannot be usefully conceived as a work process, and, further, that 'social relations' are non-existent or irrelevant. In such a case, new terms of analysis would be required, but the question of 'how does it happen to us as it does?' would still press.

In asking how it happens to us, Dorothy Smith instigates the move which marks off her sociology, and her sociology of knowledge, from all other efforts. Marx, Mannheim, and Berger and Luckmann all keep their distance from worlds and persons they study. While they talk about sensuous activity, relational standpoints, or subjective reality, these are all objects theorized and seen from above. In asking how it happens to *us*, Dorothy Smith is including herself and the reader in the field of inquiry. Where others talk of practices and members' practices, Smith talks of *our practices as members* (Smith 1990b: 91). While Marxists may identify with the interests of the working class, the working class is still Other, seen from above. Dorothy Smith's move returns us to the common ground of daily life, shared with others. The resulting sociology is knowingly done from within the world, making it just the kind of reflexive enterprise Alvin Gouldner so persuasively called for in 1970 in *The Coming Crisis of Western Sociology*. Not surprisingly, such a sociology is an activist enterprise, situated outside the relations of ruling, while problematizing them.

In turning the sociology of knowledge back into the world, Dorothy Smith has generated an enterprise with distinctive features and significant potential. Marx wished to serve the interests of the proletariat. Mannheim culled out a special place for intellectuals. Berger and Luckmann brought to centre stage the philosopher–social scientist. Now few proletarians read Marx. Intellectuals no longer use Mannheim. And only other philosopher–social scientists comprise the audience for philosopher–social scientists. Of course, scholarly fashions change. What is significant about Dorothy Smith's work is that by focusing on how things happen to us, it reaches outside academia. Through 'institutional ethnography' (Smith 1987a: 151–79), her approach provides a way for researchers to work with persons as subjects, rather than solely as objects. For example, when working with women involved in the educational process, institutional ethnography allows one to disclose to those women how matters come about as they do in their experience and to provide methods of making their working experience accountable to themselves and other women rather than to the ruling apparatus of which institutions are part (ibid.: 178).

The potential of this approach is that it can be shared outside the walls of academe. Casting her work as 'mapping social relations,' Dorothy Smith concludes a recent piece with: 'And though some of the work of inquiry must be technical, as making a map is, its product would be ordinarily accessible and usable, just as a map is. It's possible also to pass on some of what we know how to do as map makers, so that others can take over and do it for themselves' (1994: 20). Indeed, passing over the work, teaching it, as a form of organizational literacy, is taken up in the final essay in this volume.

While Dorothy Smith's work has focused on sociology from the standpoint of women, the methods and framework she has devised support inquiry from any standpoint in daily life, especially standpoints outside the relations of ruling. The essays in this collection demonstrate this point. They also demonstrate the potential of Dorothy Smith's form of sociological inquiry. We are indebted to her work and to Dorothy Smith herself. What appears between the covers of this volume is but a small payment on that debt.

James Louis Heap
December 1994
Abundance Farm
Coldwater, Ontario

Contributors

Himani Bannerji is an associate professor in the Department of Sociology at York University. She has published extensively on issues of gender, race and class, colonialism and gender, and culture and politics. She is editor of *Returning the Gaze: Essays on Racism, Feminism, and Politics* (1993) and author of *The Writing on the Wall: Essays on Culture and Politics* (1993).

Marie L. Campbell is a nurse-sociologist and a member of the Faculty of Human and Social Development at the University of Victoria, where she teaches in the Multidisciplinary Graduate Program. Her research and publications are about women's work in the human services, bringing a feminist analysis to public sector work organization.

Richard Darville is a sociologist and adult educator, currently teaching in the Department of Linguistics and Applied Language Studies at Carleton University, with long experience in the adult literacy field. His major research concerns are the genres of literacy and their significance for the politics and teaching of adult literacy, and the literacy policy process, from public discourse through the institutional regulation of programming.

Alison I. Griffith, recently appointed to the Faculty of Education at York University, has been an associate professor in the Department of Educational Leadership, Counselling, and Foundations at the University of New Orleans, where she taught sociology of education and qualitative research courses. She has published articles in the area of family–school relations and educational policy. Currently, she and Dorothy Smith are completing a manuscript exploring the social organization of mothering work for education.

Nancy Jackson is an associate professor in the Faculty of Education at McGill University, where she teaches in the areas of research methods and workplace learning. Her primary research interests are critical pedagogy of learning for work and gender issues in skills formation.

Didi Khayatt teaches at the Faculty of Education at York University. She is interested in issues of gender, race relations, and sexuality. She is the author of a number of articles, and her first book, *Lesbian Teachers*, was published by SUNY Press in 1992. She is currently involved in research in the area of sexual categories.

Gary Kinsman is involved in the socialist, gay liberation, and AIDS activist movements, and is currently teaching sociology at Laurentian University. He is the author of *The Regulation of Desire* and is working on a historical sociology of AIDS in Canada.

Liza McCoy teaches sociology at Brock University. Her current work addresses the social organization of numerical representation; she is presently completing a thesis that examines accounting texts and practice in the Ontario college system.

Ann Manicom, a former elementary school teacher, is an associate professor in the School of Education and the Women's Studies Program at Dalhousie University. Her major research interests are in teachers' work and in feminist research methodologies and pedagogies.

Gerald A.J. de Montigny teaches in the School of Social Work at Carleton University. A former social worker, his PhD dissertation was an ethnography of his practice as a front-line child protection worker and it has recently been published (1995) as *Social Working: An Ethnography of Front-Line Practice.*

Adele Mueller is an American sociologist who teaches and publishes in the area of international development.

Roxana Ng is active in the women's movement and other community activities and is an associate professor in the Department of Sociology in

Education at the Ontario Institute for Studies in Education. Her research areas include gender, race, and class as dynamic relations; anti-racist and feminist pedagogy; alternative health systems; and modes of women's organizing. Her major publications include *The Politics of Community Services* (1988) and *Community Organization and the Canadian State* (with J. Muller and G. Walker, 1990).

Marilee Reimer teaches sociology at St Thomas University in Fredericton, New Brunswick. She is a former clerical worker and studies pay equity in the public service.

George W. Smith was a research sociologist and gay rights activist who formerly worked on many research projects with Dorothy Smith at the Ontario Institute for Studies in Education.

Susan M. Turner has worked as a grass-roots organizer, sociology teacher, and consultant in community and organizational planning. She teaches in the Collaborative International Development Studies Program at the University of Guelph. Her doctoral thesis analyses the procedures of municipal land use decision making and the texts which organize people's participation in the business of land development.

Yoko Ueda originally came to Canada from Japan, and recently moved to Atlanta, Georgia. She is the director of the Japanese Studies Program and teaches sociology at Spelman College.

Gillian Walker is on the faculty of the School of Social Work at Carleton University in Ottawa. She is the author of *Family Violence and the Women's Movement* (1990); co-author with R. Ng and J. Muller of *Community Organization and the Canadian State* (1990); and co-author with S. Penfold of *Women and the Psychiatric Paradox* (1983).

KNOWLEDGE, EXPERIENCE, AND RULING
RELATIONS: STUDIES IN THE SOCIAL
ORGANIZATION OF KNOWLEDGE

Introduction[1]

One spring evening in 1977, at the University of British Columbia, about a hundred women sat around on the carpeted floor of the art gallery in the Student Union Building. It was International Women's Week. The women were gathered from the new and struggling Interdisciplinary Women's Studies Program at UBC, from community-based women's groups striving to build a broad, independent women's movement, and from a variety of left-wing political formations where women were only beginning to make their voices heard. The occasion was a public lecture by Professor Dorothy Smith entitled 'Feminism and Marxism' and eventually published with the subtitle 'A Place to Begin, A Way to Go' (Smith 1977).

Dorothy Smith began, as she often did in those days, by dissociating herself from 'any notion that what I am doing here is a performance.' Rather, she wanted her words to be heard as part of a 'political work in progress' in which others necessarily share. She was there to speak with other women about the 'extremely painful and difficult experience' of trying to be a feminist as well as a Marxist, and of trying to establish a 'grounding for a political position ... [and] a basis for working' within Marxism, for herself as well as other feminists (Smith 1977: 9). It was her first attempt to speak publically and systematically, as both an academic and an activist, about the personal journey of becoming both a feminist and a Marxist. She spoke simply and powerfully, and her words brought nods of recognition around the room. 'This began ... very personally for me as it [does] indeed for all women ... with the discovery that many aspects of my life which I had ... experienced privately as guilt, or as pathology, or that I'd learned to view as aspects of my biological inferiority – that all these things could be seen as aspects of an objective organization of society – as features that were external to me, as they were external to other women' (ibid.: 10).

This initial discovery led next, she went on to say, to the discovery of sisterhood as 'the discovery of women ... as my people ... as the people I stand with ... as the people whose part I take' (ibid.: 11). It led her also to the broad enterprise of trying to understand 'the social, economic and political relations which shape and determine women's oppression in this kind of society. What has shaped this experience of mine as a woman? What has shaped the experience of other women? What are the social and economic determinations of this?' These questions, Dorothy Smith said, carried her 'almost imperceptibly ... into an attempt to work with a Marxist framework as a way of understanding how society is put together' (ibid.: 12).

That night at UBC was more than fifteen years ago now, yet the 'work in progress' is still going on, for Smith as for many others. The language we use to name these struggles shifts from time to time with our growing understanding of the nature of the 'social and economic determinations' of our lives. But the search for a political ground from which individuals can name their experience of oppression is alive and far more broadly based now than it was in the 1970s. It is a great tribute to the work of a generation of scholars, among whom Dorothy Smith has been a significant figure, that the ground rules for defining personal and social reality – whether as sociologists, as Marxists, or as feminists – have been profoundly transformed in a lifetime. The collection of essays in this book is in part a reflection of the ongoing vitality of that transformation, as well as an expression of the profound impact of the work of Dorothy Smith in particular on a generation of scholars and activists who carry forward, in a variety of ways and contexts of struggle, the journey about which Dorothy Smith spoke that night in Vancouver.

A SOCIOLOGY THAT TALKS BACK

Dorothy Smith's innovative sociology is founded in a critique of the established sociology of North America, which she describes as 'objectif[ying] a consciousness of society and social relations that "knows" them from the standpoint of their ruling and from the standpoint of men who do that ruling' (Smith 1987a: 2). This way of naming the problem, by way of concepts that have come to be central in Smith's sociology – objectified knowledge, ruling, standpoint – was not available twenty-five years ago when Dorothy Smith was struggling along with other feminists to analyse the conditions of their lives, including in Smith's case what she came to call her 'bifurcated consciousness' as a mother and an academic. 'At the outset of the enterprise,' she writes, 'we confronted the absence of a language, an analysis, a method of thinking' (ibid.: 7).

In learning a new method of analysis, Dorothy Smith drew upon the scholars that she has called her 'preceptors': Marx, Mead, Schutz, Merleau-Ponty, Garfinkel, also Burke, Wittgenstein, Volosinov; all have served as resources in learning to think a different sociology, as taken up through the developing frame of the intellectual and cultural discoveries of the women's movement. Although Smith's work displays these intellectual roots, it is not limited to these various interpretive practices or schools. Rather, she writes, 'I learned, quite unscrupulously, from anyone whose work was of use to me in discovering an alternative to the methods of thinking I had been stuck with' (ibid.: 9).

Dorothy Smith continues to strive for a way of thinking and analysing that aims at nothing less than an overhaul of the sociological project. She is not interested in a revisionist sociology that studies women and women's issues as objects; rather, she envisions and lays the groundwork for a feminist sociology with widespread application: 'I have wanted to make an account and analysis of society and social relations that are not only *about* women but that make it possible for us to look at any or all aspects of a society from where we are actually located, embodied, in the local historicity and particularities of our lived worlds' (1987a: 8).

In contrast with the sociology that she learned as a graduate student, and which still flourishes in North America, Smith proposes a sociology that 'will look back and talk back,' a reflexive sociology, a telling about the world that can be corrected. One of the central premises of this approach is that social organization and social relations can be textually represented (written about sociologically) in ways that enable people to see how their everyday experiences come to happen. This premise has lately become a tendentious one in certain academic circles, because while Smith's work comes out of the resistance to positivism in sociology, it is now encountering the recent wave of postmodernist theory. This latter approach holds empirical research in deep suspicion; theorists claim that reality cannot be adequately represented, that multiple versions of events cannot be resolved into a single Truth. It is part of Dorothy Smith's political project to insist that now more than ever we need to be working to change our world. And that, while Truth may be an illusion, it is nonetheless possible – and urgent – to investigate and describe the relations that put our lives in place.

There has been a growing interest in this approach to sociological investigation in North America and abroad. Dorothy Smith has recently published three books of collected papers which document her work and thinking and explicate its principles and aims (*The Everyday World as Problematic: A Feminist Sociology*; *The Conceptual Practices of Power: A Feminist Sociology of Knowledge*; and *Texts, Facts, and Femininity: Exploring the Relations of Ruling*). Taken together, they offer an exciting, difficult, funny, dense, illuminating, and powerful invitation to an alternate practice of sociology.

A COLLABORATIVE PROJECT

Over the years, many students, women and men, have worked with Dorothy Smith where she taught at the University of British Columbia and then, after 1977, at the Ontario Institute for Studies in Education. Many have been attracted to this work because they could see in it a form of investigation that did not require them to step out of themselves and think about the world differently from the way they knew it in their everyday lives. It offered them a way to explore the contradictions they faced, to make sense of their experiences and their lives. Many have wanted to use this method to integrate research and political practice by doing a kind of research that would inform their activism, and vice versa. At the same time, students have appreciated that this approach is a rigorous analytic project, rooted as it is in some of the most intellectually challenging and demanding traditions in social science.

As this work is taken up by a succession of students who come from different backgrounds, and are located in different struggles, it has acquired a rich diversity. It has been taken up not only by women wishing to do explicitly feminist research, but by men and women wishing to analyse a variety of relations of power, such as the workings of racism and heterosexism and the organization of the state. And as people take up this approach to investigate the issues that matter to them, so their work contributes to the further development of the method, serving as a kind of laboratory where research problems arise and must be solved, discoveries are made, limitations are confronted, and possibilities explored.

The essays collected here are all by students and former students of Dorothy Smith who did master's or doctoral theses under her supervision. Some of the articles are drawn from this thesis work, others report on research done subsequently. The authors have worked with Smith over the range of her years as a teacher, and include some of her earliest as well as most recent students. This shared academic lineage is not, however, the only link among the authors represented here, who have collaborated on numerous intellectual and political projects (reference to which can often be found in the endnotes and acknowledgments that accompany the articles). They are also linked by sharing a method of understanding everyday life that has become for them a practice of their own, whether as teachers, researchers, or activists.

EXPERIENCE AND RULING

Smith's use of such terms as 'standpoint,' 'ruling,' 'ideology,' and 'experience' has intrigued many and spawned numerous debates.[2] While we do not directly take up these debates here, the essays in this book illustrate, and help to clarify through empirical studies, some of these complex theoretical issues central to Smith's method of understanding everyday life. Taken as a whole, they provide insight into each of these key concepts and the ways they are bound together both theoretically and empirically. Towards the end of this Introduction is a brief synopsis of each essay in the order it appears in the book. But first, in the next few sections of the Introduction, we comment on some of the key concepts, weaving together pieces from the various essays. There are, of course, many ways of making links among them, and we expect readers will construct some of their own.

Experience and ruling have a prominent place in Smith's social organization of knowledge. The essays demonstrate not only how, in a variety of sites, everyday experience is transformed into objectified forms of knowledge for the work of ruling, but also how everyday experience is an entry point into how ruling works. In this kind of research, 'experience' has both conceptual and methodological centrality. Its methodological importance is that experience provides a standpoint, a place to begin an inquiry, and a place to return to, to demonstrate its usefulness. The researcher explicitly notes the place from which she looks, acknowledging the way that her inquiry is 'situated' vis-à-vis other knowers and other ways of knowing. Beginning in experience helps the researcher identify 'whose side she is on,' while constructing an account that can be trusted.

The conceptual importance of experience lies in providing a real-life context against which, for instance, to reflect on administrative practices and their powerful effects on people's lives. In a project of this sort, the researcher explicates how administrative textual practices transform the *experienced* local and particular into standardized forms such that it can be ruled. Seeing textual practices as themselves real and experienced offers the researcher a course of practical action to explore. That is, once she sees that people follow special work processes to produce administrative texts – that opens up a different view of 'ideology.' Administrative practices can be explored as courses of organizational action that construct everyday life into something different from how it is experienced.

Smith wants us to understand ideology as not just 'the message,' but as a set of practices in which things get rewritten *in particular ways*. Of course, 'experience' is not to be mistaken as the 'pure' counterpart of ideology. 'Experience' may be and is organized ideologically through ruling practices. But, however experience is organized, we live in our bodies and experience the world from there. That experience offers us a place to stand from which to see and know.

It is not Smith's claim, nor ours, that there is 'a' standpoint from which the world can best be viewed. Instead, the notion of 'standpoint' provides a methodological direction. For those of us whose essays are collected in this volume, it describes a concrete place to begin any investigation, whether, for example, in the experiences of mothers judging the adequacy of their mothering against normative accounts produced in child development discourse (piece by Griffith), the work experiences of teachers in inner city schools confronting the health-related needs of the children they teach (Manicom), the experiences of lesbian high school students finding themselves silenced and marginalized through schooling practices (Khayatt), or the experiences of Japanese mothers managing their children's gender-differentiated entry into post-secondary education (Ueda).

These inquiries, as well as many others reported in this collection, begin in people's lived experience. The materialism of Smith's method is evident in this commitment to begin in the everyday, outside standardized forms of knowing, and to follow the course of the everyday as it is structured through standardized forms of knowing. The precise interest in the inquiry is to find out how those objectified and standardized forms of knowing are put together, how they 'work' in particular settings (often in ways not immediately visible to people in the settings, a key feature of objectified forms of knowing).

To begin in the everyday is not to claim the character of 'experience' as 'real,' but rather to trace how everyday life is oriented to relevances beyond the particular setting. As Griffith says, it is a matter of 'deliberately structuring our research ... to illuminate the social relations that ... come into view ... This fundamental link between the particularities of ... life experiences and the social relations of the society in which they/we live is our ground of inquiry.'

This commitment to beginning in experience outside regimes of ruling is not the same as the recommendation being made by some feminists to 'begin in women's experiences,' that treats experience as unmediated and women's somehow more real, more complete than other people's. The intent is *not* to understand 'experience' in a way that celebrates 'subjectivity' (or that claims to get at meanings and intentions of individuals), but rather to understand everyday experience, as George Smith puts it, reflexively. His point is that we need to see how experience is (or is shaped up to be) inextricably bound to regimes of ruling.

The various ways authors in this collection discuss ruling provide not definitions or prescriptions for how to understand ruling, but insights into how ruling works and the complexity of the struggles identified. Smith has insisted that by the late twentieth century, at least in Western industrialized societies, administration, management, and government are accomplished through work processes that rely on distinctively organized ways of knowing those aspects of the world that are to be ruled. Not only does ruling *rely on* specialized knowledge, but a central task of ruling is *to organize and generate knowledge in a form that is useful for ruling practice*. Thus, for Smith and the authors in this book 'everyday experience,' 'the social organization of knowledge,' and the 'work of ruling' are bound together. Many of the essays in the book describe different moments in this knowledge work, lodged variously in state apparatuses, academia, and professional education and practice.

Several essays, for example, offer insight into one moment of the production of knowledge for ruling – how ideological frames, abstract categories for the subsequent ordering of everyday life, are constructed and/or implemented: Ng's essay on the birth of Canadian multiculturalism, Kinsman's on the legal and medical construction of gay men as sexual offenders, Walker's on state policy development regarding battered women, Mueller's on the construction of categories for use by international development agencies, and Bannerji's on the importing of British racialized ideas about South Asians into the colonial administration of India. These essays offer insight into how conceptual and objectifying practices for knowing about people, activities, and/or events (that is, 'ruling knowledge') make it possible to put in place objective, impersonal, and extra-local methods of control and ruling action. Such frames put into place conceptualizations that form the basis of subordination, of ruling, in local, national, and global settings. These essays show documentary practices to be central to the exercise of power in advanced capitalist societies.

Many of the pieces show the processes whereby textually mediated knowledge production leaves behind 'what people know' and becomes authoritative, taking on a transpersonal and objective character. In some of the essays we see professionals (working inside sites where ruling goes on) learning to use and/or using these objectified forms of knowledge to transform their own and others' everyday local experience into standardized forms – whether it is nursing students learning to account for their work, and thereby transforming their work of caring into terms that make it accountable for instructors' work of evaluating it (Campbell); or a social worker documenting a home visit, and thereby providing for the delivery of state-mandated public services (de Montigny); or producing official photographs, drawing an individual into mandated social courses of action (McCoy). These essays show how working up individual experience so that it is objectively administrable is a practice of domination. Altered irretrievably and *subordinated* in the process is the experience of the subject about whom the professional was initially concerned. This subordination of local experience to an authorized objectified account of it touches the feminist core of Smith's writings, that the essays in this book, whatever their 'topic,' also elaborate.

Other essays show people's own work being transformed into forms through which it can be ruled, and we are able to see how these transformations mystify and distort everyday life. Jackson, for instance, describes community college instructors learning to transform their own work into objectified standardized processes as they become involved in the DACUM process for developing college curricula; invited to engage in technical tasks that reorganize a curriculum, they find the process undermining the professional control they once exercised over curriculum content. Reimer shows how the detailed managerial and policy production knowledge of clerical employees disappears in the documentary processes used in accounting for their work. Unrecognized, it forever remains unattributable to clerical employees as *their work*.

In other essays, we see community activists, located outside ruling regimes, using Smith's analysis of texts and the work of ruling to understand the peculiarly partial ways their concerns are taken up by the state. They analyse how activists' concerns become transformed into particular ideological frames within which the work of the state can proceed. Essays on this theme include Walker's on feminist activism in the battered women's movement, George Smith's on political action accessing medical treatment for people living with AIDS, and Susan Turner's on community involvement in land use planning. They show how experiences outside the relations of ruling can be better understood by investigating how the work of ruling goes on. This is key to Darville's discussion of organizational literacy as central to any concept of literacy as empowerment.

OPPOSITIONAL WORK AND THE WORK OF RULING

The essays in this collection provide illustrations of Smith's major contributions to scholarship, her theorizing of the relation between experience, texts, discourse, and the social organization of power and control. This work of ruling is conducted within relations which bind the ruled and the ruling together within textually mediated relations. Herein lies much of the complexity and the contradictions of ruling – as, for instance, when people of goodwill find themselves caught up in ruling practices or when apparently beneficial practices turn out to have negative consequences. Many of us are engaged in work that is integral to the relations of ruling. Those of us in the professions (such as nursing, education, or social work), embedded in a long tradition of radical critique of our professions, have found in Smith's approach a way of laying out more clearly how our work is bound up in relations of ruling, how our work actually enacts relations of ruling. This provides a place to begin to engage in oppositional work. The essays show us that there is no neutral place for a researcher to stand. As professionals, academics, or social activists, we participate in the relations of ruling when we undertake certain jobs and state or community responsibilities. Understanding *that* helps us decide what kind of stance we can or will take on a particular occasion. Not understanding it means that we may be 'doing ruling' in spite of our intentions to work 'on the side of the oppressed.' Darville, de Montigny, and Manicom, for example, reflect explicitly on the contradictions within their own professional work. As state workers, employed to 'help' people, they grapple with how they engage in ruling practices that limit, order, or prescribe certain behaviours. Ruling, as practised by professionals, is often done in the interest of even-handed and accountable administration. Especially when it comes to decision making and allocation of scarce resources, objective administration appears to offer useful tools. Those same tools are instruments of domination unless the work proceeds with a methodological commitment to recognizing the voices being subordinated. Doing so is likely to disorganize the ruling project, as originally conceived.

In some of the pieces, the author's stance is clearly oppositional. For instance, George Smith, Kinsman, Bannerji, and Turner analyse the methods whereby ruling effects are achieved and/or resistance undertaken in their own experiences or in the group they are writing about. In these essays the actual or potential costs of ruling to individuals are evident; in some, we are seeing the social organization of heterosexism, racism, or 'official' domination.

'Ruling,' as it appears in these essays, is not defined and preconceptualized, other than to understand how text-based social organization works to create orderliness and how pervasive in contemporary capitalist social life are these means of exercising power and authority. The essays suggest that the meaning for those involved in any particular instance of ruling is something to be discovered and understood, empirically.

Where one stands, however, determines one's perspective on ruling. One consistent message in the essays is, as George Smith puts it, that analysing ruling must begin outside ruling positions, if one is to gain insight into both what ruling is (how it is conducted) and what it accomplishes for those participants. That is what the authors, in their roles as activists, reflective practitioners, or social critics, have been attempting to do. They take a stance. Their research stance positions them to discover how people's lives are ordered, managed, *ruled* – to support *interests that are not their own.*

Troubles that arise from this kind of social organization become less mysterious when researchers understand what organizes a troublesome experience and what maintains it. We take as our premise that the world is organized in understandable ways, prior to our entering it, and that our task as researchers is to explicate that organization on behalf of those whose lives are being affected.

Having the set of skills needed to make such an analysis is, we would argue, an asset for all social activists or would-be change agents, indeed, for anyone who wants to live in equitable relations in this country, especially if one is a woman, or occupies any one of the positions outside the power bases in socially organized life that our essays discuss, or, if one wants to be engaged on the side of those people, in criticizing and changing existing policy or practice.

THE ESSAYS

While taken together the essays can be seen as laboratories where concepts central to Smith's sociology are tested and elaborated, each also stands alone as an investigation of a particular local phenomenon. The essay sketches that follow testify to the variety of ways and contexts in which Smith's methodology can be used.

In 'Accessing Treatments: Managing the AIDS Epidemic in Ontario,' *George Smith* displays the political, methodological, and theoretical significance of Dorothy Smith's work. A general problem for activists at the grass roots, he claims, is that without concrete information about the way state and ruling institutions work, it is difficult to develop effective political strategies. The need is thus for a sociology – or research strategy – that can describe the ways ruling and management are actually done. He reports how an investigation into the management of the AIDS crisis in Ontario revealed important findings that directed the work of grass-roots organizers attempting to get access to experimental treatments for people with AIDS.

Several authors examine official texts as instances of the way ruling institutions work. *Roxana Ng*, in 'Multiculturalism as Ideology: A Textual Analysis,' explores how the concept of 'multiculturalism' has been established as an ideological frame in contemporary Canadian government. In her close analysis of the 1971 parliamentary speech by Pierre Elliott Trudeau announcing the new multicultural policy, Ng uses a notion of ideology drawn from Marx and Gramsci, and inflected by Smith, that sees ideology as a work process, a method of thinking that has the inbuilt feature of covering its traces, so that ideological understandings appear as simple common sense. Multiculturalism as an ideological frame provides not only a way to think about Canadian society, but a way to prioritize and manage cultural and linguistic differences.

The study of official texts shifts to British colonial rule in India in 'Beyond the Ruling Category to What Actually Happens: Notes on James Mill's Historiography in *The History of British India*.' Here, *Himani Bannerji* examines the knowledge-producing procedures that constructed 'India' as a cultural and ruling category. The texts she studies are British accounts of Indian history and civilization which were used in drafting colonial laws meant to codify Indian tradition. Her focus on textual representations demonstrates how procedures for knowing and ruling were 'interposed ... between a people and their cultural-political past and future.'

The examination of official texts continues. In 'Violence and the Relations of Ruling: Lessons from the Battered Women's Movement,' *Gillian Walker* examines five official reports as moments in the textual construction of the 'social problem' of violence against women. Her analysis shows how an issue initially raised and dealt with by grass-roots feminist activists is reframed according to the terms of a professional social science discourse in ways that marginalize both the understandings and the efforts of feminists.

Similarly, in 'The Textual Practices of Sexual Rule: Sexual Policing and Gay Men,' drawing on Smith's approach to the social organization of knowledge, *Gary Kinsman* examines an interconnected series of official texts, in this case concerning the 'problem' of male homosexuality and the contending strategies for state regulation of gay men's sexuality that were developed in the 1950s and 1960s. Beginning from the standpoint of gay men, he takes as his problematic the ways sexual rule created frameworks for understanding and regulating gay men's active sexuality, frameworks which continue to be applied today.

Continuing the examination of conceptual practices which accomplish the work of ruling, *Adele Mueller*, in 'Beginning in the Standpoint of Women: An Investigation of the Gap between *Cholas* and "Women of Peru,"' discusses the objectifying knowledge-production procedures used by development practitioners and scholars to produce information about the category 'women in Peru.' Starting from the empirical site of Peruvian women knitting sweaters in a market square, Mueller shows how these procedures are organized by the need to manage at a distance the lives of women such as those from whose standpoint she has begun her research.

Several essays draw on institutional ethnography to explore the discursively organized links between ideological frames and categories, work in professional sites, and the everyday lives of people. In particular, a number of them examine class relations threaded through the work of mothers and teachers. The link between the work practices of educators and women's work in the home is explored in *Alison Griffith*'s 'Mothering, Schooling and Children's Development.' Working with Smith's notion of discourse as an active relation involving textually organized knowledge, Griffith identifies what she calls the 'child development' discourse as the main conceptual structure underlying and linking current educational practice and current notions about good mothering. She draws on interviews with mothers and teachers to show how mothering can be talked about, organized, and recognized in terms of the child development discourse.

In 'Corporate Wives: Gendered Education of Their Children,' *Yoko Ueda*, like Griffith, describes the work middle-class women do to manage their children's schooling. Reporting on research among the Japanese expatriate community of corporate managers and their families temporarily posted in Toronto, Ueda describes how women's complex work of managing their children's schooling coordinates the work organization in the family with the needs of the corporation and contributes to the production and reproduction of class and gendered positions.

In 'What's Health Got to Do with It? Class, Gender, and Teachers' Work' *Ann Manicom* describes an institutional ethnography on the work processes of early elementary school teachers, exploring how linkages between work processes of the home and the school are socially organized, both in discourse and in everyday experience. Drawing on teachers' accounts of their work, Manicom argues that the cumulative effects of taking time to deal with health problems, although conceptually supported by the 'whole child' discourse pervasive in contemporary education, nonetheless contribute to the construction of class differences in schooling.

In 'Compulsory Heterosexuality: Schools and Lesbian Students,' *Didi Khayatt* explores the institutional relations determining the everyday worlds of young lesbians in secondary school. Following Smith's institutional ethnographic approach, Khayatt's investigation proceeds from the standpoint of lesbian students, to study how the current organization of secondary schooling prevents lesbian students from receiving a quality education. Khayatt's informants describe how heterosexist assumptions and the suppression or distortion of information about homosexuality combine to render young lesbians invisible and unsupported.

Many of the essays in the collection examine the production and use of objectified bureaucratic processes through which everyday life is ruled. *Nancy Jackson's* study of the development of competency-based curriculum in a community college, 'These Things Just Happen: Talk, Text, and Curriculum Reform,' shows how the textual procedures used to create competency-based curricula introduce an abstracted, impersonal mode of knowing that shifts curriculum decisions away from instructors towards employers, who come to stand as the source of legitimate authority and who replace instructors as the active agents in curriculum decisions.

Liza McCoy also explores talk–text relations, only in this case the 'texts' under consideration are photographs. In her essay, 'Activating the Photographic Text,' McCoy uses Smith's notions of discourse and social relations to investigate areas of experience more usually considered the domain of 'cultural studies.' She argues that photographic meaning is not a property of the photograph waiting to be released in the act of looking, but that looking is a variable social practice through which photographs are drawn into and organize courses of action. McCoy examines 'looking' in different discourses, drawing on instances involving mug shots, identity cards, and wedding pictures to explore how viewers activate the resources of the photographic text.

An analysis of text-mediated bureaucratic processes which account for women's work is provided by *Marilee Reimer* in 'Downgrading Clerical Work in a Textually Mediated Labour Process.' Reimer draws on ethnographic research in the policy department of a government ministry to show how clerical job descriptions construct clerical work as unspecialized work routines outside the specific mandated work of the department, with the result that clerical employees' active participation in that mandated work remains officially invisible, thus, limiting their chances for promotion or job reclassification.

In another essay on textually mediated institutional practices, *Gerald de Montigny* argues in 'The Power of Being Professional' that a central feature of social work consists of common, discursively organized procedures for making sense of and reporting on clients' lives. Reflecting on incidents from his own experience as a child protection worker, de Montigny describes how he employed these discursive procedures in recognizably competent and professional ways.

Marie Campbell also looks at textually mediated administrative practices in professional work, in this case the work nurses do to make their activities visible to others through documents and records, in 'Teaching Accountability: What Counts as Nursing Education?' Reporting on her field research in a nursing diploma program, Campbell shows how current, theory-based nursing education prepares students to be competent practitioners of what she calls 'accountable' rather than 'care-centred' nursing. Students learn, she argues, to construct the appearance of adequate nursing in documents; but while this kind of training prepares students for the highly textual work process in modern hospitals, she warns, it can also work against the interests of both nurses and patients.

In 'Rendering the Site Developable: Texts and Local Government Decision Making in Land Use Planning,' *Susan Turner* analyses a process of decision making in a city council meeting where councillors are considering a developer's application for a zone change. Her investigation explores the typically unexplicated procedures for producing and reading texts that are central elements of the planning process, and that can act as an impenetrable barrier to local residents who wish to intervene in that process.

Concluding the book, *Richard Darville* provides a view of why the analyses of official texts, ideological frames, and textually mediated work processes in bureaucratic sites are important for literacy work. Many of the analyses provided in this volume help people develop what Darville calls 'organizational literacy.' In his essay 'Literacy, Experience, Power,' Darville contrasts organizational literacy with narrative literacy in his discussion of the experiences of people who are marginalized in a text-mediated society because they cannot read or write. Darville identifies two significant forms of literacy which have relevance for the field of literacy teaching: what he calls narrative and organizational literacy. He discusses these forms of literacy as constituents of social relations and argues that literacy teaching, which has hitherto stressed narrative literacy in its quest to empower the disempowered, should also assist learners to develop organizational literacy, the dominant literacy in contemporary society and an essential element of text-mediated forms of social organization.

'FEEL FREE'

The intention of the collection is to show the diversity of ways people have taken up Smith's invitation to make her work their own. It is not primarily an explication of Smith's work. The authors have all done slightly – or greatly – different readings and hearings of Smith, and they draw from different aspects of her work. Therefore, just as reading Smith requires leaving behind many standard concepts from traditional sociology, reading this collection requires dispensing with the desire for a uniform, monologic understanding of Smith's work. In this volume, the authors explain what they are taking from Smith, how they understand the relevance of her work, and especially, how they are using her concepts and notions.

That said, there is a recognizable approach to social analysis that unites the essays collected here and which will be evident to the reader. All of them are concerned with how lived experience is governed and administered – socially organized – and how that organization is achieved and mediated, particularly through texts. All of them report on empirical research into the organizing relations at work in such contexts as bureaucratic and professional work processes, education, political activism, academic research, and everyday life. All contribute, in various ways, to the project of describing the social world in ways that break with 'the standpoint of ruling and ... the standpoint of men who do that ruling' (Smith 1987a: 2).

The essays collected here report on empirical research that takes up, or is in some way inspired by, Dorothy Smith's approach to sociological investigation. In gathering them for publication, the intention is to add the example of our voices to Smith's invitation to scholars and activists to make her work their own. As Dorothy Smith writes at the end of *Conceptual Practices of Power* (1990a: 206), 'The techniques of analysis and the concepts are there for your use. Feel free.'

NOTES

1 This Introduction is a result of a collaborative effort that began at a conference in Barrie, Ontario, in February 1992 when all the contributors first presented and critiqued the essays assembled in this collection. Based on ideas offered by the group, Liza McCoy, Didi Khayatt, and Nancy Jackson prepared a first draft of the Introduction, which was subsequently revised and elaborated by the editors, Marie Campbell and Ann Manicom.
2 See, for instance, Smith's engagement with Sandra Harding (Smith 1989), and her article, 'Sociology from Women's Experience: A Reaffirmation' (1992).

Accessing Treatments:
Managing the AIDS Epidemic in Ontario

GEORGE W. SMITH[1]

For more than a decade I have been involved as a political activist working with individuals who stand outside ruling regimes that seek to manage society. From this outsider location, it is not possible to comprehend how that management works. The administrative apparatus remains opaque. This is a serious handicap for people who would change how their world is informed, ordered, and governed. I have been active in the gay rights movement in Toronto for some time and, recently, involved with AIDS ACTION NOW! (AAN!), a community-based, political-action group, concerned to improve access to treatment for people who are either infected with the human immune deficiency virus (HIV) but are asymptomatic or who are living with AIDS (PHAs). During this time, I have used political confrontation as an ethnographic resource employing a method of doing sociology proposed by Dorothy Smith (1987a).

A STUDY OF RULING

The discussion of method developed in this essay focuses on a study of the management of the AIDS epidemic in Ontario (G. Smith 1989). The study began in 1988 and is still ongoing in 1994. Its purpose was to determine why new, experimental AIDS drugs had not been available to people living with AIDS and HIV infection in Ontario. The research discovered and described the social organization of four policy lines in the management of the epidemic: public health policy, AIDS research, palliative care, and treatment. It became clear early on in the study that the government was basically concerned with public health policy, while the medical profession, organized as small, independent businessmen, was responsible for delivering treatment. Little or no basic AIDS research, as it turns out, is conducted in Canada. What passes for research is product testing of new drugs, which, again, is organized within the government's public health mandate.

Palliative care is provided by voluntary organizations governed by the concept of compassion for the dying rather than by a mandate directed at delivering life-extending treatments. The medical profession, although responsible for treatment, has generally been unable or unwilling to use new experimental AIDS drugs. This turned out to be, in part, because they are prohibited from using unlicensed treatments by public health regulations and threatened by the possibility of malpractice suits or of losing their hospital privileges should they do so. Consequently, the study's most important finding about the management of the AIDS epidemic, from the standpoint of people living with AIDS or HIV infection, is the lack of an infrastructure to manage the delivery of new experimental treatments. These findings have directed the work of AIDS ACTION NOW! in designing and in helping to put in place just such an infrastructure.

A NEW PARADIGM FOR SOCIOLOGY

The method of analysis proposed by Dorothy Smith marks a paradigm shift for sociology because of its unique epistemological/ontological grounding. Smith found herself working in a world which she saw to be materially constituted in the practices and activities of people as these are known and organized reflexively and recursively through time. This kind of ontology marks off her work from other empirical and/or radical approaches to sociology because it proposes to investigate social life in terms of how it is actually organized. The social world's pervasive reflexivity requires, in terms of traditional sociology, an epistemological shift because, as ethnomethodology has demonstrated, the sociologist cannot know her world from outside, but only from inside its social organization.[2] Thus, a neutral or disengaged position, from which the professional sociologist has traditionally launched his/her investigations, no longer exists. Smith's (1987a) inquiry into the problematic of the everyday world, on the other hand, is best understood as an effort to extend her knowledge as a member of this world to its extra-local forms of social organization.

The novel manner in which Dorothy Smith's work is grounded, the fact that it constitutes a new paradigm (Kuhn 1970) for sociology, ipso facto presents serious problems for understanding it. Although the social organization of her method starts from and thus takes up the standpoint of women, its ontology and epistemology intends a science of society which does not depend on the standard categories of feminist methodology. It seeks to explicate people's experience from their standpoint, rather than from a theoretical position, which Smith has criticized as 'ideological practice' (Smith 1990a). Smith's type of analysis is especially useful for providing a groundwork for grass-roots political action, not only because, as a matter of method, it begins from the standpoint of those outside ruling regimes, but because its analysis is directed at empirically determining how such regimes work, that is, how they are socially organized.

THE EVERYDAY WORLD AS PROBLEMATIC

Rather than starting with sociological or political theory, my study began in the everyday world with the actual experiences of actual individuals. The point of starting this way was not to engage in phenomenological analysis, but to locate the inception of these investigations with active knowers in the real world. Thus, the 'problematic' arose out of the everyday experiences of PHAs. For these individuals, their knowledge of everyday events situated them on one side of a line of fault separating them from the objective bureaucratic domain of a political–administrative regime, whose knowledge of the world is created with a view to administering it. People more or less assimilate this ideological knowledge as a form of social consciousness received as an everyday feature of their lives. Within this kind of social matrix, the conceptions (that is, the ideological practice) of a regime operate in explanatory fashion to regulate and control events in local settings. The investigation of the management of the AIDS epidemic began with just such ideological explanations used to account for the actions of a politico-administrative regime, that is, the ideology of 'AIDS as a fatal disease.' The ideology of a politico-administrative regime is ruptured when people know a situation to be otherwise on the basis of their everyday experiences. In access to treatments for AIDS, these ruptures occurred along the line of fault separating the local organization of the people living with AIDS from the objective, bureaucratic domain of a politico-administrative regime.

Because the medical treatment for AIDS was ideologically organized by the conception of AIDS as a fatal disease, palliative rather than aggressive, 'accelerated care' was the order of the day. The provincial health department, for example, basically allocated funds for hospice care and for psychosocial support for the dying. However, PHAs in Toronto knew through personal contacts and 'underground' networking with their counterparts in the United States that people with AIDS could live longer if treated aggressively. Contrary to the official prognosis of the politico-administrative regime in charge of managing the epidemic, they believed that AIDS was no longer a necessarily fatal illness in the short run.

My research began, not in the objective domain of sociological theory, but with everyday events in people's lives, and in their problems of knowing – of being told one thing, but in fact knowing otherwise on the basis of personal experience. Such 'ruptures of consciousness' provided a starting point for the research that then went on to explicate how a regime works. It called for an investigation of ideological practice extending beyond the scope of local settings. In the case of my own work, I formulated the problematic of study as 'How is the delivery of AIDS treatments in Ontario organized?'

The Epistemological Shift: The Rejection of Objective Accounts

The epistemological character of the problematic, the fact that it arises in the everyday world as a problem about knowing, sets the basic framework for the design of the research. The way Smith uses the term 'problematic' is also consistent with her analysis of language as a vehicle for organizing and coordinating the activities of people. This approach is grounded in her studies in the social organization of knowledge which make it conceptually possible to juxtapose the objective knowledge of a politico-administrative regime over against the locally organized, reflexive knowledge of individuals in the everyday world. The approach also relies on Smith's critique of ideology and of objectivity (Smith 1974b, 1990a). She treats ideology not as a mental phenomenon, but as a form of social organization dependent on texts which are organized from a standpoint, with an objective structure of relevancies located in documents, in a 'virtual' reality, outside actual local settings. Ideology operates from here as the imposition of objective, textually mediated, conceptual practices on a local setting in the interest of ruling it. The social organization of this kind of knowledge, moreover, produces the epistemological line of fault between the objective knowledge of a regime and, in this instance, the reflexive, everyday knowledge (that is, knowledge as members) of PHAs.

Dorothy Smith's use of the notion of a 'problematic' conceptualizes this line of fault as a topic of research. Her usage depends, first, on the social organization of the standpoint of actual individuals in the real world, which in turn, depends on the fact that knowing in this everyday world is reflexively, rather than objectively organized. In this view, objective knowledge is no longer 'the truth,' but a form of knowing used to rule society that contingently, but inextricably, incorporates the standpoint of men. Thus, her feminist critique of objective knowledge, and hence of standard sociology, requires an epistemological shift. This is not a shift from an objective to a subjective epistemology – which some feminists have chosen to make – but rather a move from an objective to a reflexive one, where the sociologist, going beyond the seductions of solipsism, inhabits an actual world, the social organization of which she is involved in investigating. It is precisely this epistemological shift that allows Dorothy Smith's method of sociology to embrace the standpoint of those who stand outside a ruling regime; whether this be the historical position of women in patriarchal society, the position of gay men and lesbians in heterosexual society, the location of people of colour in a racist society, or the standpoint of working people in class society – to name but a few of those individuals who often stand outside a ruling regime. In terms of my research, the epistemological shift operated in two ways: first, it meant treating informants' knowledge as socially organized and, therefore, as constituted reflexively. Second, it meant beginning reflexively from my own, actual location in the world rather than from an objective standpoint.

The Ontological Shift: The Rejection of Speculative Explanations

Developing a problematic is part of the work of putting together a research design which lodges understanding, not in a generalized world of conceptual and theoretical explanations, but in the concrete world of people's actual practices and activities. For example, with the AIDS crisis, people living with AIDS blamed a lack of access to treatments on the homophobia of the Tory minister of health, or more generally on bureaucratic red tape. In each and every case, the impugning of these kinds of causes was organized conceptually, theoretically, as an interpretation of events that depended on the standard shibboleths of political theorizing, especially among gay men. There was little interest in investigating empirically how people's treatment by the AIDS bureaucracy came about. Rather than criticizing the ideological practice of these politico-administrative regimes as a method of determining how things happen, activists usually opted for speculative accounts. The touchstone of these explanations was the attribution of agency to concepts such as 'homophobia' or organizational glosses such as 'red tape.' These became the 'causes' of action or inaction by a regime. Instead of events being actively produced by people in concrete situations, they are said to be 'caused' by ideas such as 'AIDS phobia.'

These kinds of explanations preclude understanding how the world actually works. While they often have a certain force in organizing political reactions to the activities of a ruling regime, these kinds of self-activating conceptions obfuscate how things are actually organized. Unfortunately, because it does not have a concrete grip on how things function, this kind of theorizing is not of much help in effectively challenging or changing the workings of a regime. In contrast to these kinds of procedures, research undertaken in a materialist mode produces a different kind of result.

The study of the AIDS epidemic revealed that no level of government – federal, provincial, or municipal – had a mandate to manage the delivery of new, experimental treatments to people living with the disease. This lack of a treatment-delivery infrastructure both provided for and hence succumbed to the conception of AIDS as a fatal illness. The situation was viciously circular. The problem of government bureaucracy, in this instance, was not so much a matter of 'red tape' and homophobia as it was a lack of a mandate and a managerial infrastructure to deal with the delivery of treatments. What became politically necessary, consequently, was the establishment of a treatment-access infrastructure that supported the efforts of physicians responsible for the delivery of new experimental therapies to people living with AIDS. The political work of AIDS ACTION NOW!, in combating the 'AIDS as a fatal disease' ideology, became the creation of this kind of a treatment-delivery infrastructure, including: the relaxation of the regulations governing the federal Emergency Drug Release Program, the publication of Treatment Update, a newsletter for doctors documenting recent medical advances in treatments, and campaigning for a government-run AIDS treatment registry. The move away from idealist theorizing and speculation to investigating empirically the everyday world is what is meant by the 'ontological shift' in the research. This shift is the basis of the critique of speculative accounts, and a necessary condition for the formulation of people's experience of an everyday world as research problematic.

A REFLEXIVE-MATERIALIST RESEARCH METHODOLOGY

The fact that Dorothy Smith's method of sociology eschews the use of explanatory theories as a basis for understanding how politico-administrative regimes work is not to suggest that this kind of research is not conceptually coordinated; on the contrary. However, the conceptual basis of the research is reflexively organized within a materialist understanding of a world that is put together in people's practices and activities. It follows, for example, that the ethnographer's language not only coordinates his/her investigative activities, but also the work, down the road, of writing up the analysis as sociological description. It is not used in explanatory fashion to construct variables as 'causes' of social action, or to produce objective accounts. To implement the epistemological and ontological requirements of a reflexive-materialist methodology requires considerable inventiveness. The problem is always one of explicating and describing the reflexive, social ontology of the everyday world.

'Social Relations': A Device for Investigating Social Organization

The everyday world as problematic formulates inquiry as focused on describing the extra-local, ideological determinations of local events. Examining these kinds of determinations requires a method of work that can study social organization as this is coordinated and concerted, reflexively and recursively across space and time, in the practices and activities of individuals. Dorothy Smith's device for doing this is the concept of 'social relations.' The notion of 'social relations' is employed in a practical manner to talk about and to investigate the actual practices of individuals, articulated to one another, in courses of action where 'different moments are dependent upon one another and are articulated to one another not functionally, but reflexively, as temporal sequences in which the foregoing intends the subsequent and in which the subsequent "realizes" or accomplishes the social character of the preceding' (Smith 1983: 319). Also, the notion of 'social relations' is involved in discovering the recursive properties of spatial–temporal forms of social organization, especially those that take a textually mediated form (Hofstadter 1980: 127f). Texts as active constituents of social relations can iterate the particular configuration of their organization in different places and at different times, thereby conceptually coordinating and temporally concerting a general form of social action. Recursion, consequently, is also discoverable in how particular, textually organized, local experiences of people have the same social configuration as the experiences of others, organized extra-locally through the same text, at other times and places.[3]

The notion of 'social relations,' within this context, provides a method of looking at how individuals organize themselves vis-à-vis one another. It is not a thing to be looked for in carrying out research, rather, it is what is used to do the looking. Documents are an important resource, playing an active role in coordinating and organizing people's activities (Smith 1984). This discovery provides for the sociologist's ability to investigate and describe networks of textually co-ordered activities going forward simultaneously across a number of distinct sites of social action. The concept of social relations thus operates to enter the social world into the sociological text by helping the ethnographer formulate his/her description of it.

'Regime' as a Technique for Investigating a Ruling Apparatus

I have adopted the notion of regime as a mechanism for facilitating an investigation and description of how ruling is organized and managed by political and administrative forms of organization. An everyday feature of our society is how these various institutional sites of regulation and control are merged together to create what I have called, borrowing some terminology from regulation theory (for example, Aglietta 1979), a politico-administrative regime. These kinds of regimes usually have two interrelated pieces of organization: a political apparatus and a bureaucracy.

Like 'social relations,' 'regime' is not treated as a reified, theoretical entity that causes social phenomena. It does not tell us anything, consequently, about how governing and ruling practices work, except to provide for investigative procedures that go beyond what is meant by 'the state' to include multiple sites of administration following a distinctive mode of regulation. The notion of a politico-administrative regime operates as a heuristic device for investigating empirically how ruling works; how the lives of people are regulated and governed by institutions and individuals vested with authority. This is not to suggest that there is a uniformity to the work of ruling. The study of the management of the AIDS epidemic was not intended to produce a theory about the political economy of health care (for example, McKinlay 1984). Rather, describing the managerial or administrative response to the AIDS epidemic was an empirical matter. It was necessary to look and see to find out just how these regimes worked.

The Concept of the Materialist Epoché

The notion of an epoché is taken from Schutz's (1973) procedures for grounding phenomenological sociology by bracketing the everyday world in order to abstract and analyse social phenomena. What is being recommended here is precisely the reverse: a bracketing of sociological theory, political ideology, and other abstract and abstracting practices of traditional sociology so as to leave social phenomena, for the purpose of analysis, concretely embedded in the social organization of the everyday world. The materialist character of these procedures follows from Marx's social ontology (Lukacs 1978; Gould 1978).

Marx, of course, was interested in investigating particular social forms of economic organization such as the social relations of production and capital. Where the procedures of the materialist epoché deviate from Marx's method is in the way in which they take up the everyday world as reflexively, recursively organized. In particular, they insist that investigation begin from inside an actual world with the intention of making sense of it in its own terms.

ACCESS TO THE FIELD

The work of the activist/ethnographer, organized by the everyday world as problematic, is to explore and to describe the extra-local organization of the problems of those whose lives are at issue. It is the various sites of this extra-local organization that constitute the terrain of the fieldwork.

A Standpoint Outside a Politico-administrative Regime

In beginning from the local historical setting of people's experiences, the ethnographer must start in a reflexive fashion from inside the social organization of not only his/her own world, but by extension the social world he/she intends to investigate. The latter is not bounded by the walls of a local setting, but extends beyond the purview of the everyday. In investigating this extra-local realm it is the local experiences of people that determine the relevancies of the research. In the case of my own work, my research was given direction by the ongoing confrontation with the authorities. It was this that determined what piece of the puzzle I should study next. The first step in the research, consequently, was not a study of the relevant sociological literature. Nor did I start by trying to construct a bird's-eye view of a regime. I never collected data in general using a standard protocol with the intention of making sense of it later. Nor was my access to the field organized from within a politico-administrative regime, using university affiliations or organizational structures close to hand.

Let me elaborate further this issue of confrontation and its determination of research priorities: it was the frustration over the lack of experimental treatments for people living with AIDS that led, first, to the investigation of government activities, and second, to the discovery that government intervention in the epidemic was first and foremost grounded in public health legislation. With the discovery that the government had no legislative mandate to provide new, experimental treatment for individuals, public health relations came into view for me as the preoccupation of the politico-administrative regime managing the epidemic. It was this preoccupation that resulted in the government being concerned almost entirely for the uninfected and about the spread of the disease, on the one side; and on the other, doing precious little for those who were already infected, sick, or dying – apart, of course, from some financial support for palliative care.

This discovery did two things: first, it identified a major source of the problem of access to new treatments; and second, it raised the question of what other social relations were involved in the management of the epidemic. These discoveries had the effect of focusing the politics of AIDS ACTION NOW! very concretely on the delivery of treatment. That political interest kept the research on track. Organizing entry to the field from the standpoint of PHAs meant that apart from the realization that the government's preoccupation with 'public health' was detrimental to PHAs, the social organization of this policy, for instance, did not become a topic of research.

Contemporary Politico-administrative Regimes Provide
Access to Sites of Official Activities

Starting from the standpoint of PHAs, that is, from outside a politico-administrative regime, raises the question of how to get access to the field. Politico-administrative regimes in Canada have developed an increasing capacity, mainly as a result of changes in administrative practice, to involve the public in policy decisions. The consensus conference on AIDS organized by the Province of Ontario is a typical approach by corporate liberal governments for involving groups that are protected and legitimated by human rights legislation. Recently in Ontario, these rights have been extended to homosexuals. Nonetheless, access to a regime is still a very slippery terrain shaped by practices of confrontation and negotiation.

Regimes legitimate cadres of local leaders as 'representatives' of various local community organizations. In this process, community groups often end up functioning as the local extension of the management system of government (Ng 1988), at least to the extent that government makes them party to its policies and funds their activities. For me as an activist interested in conducting an ethnographic study of the AIDS bureaucracy, these participatory forms of administration provided a practical entry point to the field from the standpoint of those whose everyday lives are at the mercy of this kind of politico-administrative regime.

My inquiry into the AIDS bureaucracy began with the experiences of PHAs and with efforts to trace the social relations organizing their experiences beyond the boundaries of the local, everyday settings of their lives. Professionals, in this case doctors working with PHAs, helped sketch the social infrastructure of the local organization of the AIDS bureaucracy, for example, the relations between family physicians and medical specialists and researchers in hospitals, or how the budgetary organization of hospitals worked. Some of the early political activities centred on the ethics of placebo-controlled trials, and involved communicating, for example, with the institutional review board of the University of Toronto and the College of Physicians and Surgeons of Ontario to demand that patients not be forced into clinical trials to get treatment. This was the second focus of the research.

Third, there were meetings with government officials such as the deputy minister of community health, and later participation in a province-wide consensus conference on the management of AIDS in Ontario. Knowledge of the organization of the AIDS bureaucracy also came from other community-based groups during meetings, for example, to establish our bases of unity and thus to set our common political agenda.

Fourth, entry to the AIDS bureaucracy was secured through meetings with officials from the health protection branch of the federal government, and through presentations to the Toronto Board of Health and to the federal minister of Health and Welfare. Lastly, the organization of the management of the epidemic was accessed through textbooks on topics such as biomedical ethics (Levine 1986), the design of clinical trials (Spilker 1984), the AIDS bureaucracy (Panem 1988), and the history of the medical profession in the United States (Starr 1982). The Guidelines on Research Involving Human Subjects put out by the Medical Research Council of Canada helped distinguish between the social relations of treatment and those of the AIDS research involved in testing pharmaceutical products (Medical Research Council of Canada 1987).

In general, access to the field was negotiated outward from the local circumstances of PHAs to the various work sites of the AIDS bureaucracy. I never set up separate, formal interviews with bureaucrats, politicians, and professionals, or people living with AIDS in order to collect the data. Rather, the route of access was determined by the course of confrontation, which in turn was determined by the analysis of the data. Data gathering was a reactive rather than a proactive process. In every instance, the research constituted an exploration of the administrative and political sites of a particular regime, starting from my location in the everyday world.

Meetings, Events, and Conversations as Access to the
Social Organization of a Regime

The data collection did not involve standard ethnographic practices like interviewing subjects, although individuals working in a regime were treated as knowledgeable informants. Meetings, events, and conversations usually stood in for interviews providing opportunities for data gathering. Some were held with professionals who saw themselves on the side of ordinary people. Others were held with bureaucrats, professionals, and politicians who, although often perfectly well intentioned, took up the standpoint of the regime as an ordinary feature of their work. An example would be the meetings of the treatment and clinical trials working group responsible for creating a position paper for the Ontario AIDS consensus conference. The latter included federal and provincial government bureaucrats, representatives from the pharmaceutical industry, AIDS researchers, primary-care physicians treating people with HIV infection, PHAs, and myself as a representative from AIDS ACTION NOW!. I learned from their knowledge and action how to understand the social organization of the regime.

Conversations with individuals working within a politico-administrative regime took place sporadically, mostly with professionals giving accounts of what was taking place with a view to proffering their own strategy of what should be done. These conversations could be quite insightful. One victory which AAN!, in part, took credit for was the change in the federal government's Emergency Drug Release Program (EDRP) – designed to provide compassionate release of unlicensed drugs – to include new, experimental AIDS treatments. Among AIDS activists this change represented just a modification in the government's attitude – a little less homophobia, or AIDS-phobia, perhaps – nothing more. A former Dean of Medicine gave me a different account, saying that the regulations of the department had been 'relaxed' to accommodate access to new AIDS treatments. PHAs were getting a kind of service that other individuals in Canada with serious ailments had heretofore not been able to get. The questions I then set about trying to answer on the basis of this conversation were 'What were these organizational changes?'; 'How did the EDRP really work?'

Documents as Access to the Social Organization of a Regime

Investigating how a politico-administrative regime works, involves more than just face-to-face methodologies, such as attending meetings or speaking with officials. It also requires treating texts as actively coordinating social relations (Smith 1982, 1987a), especially extra-local forms of organization like those that coordinate the operations of an AIDS bureaucracy. To recover these ontological properties of documents it is necessary to read them not for their meaning as such – although this is important – but for how they organize people's lives. This meant examining how the language of documents operates as a conceptual coordinator of social action. For example, the notion of 'the general public,' embodied in the Health Protection and Promotion Act of Ontario with its conception of 'the health of the people of Ontario,' coordinates the social relations of public health which exclude the interests of those who are already infected or ill. It was this form of extra-local social organization that gave credence to the charge of government homophobia in the treatment of PHAs. Official documents, if they are read differently, that is, to reveal the organization they coordinate, provide access to the social relations of a politico-administrative regime. The letterhead from the Ontario Ministry of Health, for example, indicated that the 'AIDS Section' is part of the 'Public Health Branch' of the 'Ministry of Health.' This is where the provincial AIDS coordinator has her desk, and from where the provincial assault on the epidemic is coordinated. The Ontario Health Protection and Promotion Act makes it clear that this section, given its location in the bureaucracy, has no mandate to deliver new, experimental treatments to PHAs.

The organization of the media also provided an entry to politico-administrative regimes, particularly as their work was integral to how the confrontation between a regime and those whose lives it sought to administer is constituted. Reporters covering the AIDS beat often asked questions of individuals in the AIDS bureaucracy that helped solve puzzles for me posed by its opacity. Part of the political confrontation with a regime is managing the media and both 'sides' of a confrontation work at this. It took a long time for AAN!'s media committee to get the print, radio, and TV media to move from a palliative care frame (that is, human interest stories on the dying) to the issue of access to experimental treatment. It goes without saying that the study of the media's treatment of the AIDS issue was itself part of the investigation of the regime's management of the AIDS epidemic.

DATA COLLECTION AND ANALYSIS

The constant political confrontation between AIDS ACTION NOW! and its respective, politico-administrative regime, often designed on the basis of the analysis as it had so far developed, continued to orient my collection and examination of data. The ongoing analysis of the data was intended to extend my working knowledge of a regime. In every instance, this involved the acquisition of the knowledge people working in the setting had, with the kind of reflexivity that entailed. My ethnographic work, in this respect, was intent on describing, from inside, the social organization of a world that was constantly emerging, and one of which I, too, was a member. As I investigated this world, it was common to come upon gaps in the reflexive properties of my knowledge. This was a little like coming across a word in a sentence that did not make sense. Situations like this usually occurred when someone said something that failed to fit properly with my understanding of how things worked. Needless to say, it involved an acquired ability to 'see' organization in people's talk and in the text of institutional documents. The procedures I used to demarcate the limits of my understanding depended, first, on invoking the materialist epoché whereby both political and sociological theory were bracketed so that I had to make sense of settings on their own terms; and, second, treating people who worked in the regime as knowledgeable informants. It was always important to remember that simply in order to hold their jobs they had to know their way around the regime that I was interested in investigating and describing, but knew little about. These procedures, however, did not require me to believe the ideological accounts produced by a ruling apparatus; what it did require was to be able to sketch the form of social organization that produced them.

The materialist epoché that places emphasis on acquiring members' knowledge was also necessary in reading documents. Data collection procedures that retained the reflexivity of the setting were needed to give a document its intended (or members') reading from inside the professional or governmental agency that produced it (Garfinkel 1967b: 186–207). In reading documents, an important assumption was that a document had an intended reading that was reflexively related to the forms of social organization it helped coordinate, for example, seeing the operations of the provincial Ministry of Health as reflexively organized in relation to the Ontario Health Protection and Promotion Act. The reflexive technique in handling documents was to treat them as active constituents of social relations (Smith 1982). While there are important physical aspects to the social organization of the management of the AIDS epidemic – for example, buildings, offices, labs, technical equipment, and computers – the genesis of this social organization was produced and reproduced in language, either as talk or text. In every instance, language was social organization. Thus, the study of a form of social organization became, in part, a study of its language.

In the later stages of writing up my research, it was possible to embed the data in a wider set of social relations by reading the relevant documents and/or sociological literature. Instead of starting with the usual review of the literature as a way of structuring the research, the examination of relevant documents was left to the end so that the analysis of the data could provide a structure of relevance for the reading, rather than the other way round. For example, my ability to understand the social relations of treatment in researching the management of the AIDS crisis was enhanced by reading an interview with the new head of the Human Subjects Review Committee at the University of Toronto which described this distinction between treatment and research in some detail.

The ability to embed the description of people's activities in a wider set of social relations depends, as I have already pointed out, on an important ontological property of social courses of action – their recursivity. The legislation organizing the government's role in the provision of health services provided for forms of public health management in local settings that disregarded the need for experimental treatments of people infected with HIV. Again, this was true in multiple settings across Ontario. Local medical services operated as a copy of the social form of the service envisaged by the legislation. The organization of these social relations, consequently, was recursive. This ontological property of social relations makes it possible, in examining a particular instance at a local level, to move to a description of a general form of organization, to social relations as general course of action coordinated by texts. Methods of traditional 'objective' sociology depend on the procedures of inductive statistics to accomplish this level of generality.

CONCLUSIONS

I think of investigating a politico-administrative regime as an ordinary part of the day-to-day work of challenging and transforming a ruling apparatus. But it does not, in itself, produce a political analysis or a 'political line.' Doing this kind of research is not the practice of vanguard politics. On the contrary, research studies of this sort are designed to be written up, published, and made available to all members of a grass-roots organization for their political consideration. They are intended to provide, on a day-to-day basis, the scientific ground for political action. Because the problematic arises along the line of fault between a politico-administrative regime and the local everyday settings of people's lives, it also lies along the disjuncture of class relations in our society.

The results of this study place in perspective some of the things already known about the management of the AIDS crisis in Ontario. They provide, however, for a systematic understanding of these insights. They give the political work of activists a scientific basis. My analysis, for instance, provided a basis for an AIDS politics that systematically took up the work of putting in place a health care infrastructure that would actually meet the challenge of AIDS and HIV infection. When political strategies are grounded in theory – sociological or political – there is a strong tendency for them to misfire, or worse yet, backfire. Grass-roots organizing is better based on a sociology committed to describing how society actually works.

NOTES

1 An earlier version of this essay was prepared for presentation at the Qualitative Research Conference, York University, 15–16 May 1990, and was later published as 'Political Activist as Ethnographer' in *Social Problems* 37 (4) 1990. The present version appears here with permission of the University of California Press.

2 The notion of reflexivity that I am using is rooted in ethnomethodology. It points to the social organization of the use of language, and hence of consciousness, as coordinating, and so as integral, to a social course of action (Heritage 1984: 150). The documentary method of interpretion understood as arising out of and going on to accomplish a particular form of social organization is paradigmatic. This mode of analysis, by insisting that language and consciousness always have a social context, undermines the possibility of objective knowledge.

3 Hofstadter (1979: 127) in his discussion of recursive processes gives a couple of examples that are useful here. First, he described recursion as nesting and variations on nesting. The concept is very general. (Stories inside stories, movies inside movies, paintings inside paintings, Russian dolls inside Russian dolls (even parenthetical comments inside parenthetical comments!) – these are just a few of the charms of recursion.) What is important to emphasize here is how a story inside a story, for example, is part of the larger story and therefore has something of the same form. Here is another example from Hofstader (ibid.: 128): 'When you listen to a news report on the radio, oftentimes it happens that they switch you to some foreign correspondent. "We now switch you to Sally Swumphly in Peafog, England." Now Sally has got a tape of some local reporter interviewing someone, so after giving a bit of background, she plays

it. "I'm Nigel Cadwallader, here on scene just outside of Peafog, where the great robbery took place, and I'm talking with ..." Now you are three levels down. It may turn out that the interviewee also plays a tape of some conversation. It is not too uncommon to go down three levels in real news reports, and surprisingly enough, we scarcely have any awareness of the suspension.' Again, each level of this news report is about the same story. This is a requirement for each level to be nested in the next. Otherwise the report would be incoherent.

Multiculturalism as Ideology: A Textual Analysis

ROXANA NG[1]

ROXANA NG[1]

MULTICULTURALISM: AN IDEOLOGICAL FRAME

Since the 1970s multiculturalism has become a fact of life in Canadian society. Debates around multiculturalism range from the liberal perspective that the federal policy of multiculturalism is inadequate to address Canadian diversity, to the ultra-conservative perspective (such as that held by the Reform Party of Canada) that the policy has disrupted Canadian unity. Much scholarly literature on the subject is devoted to a critique or reconceptualization of the policy.[2] For all intents and purposes, multiculturalism is a taken-for-granted social fact; that it was invented out of the bureaucratic and ruling relations of Canadian society has been eclipsed.

This essay deviates from the standard debates. I argue that multiculturalism is not a naturally occurring phenomenon; it is an 'ideological frame' put in place by the Trudeau government, in 1971, to reorder a society away from Anglo-conformity to govern a new reality – a society with a diverse minority population which had become increasingly vocal and militant in their demands for equitable or special treatment. Thus, multiculturalism is through and through an artifact *produced* by the administrative processes of a liberal democratic state in a particular historical conjuncture to re-conceptualize and reorganize changing social, political, and economic realities.

In this essay I provide an in-depth textual analysis of the policy pronouncement by Prime Minster Trudeau in the House of Commons on 8 October 1971 to show how the concept was constructed and articulated to a bureaucratic process so that it is treated as a fact. This speech is vital in the ideological construction of multiculturalism because it pronounced multiculturalism as a social fact and made feasible its implementation as state policy.

The term 'ideology' is used commonly in the social sciences to refer to a system of political beliefs or values, or to identify biases in sociological perspectives or statements pertaining to special interests. I use the term 'ideological frame' here to draw attention to the *accomplished* character of ideological thinking and processes. 'Ideological frame' does not simply refer to a bias or a set of beliefs. It identifies ideologies as processes that are produced and constructed through human activities. They are ways in which capitalist societies are ruled and governed (see Marx and Engels 1970; Gramsci 1971). Once an ideological frame is in place, it renders the very work process that produced it invisible and the idea that it references as 'common sense' (Gramsci 1971). That is, the idea(s) contained within the ideological frame become normalized; they become taken for granted as 'that's how it is' or 'that's how it should be.'[3]

I argue here that multiculturalism as an ideological frame has reoriented our understanding of Canadian society in definite ways (that is, Canada is a multicultural, rather than an English and French, society). However, as my analysis will show, multiculturalism is not a free-standing phenomenon; it is developed within the framework of national unity. Its purpose is to contain the competing claims of different groups which emerged at a particular time in Canadian history. As an ideological frame (within the state's overarching concern of national unity), multiculturalism provides for ways of managing a society with multi-ethnic and multiracial groupings away from Anglo-conformity. The policy pronouncement sets up the parameters of what is relevant and irrelevant for bureaucratic state action.

The strategy taken here is textual analysis, following the method developed by Dorothy E. Smith (1990a, 1990b). Analyses of texts frequently treat them as givens; the purpose is to discover their meaning through different kinds of interpretive practices (Smith 1990b: 120–5). Instead of treating the policy as an independent document that can be subjected to multiple and competing interpretations, my analysis treats it as part and parcel of a social organization having to do with how Canadian society is regulated by the state. It is taken to be a constituent in a coordinated course of state action which governs the kind of society in which we live (ibid.: 121–2). This is how Smith puts it: 'In taking up a text as a constituent of a social relation, we are constrained not only to understand it as a moment in a sequence, but also to recognize that the interpretive practices which activate it are embedded in a relational process. Textual practices are operative in the work of accomplishing the social relations in which texts occur' (ibid.: 125).

As the prime minister's pronouncement, the text analysed here is an essential piece in an administrative course of action, and has played a determinate role in the reframing and reorganization of Canadian society in the 1970s. My presupposition is that as a policy pronouncement that is entered into *Hansard*, it intends a particular interpretive schema which is embedded in and articulated to the ruling relations within the bureaucratic state apparatus. This interpretive schema can be recovered from the analysis: the 'analysis will display *how* the text makes sense' (Smith 1990b: 121). Thus, the 'correct'[4] analysis will display how multiculturalism is to be conceptualized and implemented.

CONTEXTUALIZING MULTICULTURALISM AS STATE POLICY

Reconceptualizing Canadian society as multicultural was not merely a prime minister's whim. The seed for the idea of a society based on the coexistence of ethnic groups for the cultural enrichment of Canada – multiculturalism – was planted in the social and political milieu of the 1960s. It was the culmination of the federal government's responses to a series of national crises that threatened Canadian unity. The processes leading up to its promulgation as state policy involved an elaborate division of labour with the intelligentsia playing a major role.

The 1960s was a decade of economic prosperity and social upheaval in the Western world. In spite of the postwar boom of the 1950s, which was believed to have eliminated classes, especially in North America, sociological studies showed that economic and hence social inequality persisted in the 1960s (Edwards and Batley 1978). In their analysis of the 'positive discrimination' program in England, for example, Edwards and Batley (1978) found that the rediscovery of poverty during this period was indeed a source of social discontent and unrest in the West generally. In North America, the civil rights movement in the United States drew attention to the persistence of inequality along economic and racial lines.

In Canada the historical animosity between the Francophones and the small but powerful English elite in Quebec was exacerbated by deteriorating economic conditions in that province. The separatist movement was gaining momentum. The Quiet Revolution, which became increasingly strident, culminated in the FLQ crisis in October 1970.[5] The crisis in Quebec, not to mention the growing militancy of the aboriginal people and other dissident groups (such as youths), posed a serious threat to Canadian federalism and the hegemony of the state, which was grappling with new ways of managing a changing society (Panitch 1977).

Indeed, it was the growing antagonism between Quebec and English Canada that prompted the federal government, in July 1963, to appoint the

Royal Commission on Bilingualism and Biculturalism to inquire into and report on the existing state of bilingualism and biculturalism in Canada and to recommend what steps should be taken to develop the Canadian Confederation on the basis of equal partnership between two founding races, taking into account the contribution made by other ethnic groups to the cultural enrichment of Canada and the measures that should be taken to safeguard the contribution (Canadian Royal Commission on Bilingualism and Biculturalism 1965: 15). In effect, the establishment of this commission proclaimed the existence of a national problem with which the state had to deal (see Chua 1979: 47).[6]

In looking at the work of the Commission on Bilingualism and Biculturalism, we begin to appreciate the extensive division of labour among seemingly autonomous groups in the activities of ruling in modern capitalist societies. Ruling does not only involve politicians and government officials; it occurs in many sites simultaneously, involving vast numbers of people who do not consider themselves part of 'the government' (see Ng, Walker, and Muller 1990). Of particular import here is the fact that the intelligentsia was central to the inquiries conducted by the Commission on Bilingualism and Biculturalism and to conceptualizing a new social arrangement other than Anglo-conformity. Whereas initially the commission was mandated to examine the relations between the French and the English in Canada, volume IV of the commission's report (1965) and its recommendations made clear that Canada needed a new cultural policy to recognize and contain the competing claims of other ethnic groups.

As the subsequent analysis will show, the multiculturalism policy was embedded in the unique social and political relations described above. As a state policy, it both referenced and instructed other work processes pertaining to the state.

TEXTUAL ANALYSIS

What follows is an analysis of the policy pronouncement by Prime Minister Trudeau in the House of Commons on 8 October 1971. The text employed for the present analysis is abridged from *Hansard*, reprinted in Howard Palmer's *Immigration and the Rise of Multiculturalism* (Palmer 1975: 135-7). Although this is not the complete text, it suffices for my purpose because the intent of the policy is fully available in this version.

For this analysis I have divided the speech into four parts. The text is identified by consecutive line numbers as it appears in Palmer (1975). This discussion will focus on the first three sections, since they are most salient in the accomplishment of multiculturalism as an ideological frame and how this cultural policy was to be implemented.

A close examination of the text reveals that there is a progression from a general description and definition of multiculturalism, to specific instructions of its relation to different departments and bureaucratic processes within the state.

Section I: 1-36

1 Right Hon. P.E. Trudeau (Prime Minister): Mr. Speaker, I am
2 happy this morning to be able to reveal to the House that the
3 government has accepted all those recommendations of the
4 Royal Commission on Bilingualism and Biculturalism which
5 are contained in Volume IV of its reports directed to federal
6 departments and agencies. Hon. members will recall that the
7 subject of this volume is "the contribution by other ethnic
8 groups to the cultural enrichment of Canada and the measures
9 that should be taken to safeguard that contribution."
10   Volume IV examined this whole question of cultural and
11 ethnic pluralism in this country and the status of our various
12 cultures and languages, an area of study given all too little
13 attention in the past by scholars.
15   It was the view of the Royal Commission, shared by the gov-
16 ernment and, I am sure, by all Canadians, that there cannot be
17 one cultural policy for Canadians of British and French origin,
18 another for the original peoples and yet a third for all others. For
19 although there are two official languages, there is no official
20 culture, nor does any ethnic group take precedence over any
21 other. No citizen or group of citizens is other than Canadian, and
22 all should be treated fairly.
23   The Royal Commission was guided by the belief that
24 adherence to one's ethnic group is influenced not so much by
25 one's origin or mother tongue as by one's sens [sic] of belonging to
26 the group, and by what the Commission calls the group's "col-
27 lective will to exist." The government shares this belief.
28 The individual's freedom would be hampered if he were
29 locked for life within a particular cultural compartment by the
30 accident of birth or language. It is vital, therefore, that every
31 Canadian, whatever his ethnic origin, be given a chance to learn
32 at least one of the two languages in which his country conducts

33 its official business and its politics.
34   A policy of multiculturalism within a bilingual framework
35 commends itself to the government as the most suitable means
36 of assuring the cultural freedom of Canadians ...

This section of the text sets up multiculturalism as an ideological frame of how the public is to think about Canadian society in the 1970s. Procedurally, Trudeau begins by accepting the recommendations of the Commission on Bilingualism and Biculturalism, thereby legitimizing its work. However, he also makes a separation between the commission and the government of Canada: 'the view of the Royal Commission, shared by the government' (ll. 15–16). The commission is an extra-governmental body. By implication, the views expressed by the commission, derived from research findings and scientific investigation by members of the intelligentsia, are objective and unbiased. Since the commission travelled across the country soliciting input from Canadians, the findings also reflect the views of Canadians.[7]

Trudeau then proceeds to define the parameters of multiculturalism. While the commission was mandated to investigate the state of bilingualism in Canada, it also discovered the contributions of other ethnic groups, and concluded that 'there cannot be one cultural policy for Canadians of British and French origin, another for the original peoples and yet a third for all others' (ll. 16–18). Thus, multiculturalism has to do with the question of cultural and ethnic pluralism in Canada: 'although there are two official languages, there is no official culture, nor does any ethnic group take precedence over any other' (ll. 19–21).

From the very beginning of the pronouncement, a distinction between cultural and language issues is made. This is important because it is in the area of 'culture,' defined specifically apart from language (and in support of national unity, as we shall see later), that individuals have a claim to equality: 'adherence to one's ethnic group is influenced not so much by one's origin or mother tongue as by one's sens [sic] of belonging to the group, and by what the Commission calls the group's "collective will to exist"' (ll. 24–7). Notice here that multiculturalism is not a free-standing policy; it is located within the framework of bilingualism (l. 34) (and the overriding concern of national unity as we shall see later). Culture has less to do with one's origin or mother tongue (l. 25) than with one's sense of belonging to the group (ll. 25–6).

The pronouncement is very clear as to where Canadians can make a claim to freedom: not in the areas of language, official business, and politics (which come under the jurisdiction of the policy of bilingualism), but in the area of 'culture' defined in the way specified in this text: 'It is vital ... that every Canadian, whatever his ethnic origin, be given a chance to learn at least one of the two languages in which his country conducts its official business and its politics' (ll. 30–3).

Although the policy is not named until line 34, 'A policy of multicultur-alism within a bilingual framework commends itself to the government as the most suitable means of assuring the cultural freedom of Canadians ...' (ll. 34–6), the parameters of the cultural policy, and how individuals can lay claim by means of it, are established from line 15 onward. What is being put in place, from lines 1 to 52, is a reconceptualization of a society with a multi-ethnic population away from the former model of Anglo-conformity (see Palmer 1975).

Section II: 37–52

37   In implementing [this] policy, the government will provide
38   support in four ways.
39   First, resources permitting, the government will seek to assist
40   all Canadian cultural groups that have demonstrated a desire
41   and effort to continue to develop a capacity to grow and contri-
42   bute to Canada, and a clear need for assistance, the small and
43   weak groups no less than the strong and highly organized.
44   Second, the government will assist members of all cultural
45   groups to overcome cultural barriers to full participation in
46   Canadian society.
47   Third, the government will promote creative encounters and
48   interchange among all Canadian cultural groups in the interest
49   of national unity.
50   Fourth, the government will continue to assist immigrants to
51   acquire at least one of Canada's official languages in order to
52   become full participants in Canadian society.

This section of the text moves the cultural policy from a set of ideas to the specifics of its implementation. It spells out the government's responsi-bility vis-à-vis the individual's or group's obligations. The government is responsible for providing funding (resources permitting) and services in four areas:

1. Helping *cultural* groups who have demonstrated a desire and effort to

develop a capacity to grow and contribute to Canada (ll. 39–43) (my emphasis);

2. Helping individuals within *cultural* groups to overcome cultural barriers to full participation in Canadian society (ll. 44–6) (my emphasis);
3. Promoting creative encounters and interchange of all cultural groups *in the interest of national unity* (ll. 47–9) (my emphasis); and finally,
4. Assisting immigrants to acquire at least one official language so that they can participate fully in Canadian society (ll. 50–2).

Although not revealed earlier, it becomes clear, in this section of the speech, that the central intention of the government in reconceptualizing Canadian society is not so much concerns for individual rights and freedom as the interest of national unity (l. 49). 'Culture,' as can be seen here, is always defined in relation to national unity: only individuals and groups who have *demonstrated* a desire and effort to contribute to and to participate in Canadian society will receive funding (ll. 39–46). Language training in English or French will be made available to immigrants to enable them to participate in Canadian society (ll. 47–9). All these activities are aimed at forging a new unity and sense of belonging among Canadians whose origins are neither British nor French (l. 17).

Taking the text from the beginning to line 52, a hierarchy of government priorities emerges: national unity is the overriding concern. Within this overarching framework, we see the development of two policies to address the historical and contemporary tensions of Canadian society. Bilingualism, Canada's language policy, recognizes the two founding peoples, English and French. This is the framework within which official business and politics are conducted (ll. 32–3). Multiculturalism as a cultural policy is designed to appease the minorities who have become an integral part of Canada's social, political, and economic reality as Canada developed from a colony to a modern nation-state. It is at the level of 'culture,' with the specific characteristics described in this speech, that individuals may seek equality within Canadian democracy.

I have argued that this announcement is not just political rhetoric, which is one interpretation of the multiculturalism policy (for example, Peter 1981). It articulates multiculturalism to a bureaucratic course of action. As such, this text is an essential constituent in the social relations of ruling (see Smith 1990a; Ng, Walker, and Muller 1991: 314–15). The intent of this policy becomes clear in this section of the speech, which connects the concept to the resources of the state.

One of the key functions of the modern nation-state is the allocation of resources, notably financial resources, within specific political boundaries. In stating the parameters of government support (l. 38), we see that multiculturalism is fully embedded in and connected to the administrative processes of the state: money will be allocated for certain activities. The qualifier, resources permitting (l. 39), is noteworthy. While the federal government is willing to allow minority groups some claims to the resources provided by the state by reordering some of its programs and priorities, the pronouncement is very clear that cultural freedom is not the only concern of the government. It will not be practised to the extent of drastically altering existing resource allocation or depleting the finances of the state.

In Section III of the text, we see further the way that a cultural policy is being articulated to the bureaucratic processes of the federal government for its implementation.

Section III: 53–85

[Translation]
53 Mr Speaker, I stated at the outset that the government has
54 accepted in principle all recommendations addressed to federal
55 departments and agencies. We are also ready and willing to
56 work cooperatively with the provincial governments towards
57 implementing those recommendations that concern matters
58 under provincial or shared responsibility.
59   Some of the programmes endorsed or recommended by the
60 Commission have been administered for some time by various
61 federal agencies. I might mention the Citizenship Branch, the
62 CRTC and its predecessor the BBG, the National Film Board and
63 the National Museum of Man. These programmes will be re-
64 vised, broadened and reactivated and they will receive the addi-
65 tional funds that may be required.
66   Some of the recommendations that concern matters under
67 provincial jurisdiction call for coordinated federal and provin-
68 cial action. As a first step, I have written to the First Ministers of
69 the provinces informing them of the response of the federal
70 government and seeking their cooperation. Officials will be
71 asked to carry this consultation further.
72   I wish to table details of the government's response to each of
73 the several recommendations.
74   It should be noted that some of the programmes require pilot
75 projects or further short-term research before more extensive

76 action can be taken. As soon as these preliminary studies are
77 available, further programmes will be announced and initiated.
78 Additional financial and personnel resources will be provided.
79 Responsibility for implementing these recommendations has
80 been assigned to the Citizenship Branch of the Department of the
81 Secretary of State, the agency now responsible for matters affect-
82 ing the social integration of immigrants and the cultural ac-
83 tivities of all ethnic groups. An Inter-Agency Committee of all
84 those agencies involved will be established to coordinate the
85 federal effort.

What follows after line 52 are specific instructions for how the recommendations of the royal commission, now in the form of an official cultural policy, will be given shape. This section of the speech provides a framework for refocusing the work of the government departments, thereby entering multiculturalism into the bureaucratic processes of the state.

As a federal state, the Canadian government was circumscribed at the time, by the British North America (BNA) Act, which spelled out the jurisdictional boundaries of the federal and provincial governments (see Maxwell 1969: 30–5). This is acknowledged by the prime minister: 'We [the federal government] are ... ready and willing to work cooperatively with the provincial governments' (ll. 55–6). He further discloses that he has written to the first ministers informing them of the intent of the federal government and requesting their cooperation (ll. 68–9). Thus, the protocol of policy implementation has been followed.

The prime minister also states that, although not carried out under the framework of multiculturalism, there are existing programs that are responsible for the 'cultural' activities of the nation – the National Museum of Man and the National Film Board, for example (ll. 62–3). These programs will be revised to bring them into line with the new policy. More importantly, additional funding will be allocated for this purpose: 'Some of the programmes endorsed or recommended by the Commission have been administered for some time by various federal agencies. I might mention the Citizenship Branch, the CRTC and its predecessor the BBG, the National Film Board and the National Museum of Man. These programmes will be revised, broadened and reactivated and they will receive the additional funds that may be required' (ll. 59–65).

The agency responsible for implementing the policy is named: the Citizenship Branch of the Department of the Secretary of State (ll. 79–81). This is in accordance with the intent of separating 'culture' from political and economic matters: multiculturalism comes under the jurisdiction of this department rather than the Department of Employment and Immigration, for instance, which deals with immigrants as a labour and economic matter.

Other programs will be set up pending completion of research already taking place (ll. 74–8). Finally, a coordinating body – an Inter-Agency Committee – will be established to oversee the implementation of the multicultural policy. While the mandate of this last committee is not spelled out in the text, it provides sufficient direction for those implementing the policy to go forward with this instruction. As a point of interest following from this analysis, the Consultative Council of Multiculturalism was established in 1973, consisting of leaders from different ethnocultural communities, to advise the federal government about how to put multiculturalism into administrative reality (see CCCM 1975).

The fourth section of the speech reiterates the pronouncement of the multiculturalism policy within a bilingual framework, and restates rhetorically the basis for Canadian democracy. What is especially revealing in this last passage is the prime minister's acknowledgment that multiculturalism is not a chance occurrence. It is a conscious choice (that is, it is constructed) and a managed reality (through state initiative and support).

[English]
86 In conclusion, I wish to emphasize the view of the government
87 that a policy of multiculturalism within a bilingual framework is
88 basically the conscious support of individual freedom of choice.
89 We are free to be ourselves. But this cannot be left to chance. It
90 must be fostered and pursued actively. If freedom of choice is in
91 danger for some ethnic groups, it is in danger for all ...

CONCLUSION

In the above analysis, I have shown that far from being a naturally occurring phenomenon, multiculturalism is an ideological construction. By analysing the Trudeau speech on the multiculturalism policy and situating it in its social, political, and historical milieu, I have demonstrated that this pronouncement served a key function in an ideological process in two ways.

First, the text accomplished the facticity of multiculturalism. That is, it introduced and officiated the concept of multiculturalism as currency in public and scholarly discourses. Multiculturalism became available for researchers, journalists, politicians, bureaucrats – in short, the Canadian 'public' – to describe and think about Canadian society in particular ways after this time. That is, as a multicultural society, individuals and groups, regardless of their ethnic origins, should be treated fairly (l. 22); no groups may take precedence over any other (ll. 20–1).[8] Immigrants will be assisted to acquire one of Canada's official languages (ll. 50–1). All groups can receive government funding to pursue activities that promote Canadian unity and assist their members to overcome cultural barriers to enable their full participation in Canadian society (ll. 39–49).

While Canadians may debate whether the federal policy (enshrined as law by the Progressive Conservative government in 1988) has gone too far or not far enough to fulfil the ideal of multiculturalism, that Canada is a multicultural society is beyond debate. It is 'common sense' knowledge. This is what I mean when I argue, following Marx's and Engels' analysis (1970) of ideology in nineteenth-century German society, that an ideological frame has the characteristic of rendering the processes that produce it invisible. Indeed, it has become 'normal' to think about Canadian society as multicultural.

Second, the prime minister's pronouncement was an essential constituent in the relations of ruling in that it served to organize the relations between ethnic groups and the bureaucratic and administrative apparatuses of the state. This speech gave instructions for how programs and services would be reorganized in accordance with a new ideological frame. The fact that the policy was announced in the House of Commons and documented in *Hansard* is noteworthy: it became a matter of public and state record. As I and others (Ng 1988; Ng Walker, and Muller 1990; Smith 1990a, 1990b) suggest elsewhere, documentary processes are crucial to the relations of ruling in advanced capitalism because they serve to encode and coordinate administrative processes through time and space, thereby 'holding' bureaucratic practices in place.

In the beginning of this essay, I alluded to the central role played by members of the intelligentsia in conceptualizing a new social arrangement for the purpose of managing a diverse population in the 1960s. This is an instance of how we, as members of the intelligentsia, participated in the creation of ideology. The analysis undertaken here shows that we also have the conceptual and analytical tools to unpack ideological formations, so that we can participate in and/or struggle against state processes in informed and proactive, rather than ad hoc and reactionary, ways.

NOTES

1 Ideas for this essay were conceived in Dorothy E. Smith's graduate seminar on 'Textual Analysis' in 1979. Previous versions were presented at a conference on

'The Social Organization of Knowledge' (Barrie, Ontario, 20–2 March 1992) and the American Anthropological Association annual meeting (San Francisco, California, 2 December 1992). I am grateful to extensive feedback from colleagues in the former conference. For this version of the essay, I thank Gary Kinsmen, Adele Mueller, Dorothy Smith, and the editors for their comments.

2 Some examples are Palmer (1975), Lupul (1977), Troper (1979), Peter (1981), Burnet (1988), and Moodley (1983). Roberts and Clifton (1990) attempt to provide a typology of multiculturalism and suggest where the Canadian policy fits in. In their most recent work, Fleras and Elliott (1992) trace the history and development of multiculturalism in Canada.

3 This taken-for-granted character of ideology is what Gramsci calls 'common sense.' He uses this terms to refer to the 'uncritical and largely unconscious way of perceiving and understanding the world that has become "common" in any given epoch' (Gramsci 1971: 322). I prefer this term to 'ideology' because it draws attention to the taken-for-granted character of ideological thinking, and it extends the notion of ideology to include, not only ideas, but practices which have become 'normal' ways of doing things (see Ng 1993). In a seminar on 21 March 1993, Collin Leys pointed out that when an ideology becomes completely normalized, it is embedded in language. To describe Canadian society as multicultural pinpoints precisely the normalization of this ideological frame.

4 By the 'correct' analysis, I mean that the validation of the analysis lies not in an abstract theoretical framework, but in the processes that the text references and of which it is a part.

5 This is a rather cursory discussion of the complex historical unfolding of English and French relations dating from the early period of colonization in the sixteenth century. For a more detailed discussion, see Rioux (1971) and Milner and Milner (1973). My lack of proficiency in French made it impossible for me to consult French materials, which discuss these relations from another perspective.

6 Royal commissions are not part of the regular bureaucratic apparatus. They are appointed by the governor-in-council, and their primary task is to investigate a problem and recommend or ascertain the most feasible solutions (Maxwell 1969: 41; Maxwell and Maxwell 1984). They have no mandate to enforce their recommendations, which are made public by being tabled in the House of Commons (Maxwell and Maxwell 1984: 4). Maxwell observes that, because of the apparent neutrality and detachment (from the formal state apparatus) of royal commissions, they are one way to introduce change into the system with minimal disruption. I thank James Maxwell here for making available his dissertation and unpublished materials.

7 In his analysis of the preliminary reports of the Bilingualism and Biculturalism

Commission, Chua (1979) shows how a social problem, in this case the problem of language and culture, was 'secured.' That is, the 'problem,' having the specific character described in the report, was produced by the selection and ordering of the information received. He argues that the commission did not merely describe the problem; it was constructed through the investigation process (as I argue here that multiculturalism is constructed in the Trudeau speech). Chua further argues that one of the ways in which a democratic capitalist state displays its democratic commitment is to set up task forces and commissions independent of formal governmental organs to report on public opinions on a particular social situation and to recommend appropriate state activities. He demonstrates in his analysis how this kind of objectivity is accomplished and argues that this openness in no way guarantees the democratic disposition of commissions.

8 I remind the reader that not all modern nation-states in the West operate according to this model of society. An obvious example of a liberal democratic state operating with a different model is Germany. In spite of its long history of being populated by vast numbers of different groups (the Jews, the gypsies, and Turkish immigrants to name a few), Germany defines its citizenry in terms of blood line. Those whose ancestry is not 'Germanic' are considered foreigners (see Rathzel 1990). This is another construction of social reality.

Beyond the Ruling Category to What Actually Happens: Notes on James Mill's Historiography in *The History of British India*[1]

HIMANI BANNERJI

> Our knowledge of contemporary society is to a large extent mediated to us by texts of various kinds. The result, an objectified world-in-common vested in texts, coordinates the acts, decisions, policies and plans of actual subjects as the acts, decisions, policies and plans of large-scale organizations.
>
> D.E. Smith, *The Conceptual Practices of Power*

The concept of tradition is always with us, even though, and perhaps because, we live in North America or Europe, coded as the West. Associated with certain parts of the world, their peoples and cultures, characterizing them as 'others' not 'us,' tradition and its conceptual satellites appear in an automatic gesture of comprehending and creating difference. Tradition serves as an interpretive and constructive device, providing a discursive staple for newspapers and television, scholarly texts, feminism and fashion magazines, development policies, and UN sanctioned bombing of Iraq. Sections of the world, variously called 'the East,' 'the South,' or 'the third world,' contrasted to 'the West,' 'the North,' or 'the first or developed world,' have been designated as domains of tradition.

Edward Said, very early in a long line of critics of colonial discourse, noted a historical knowledge-power relation encoded in the category 'the East' or 'the Orient.'[2] He drew our attention to an essentialist, homogenizing representational apparatus which levelled with its imperial gaze diverse non–European regions into imaginary geographies and vast historic–cultural blocs. One of the interpretive devices that helped to accomplish this task was 'tradition.' The adjective 'traditional' (relatedly underdeveloped, backward, as opposed to 'modern,' progressive, advanced or developed) seems to synthesize disparate cultural characteristics to the satisfaction of the West.[3] Associated with stereotypes of mysticism and spirituality, dowry, wife-burning, female infanticide, overpopulation [*sic*], primitive technology, peasants and villages, India in particular has been projected as a 'traditional' society. It has long held a binary relationship to the West's self-representation, ramified through its package of science and rationality, technological–economic development, 'open society,' and political freedom.[4]

Deconstructing this traditional India as an ideologically representational category by unpacking the constituent social relations and epistemological method of its production implies an examination of the notion of tradition as a mode of reification. Furthermore, to return this imagined India to the realm of history, necessitates its disarticulation from the notion of tradition which dehistoricizes the cultures of Indian peoples.[5] This essay attempts a part of that task by examining the epistemological mechanism, the social relations embedded within that, and the resulting representational character of India as produced by James Mill in *The History of British India* (which first appeared in 1817). The importance of this book in terms of representing India in the West, and also in India itself, is difficult to exaggerate.

TEXT, RULE AND IDEOLOGY

Knowing is always *a relation* between knower and known. The knower can not be collapsed into the known, cannot be eliminated; the knower's presence is always presupposed. To know is always to know on some terms, and the paradox of knowing is that we discover in its object the lineaments of what we know already.

D.E. Smith, *The Conceptual Practices of Power*

We could, I imagine, be easily asked, why ascribe a single text such importance, and what power can conceptual practices have in the creation of hegemony? What, in short, is a written text or epistemology to ruling?

The answer to these questions lies in a Gramscian understanding of the concept of hegemony. According to this, even though force is the fundamental content of hegemony, it does not reside only in physical brutality or a machinery for direct coercion. The initial moment of conquest has to be translated or mediated into an administration of power. The work of intellectuals who interpret the reality to be ruled and inscribe this into suitable categories, provides the administrative basis for a sustained, reproducible ruling (Said 1978).[6] In the case of India, Orientalist scholar–administrators of the East India Company, along with those of the colonial state, provide this conceptual or categorical framework.

On this basis an India is constructed from the standpoint of European and colonial rule. It consists of a set of 'virtual realities vested in texts and accomplished in distinctive practices of reading and writing' (Smith 1990a: 62). The ruling nature of this construction is evident from the fact that it tells us less about that country than about the social imperatives of the producers of that knowledge (Said 1978: 4–9). The importance of texts which transmit knowledge, especially about 'distant amorphous' places (ibid.: 9), to the West from whence also colonialism and imperialism spring, must always be kept in mind. They provide the building blocks for cultural and ideological representation of these areas. Sociocultural relationships between these spaces are conducted mainly through what Smith calls 'the textual mode' (Smith 1990a: 61–5, 83–8). Furthermore, these constructed 'objects of knowledge' claim authority for neutral or unbiased representation. No allowance is made for the possibility that the knower's, for example, Mill's, location in relations of ruling or intention is implicated in the types of discourse deployed and developed (Smith 1990a: 14–18).[7]

This epistemological erasure of the social, through the adoption of a metaphysical mode entailing occlusiveness, displacement, and objectification, is named as ideology by Marx in *The German Ideology*. Here ideology is not solely the *content* or a collection of particular ideas and stereotypes, but also, and mainly, *an epistemological method*. A close reading of *The German Ideology* shows that not only are the 'ruling ideas of any age ... the ideas of the ruling class,' but also how these ideas are implicated in forms and products of social relations necessary for ruling (Marx and Engels 1973: 5). We begin to see constructive and reflexive relations between the apparatuses of ruling and knowledge.

This ideological method which degrounds and obscures the historical and material dimension of ideas naturally postulates a superordinate and separate realm for them. In 'Ideological Practices of Sociology,' Smith transposes Marx's critique of philosophy to the standard knowledge procedures of conventional (bourgeois) sociology and insists that they are neither 'objective' (except reificatory) nor 'pure' (see Smith 1990a: 14–16, 66–70). The productive tools and impacts of these procedures, when queried on the ground of everyday life, amount to a categorical and segregated organization of relations of ruling, involving specific semiotic systems. They are, for her, 'isomorphic with relations of ruling,' and necessarily invert the actual lived subject/object relations. They write over subjectivities, experiences, and agencies of peoples in history (Smith 1990a: 83–8).

Smith's Marxist critique of sociology as ideology can be extended to historiography of colonial history. I have chosen James Mill's *The History of British India* for an exploration of its epistemological processes with the intention of uncovering how Mill's India is an ideological constellation, which Ronald Inden (1990) calls an 'imagined India.'

MAKING INDIA BRITISH: JAMES MILL AND COLONIAL HISTORIOGRAPHY

It is certain that the few features of which we have any description from the Greeks, bear no inaccurate resemblance to those which are found to distinguish this people at the present day. From this resemblance, from the state of improvement in which the Indians remain, and the stationary condition in which their institutions first, and then their manners and character, have a tendency to fix them, it is no unreasonable supposition, that they have presented a very uniform appearance during the long interval from the visit of the Greeks to that of the English. Their annals, however, from that era till the period of Mahomedan conquests, are a blank.

James Mill, *The History of British India* (1968)

Mill's *The History of British India* has stood in for 'Indian history,' even though Mill encapsulates his real project in the very title of his study. The title holds, as does the book, an actuality and an ambition within one cover. India at the time of his writing (1805–17) was not fully under British control, either in terms of occupation of territories or in terms of knowledge. A comprehensive task of creating knowledge for ruling had been already undertaken by the Orientalists in the eighteenth century, but an India equal to the task of colonial rule had not yet been fully formulated. Besides, both in England and India there were many turns and reversals in political philosophy of governing and practical politics. The notion of 'British India,' therefore, projects both a partial actuality and a desire of full domination, as well as their conceptual bases (Mill 1968: 118–19). Mill's India is thus an ingested and aspired to social space for colonial rule. The book's towering status as a colonial text is evinced in securing Mill the job of the Chief Examiner of India House, the highest post in England of the most lucrative instrument of colonial rule. Administrators, legislators, missionaries, and businessmen engaged with India, among others, read this book as a compulsory text. An important footnote is John Kenneth Galbraith's preface to the 1968 edition. He read Mill's history book before venturing out as American Ambassador to India. The preface to it he wrote subsequently abounds in admiration of Mill for giving the modern reader a fundamental grasp on Indian reality.

Galbraith's preface supports Mill's claim that *The History of British India* would stand as an enduring representation of India for the West. An assessment, then, of this crucial text as ideology should be conducted along the following lines:

1 The epistemological method and historical context, including the social positionality of the author;
2 The particular content with regard to ascriptive stereotypes of concepts and images;
3 The overall political implications of these textual and conceptual practices with regard to the type of social subjectivity or historical agency ascribed to the Indian people.

Speaking of context, James Mill is primarily known as the apostle of Bentham's utilitarian philosophy and its application to matters of government. It is less known that in earlier life Mill was an evangelical preacher, and he remained close to Wilberforce and the Clapham sect. He was admired by William Bentnick, the governor general of Bengal, and by important parliamentarians such as Thomas Babbington Macauley. For his formulation of 'British India' Mill relied on the archival compilations of the East India Company and translated resources of the Orientalists. But his particular interest, unlike theirs, did not lie in the antiquities and their revival, and he successfully ejected parts of the earlier approach which combined a negative cultural–moral judgment of contemporary Indian society with a respect for India's ancient civilization.

Mill's history project, and thus his historiography, obviously stems from the standpoint of a colonial empire. It is not in 'discovering' India as an historical entity, but in vindicating the moment of colonial rule that he found his intellectual motive force. His purpose was to unfold the implications of events which marked the 'commencement of the British Intercourse with India; and the Circumstances of its Progress, till the Establishment of the Company on a durable basis of Act of Sixth of Queen Anne' (Mill 1968: 1). The scope of the three-volume project consists of

recording the train of events, unfolding the Constitution of the Body, half political, half commercial, through which the business has been ostensibly performed; describing the nature, the progress and effects of its commercial operations, exhibiting the legislative proceedings, the discussions and speculations, to which the connexion of Great Britain with India has given birth, analyzing the schemes of government which she has adopted for her Indian dominions, and attempting to discover the character and species of relation to one another in which the mother country and her eastern dependencies are placed. (Ibid.: 2)

The attempt consisted of situating and legitimizing British colonial rule in a pattern of ruling successions in India. Emphasizing force and repeated invasions by foreigners, characterizing the Mughal empire in particular as foreign rule, and portraying the Mughals as despotic and a degenerative influence on the Hindus, Mill argued for the necessity of an English empire in India. It was as a rule of reason and a civilizing mission that he justified it. Throughout his first chapter, on the English mercantile companies and the foundation of the colonial empire in Bengal, Mill presents an innocent commercial history. All European atrocities of conquest and commerce, including slave trade, are erased while presenting English achievements and superiority in 'the spirit of commerce.' The only moral judgment is levelled at the Dutch for executing nine Englishmen in the 'massacre at Amboyna.' The Mahomedans, however, attract heavy condemnation on the ground of savagery and ruthlessness, while 'that brilliant empire, established by the English ...' was entirely legitimated in India (ibid.: 33). It was even portrayed as sanctioned succession, as in the following statement: 'A firman and decree of the Emperor, conferring [these] privileges was received on the 11th of January, 1643; and authorized the first establishment of the English on the continent of India, at that time the seat of most extensive and splendid monarchies on the surface of the globe' (Mill 1968: 21). The 'recording of train of events' was thus no neutral narrative venture for Mill. *The History of British India* had but one main objective, to project and promote British rule in India.

This objective required a representational characterization of the object of rule – namely, Indian peoples. The remainder of the three volumes is dedicated to this enterprise, the construction of a definitive sociomoral version of India, beginning with the most extensive chapter on 'manners, morals and customs of the hindoos.' This is followed by a temporal history, also laced with moral and cultural judgments. Together they contained both justification and direction for the development of the colonial state.

Mill's history consciously eschews any archival or empirical research, including the knowledge of local classical or vernacular languages and texts. Thus, it is not impeded by or accountable to information that may not fit in the introjected ideological schema. This colonial historiography is distinct from that of writing European history, where the historian attempts a direct familiarity with the sources and records events in time. In colonial historiography however, the historian, according to Mill, plays the role of a judge who is faced with a crime and a set of circumstances and testimonies of witnesses. These he must construe as 'evidences' of a typical event, as well as decide on the credibility of the witnesses.[8] He must then read or hear the testimonies, etc., with the legal provisions pertaining to this crime. Whether something is an evidence at all will depend on what it is an evidence of, that is, on the pre-existing legal construction of that crime. This legal discourse of Mill's contains explicit epistemological principles and statements. Beginning with the premise that he 'knows' India (the crime) even before he undertakes his task, he employs a principle of relevance and logic in selecting and sorting evidences for this preconceived knowledge which originates outside his research. Thus, the text is a fully fleshed version of his presuppositions, details of which are to be read as illustrations of his preconceptions of Indian history and society. The attempt results in a seamless 'imagining' or construction of India, unaccommodating of complexities which might have problematized this construction.

Mill's proudly stated historiography, which adopts a metaphysical mode as a tool of social research, could be termed an idealist rationalism. This method was critiqued by Marx as the epistemological method of ideology. Discrediting the need for a material basis or actual research for writing history, Mill starts with an essentialist version of a 'real India' as opposed to the phenomenal, which is qualitatively different from and unaccountable to the empirical and social. Logical deductions and interpretations rely, thus, on this prehistorical and essentialist notion of the 'real.' Merging the formality of logic with the universal claims of metaphysics, Mill purports to provide his readers with the 'real truth' about India. He never questions his presumptions about India, their sources, or the existing social relations between a colonial investigator and a colonized reality. Totally unselfconscious, he characterizes his method as that of 'positive science,' resting on notions of 'true' and 'false' causes, 'witnesses' and 'evidences' in order to come to the right sociomoral judgments about India (ibid.: 6–7). However, in this process Mill creates not only moral judgments; these also become 'facts' about India which function as metaphysical and foundational categories for classifying, judging, and administering Indian peoples and societies. Thus, the writing of history becomes a production of ideology, content, and epistemology matching each other, occluding constructive relationships between consciousness and society. Unlike the sciences, Mill's method dispenses with verification, with the obligation to test preconceptions, and so forth against the archival, empirical sources, both vernacular and European. He discourages new research, since he considers that a 'sufficient stock of knowledge was already there' (ibid.: 5).

The standpoint of domination is also implicit in the fact that Mill never considers the ability or the right of Indians to define and represent themselves. His text as a whole is both a device and a justification for that silencing. The only voice and image permitted to 'the native' would be those he/she would acquire in the course of the colonial narrative.

The ideological character of Mill's enterprise, which fears any threat to his ideal type, emerges in his complex intertextual relationship with the English Orientalists.[9] Since no narrative even remotely resembling a history could have been written without previous records and translations, Mill was highly dependant on the Orientalist archive. Though he did not in all points share their view of India, the lineaments of what they already knew provided the pedestal for his project. But he resorted to a strategy of abstraction to decontextualize and incorporate previous research and interpretations and manipulated stereotypes and attitudes as he needed them.

Mill's major debt to the Orientalists for an ideological version of India lay in the polyvalent concept of tradition. It is this grab-bag category of cultural interpretation and representation which provided Mill's staple or modality for constructing difference. It created a ground for essentialism and thus generalization, since everything found in or about India could be read in light of this pre-established concept. The peculiar relationship held by this concept to time and social agency, bespeaking an arrested time, fixity, and repetition, allowed any reading of India through the lens of tradition as both chaotically mobile and rigidly fixed. This imputed changeless, passive lack of agency was then put forward as an intrinsic characteristic of Indian peoples and their histories. Caught in the conceptual grip of 'tradition,' events and changes of a few thousand years could then be seen as 'blank annals' (ibid.: 118–21) or an eternal repetition.

The deployment of the concept of tradition, which did not originate in the colonial encounter or Mill, but pre-existed in Europe for other and similar sense-making purposes, became a major device for constructing both the 'crime' and the evidence for the historian–judge Mill. Orientalist scholar–administrators such as William Jones had already established traditionality as an essence of Indian society, and of the 'hindoos' in particular. In fact from the era of Warren Hastings in the 1770s to the time when Mill was writing his book, colonial civil legislation in India continually assumed and constructed tradition through translation of Hindu and Muslim scriptures and a selective compilation of their personal laws.[10]

The concept of tradition, when deployed in the 'otherization' of India, entailed the related notions of civilization and antiquity. While concepts such as 'tradition,' 'antiquity,' and 'civilization' were invested with positive connotations for the colonial conservatives of the eighteenth century, they also served as conduits for varying moral judgments about colonized societies at each stage. What was meant by civilization or its importance at each stage decided whether a country with an old history and complex sociocultural organizations could be called civilized. Thus, the attitude towards civilization and traditionality, as well as the ascribed types of traditions, decided whether a country was civilized or barbaric or savage. And those who had power and the need to define the truth about India, claiming self-transcendence, had decided that it was a traditional country. Thus, it was at once in and out of time and history, replete with peculiar barbaric traditions. Mill also went by these categorical formulations of India already accomplished by the India Office, but unlike the Orientalists, denied either the value or the existence of an ancient civilization in India. As a utilitarian and Malthusian economic liberal he not only had little interest in traditional societies or ancient civilizations, but even less in Eastern ones.

Mill's book therefore begins by disputing the Orientalist ascriptions of antiquity and civilization to India. His version of this country is projected in no uncertain terms at the very outset: 'Rude nations seem to derive a peculiar gratification from pretensions to a remote antiquity. As a boastful and turgid vanity distinguishes remarkably the oriental nations, they have in most instances carried their claims extravagantly high' (ibid.: 107). He goes on to criticize Orientalist accounts of Hindu creation stories and the Hindu methods of record keeping and chronicle writing. Dubbing the Orientalist acknowledgment of Hindu claims to antiquity as duped submission to the 'national pride of barbarians,' he dismisses indigenous records, literature, and other archival sources as worthless for writing 'history' (ibid.: 118–19). Judging the sources and witnesses in this peremptory way, Mill simultaneously displays his power location as a reader of Indian reality and manipulates, controls, and constructs sociocultural facts about India according to his own discursive organization.

This disregard for matters indigenous to India, echoed later by Macaulay, in his influential 'Minute on Education for India' (Curtin 1971), pits Mill often against the Orientalists. He is particularly dismissive of their impartiality and accuracy, since they knew Indian languages, lived there, and enjoyed the literature that they found. Thus, they lacked the necessary detachment which Mill considered essential for a judge–historian, and he found himself eminently suitable for this task on the very ground of lack of knowledge of languages and lack of direct connections with or experiences of India.

H.H. Wilson, on the other hand, an Orientalist scholar–administrator, who went on to become Boden Professor of Sanskrit at Oxford, subsequently edited *The History of British India* and provided extensive footnotes correcting Mill's 'errors' in representing Indian culture or history. Asserting that Europeans cannot know India without learning its ancient and modern languages and reading extensively to develop a cultural literacy to be complemented by life experiences and discussions with Indians, Wilson offered in his 'corrections' a parallel text to Mill's.

Wilson's footnotes and commentaries highlight Mill's enormous ignorance of India and his even greater arrogance that his very ignorance was a prerequisite for knowledge. Mill was one of the earliest propagators of the notion that India did not have a history, a notion that was to be found from William Jones to Marx to modern times. For Mill, India lacked history both in terms of an intellectual discipline and a social progression or evolution in time, expressive of agency and originality. Presenting Hindus both as infantile liars as well as the real 'natives' of India, caught in fantasy and blind to the difference between fact and fiction, and Indian Muslims as foreign invaders who only kept minimal records, Mill regarded European historians such as himself as the real historians of India.

Mill's view of himself as the definitive historian of India, while denying India any history, creates crude inconsistencies in his text. On the one hand, his own lack of willingness and ability to do primary research on India makes him reliant on early Greek and later European sources. He is thus constrained to say that Orientalists 'had studied the Indian languages' and 'acquired the means of full and accurate information' (Mill 1968: 118). On the other hand, they were seduced by that very knowledge into a positive view of India, especially of the Hindus. Mill draws instead upon the Greeks for denigrating social features which 'bear no inaccurate resemblance to those which are found to distinguish this people at the present day.' Consequently he states in the same breath that 'we have no reason to suppose that their knowledge of the hindus [*sic*] was valuable' (ibid.: 118). Mill's double project is to degrade and deny Indians any worthwhile historical and cultural agency and thus any history of its expression. His ultimate aim seems to have been the establishment of an empty historical-cultural slate for India inscribed with barbaric traditions. He shares with the evangelical missionaries the conviction that Indians (mainly Hindus) are essentially degenerate and full of 'insincerity, mendacity, venality and perfidy' (Niranjana 1990: 776–7).[11]

Mill's pathological dislike of Indians, and the colonial context and the content of his book, are secured by his manipulation of categories such as 'tradition,' 'civilization,' 'barbarism,' and 'savagery.' He constructs simultaneously a social space which is rigidly ordered and enclosed, and yet formless and primeval. A telling example of this is to be found in his reading of the caste system, which he sees both as atavistic or irrational and forged with 'iron laws' (Mill 1968: 153). Wilson's extensive footnote on this topic, however, not only shows up Mill's scanty reading and reliance on rumour, but also illustrates the complexity of caste as a form of fast mutating social practices and organization, rather than a mere discourse of tradition (Mill 1968: 125, n. 1). Mill's ascriptive confidence actually rests on the a priori notion of European social superiority over conquered 'others.'

What also becomes evident from the struggle between the text and the footnotes is that the modalities of colonial rule vary in historically specific moments. The goals and practices of a mercantile monopoly (East India Company) differ substantially from ideological aspirations of the rising colonial state. Thus, Mill's dismissal of the need to research Indian history can be contrasted to Wilson's view that research on India was in 'the veriest of infancy,' or that Mill's opinions of Indian society, 'to say the least of them,' were 'premature.'[12] Wilson's view of India as 'traditional' was coherent with a positive ascription of 'civilization,' qualifying its decline. But for Mill a steep decline follows the Aryans, whom he erroneously sees as 'aboriginal' to India. After the Aryan 'golden age' India becomes a static yet chaotic society. Further degenerating under Muslim invasions and rule, it remains stagnant and decadent until the arrival of the British (ibid.: 113). Thus, Mill creates his own 'Robinsonade' (Marx 1977: 83–5) through this teleology of European and Indian history moving towards capital and colonization, using enlightenment notions of civilization and humanism together with the moral lens of evangelicalism. That is to say, he creates a history of India as a part of an overall current political and ideological project.

As such Mill denies or distorts all political developments within India, particularly that of a state formation and the development of social government and legislation. He invents a nomadic stage of Aryan pastoralism which he inlays with an English nuclear family form (Mill 1968: 122). This happy pastoral stage, according to Mill, is followed by a tortuous route of decline. But Orientalist and other European insistences force him to impute to India a highly qualified form of barbaric civilization. 'The first rude form of a national polity' is to be found in 'fully as early a period as any portion of the race' (ibid.: 122). But he also adds that the 'cautious inquirer will not probably be inclined to carry this era very far back' (ibid.: n. 1). The legislative texts of the earlier periods, such as Manu's *Dharmashastra*, translated by the Orientalists, are seen by Mill (1968: 124) as exceptional achievements of 'superior spirits,' rather than as the result of a general development of political and social government. According to him:

The first legislator of the Hindus, whose name it is impossible to trace, appears to have represented himself as the republisher of the will of God. He informed his countrymen that, at the beginning of the world, the creator revealed his duties to man, in four sacred books, entitled Vedas; that during the first age, of immense duration, mankind obeyed them, and were happy; that during the second and third they only partially obeyed, and their happiness was proportionately diminished; that since the commencement of the fourth age disobedience and misery had totally prevailed, till the Vedas were forgotten and lost; that now, however, he was commissioned to reveal them anew to his countrymen, and to claim their obedience. (Ibid.: 125)

Wilson's comment on this is telling: 'The whole of this is imaginary; there is no such legislation, there are no such assertions in Hindu tradition' (ibid.: 125, n. 1). Flying in the face of all available evidence encoded in *Dayabhaga* property laws, Mill also claimed that there was no private property, revenue, or justice system in India, nor a system of public finance and public works, nor a knowledge of the art of war. For this lack he resorted to explanations based on the 'laziness of the hindus [*sic*]' (ibid.: 133, n. 1). Wilson's comments, therefore, establishing his difference from Mill, allow for variant readings of a colonized society from within the very precincts of colonial rule. These debates from within also expose at their clearest the articulation between knowledge and social relations of power, and their historical specificities.

All disagreements notwithstanding, the overall colonial project comes out loud and clear when we see that Mill develops as a key in his history one Orientalist theme to its fullest – that of Asiatic despotism, which should be distinguished from European enlightened despotism. In this formulation converged negative perceptions of the 'two peoples' of India. The sources of this despotism were traced to both caste-bound, 'traditional' Hindus (with their self-enclosed village societies) and Muslims, already renowned in post-Crusade Europe as absolute despots, with racial and religious propensities in this direction (Said 1981). Unlike Europe, 'Asiatic' political institutions and economies are claimed to be sustained by brute force, superstition, authoritarianism, and tradition (Mill 1968: 141). Mill projected this stance through the conflation of the typology or the iconography of the monarch and the actual or practical system of government in different historical stages. Taking statements from Manu literally, oblivious to similar European iconography of the monarch, for example in Hobbes's *Leviathan*, Mill posited a monstrously totalitarian system of government for India, as an intrinsic expression and requirement of the peoples (Mill 1968: 141).

The Eurocentrism or racism inherent in the concept of Asiatic despotism is a manipulation of the concept of 'traditional society.' This is exposed through Mill's and Wilson's contradictions with each other, as well as through the contradictions within Mill's text. For example, the rigidity of this notion and Mill's ascribed chaos and formlessness of Indian cultures and polity are both accommodated by 'tradition,' and as a whole play condemnatory roles. Wilson's copious footnotes also signal the complexity of actual political practices, in sharp contrast to Mill's construction of symbolic fixities. Wilson questions both Mill's claims that the government which 'almost universally prevailed in the monarchies of Asia ... was contrivance extremely simple and rude' (ibid.: 142) and that the Hindu king or sovereign combined all functions of the state in himself (ibid.: 143). Instead he draws attention to the similarities between European and Indian governing systems, remarking that 'in the more skilful governments of Europe, officers were appointed for the discharge of particular duties in the different provinces of the empire ... All together act as connected and subordinate wheels in one complicated artful machine' (ibid.: 145). The notion of Asiatic despotism in India should therefore be seen as less descriptive than ascriptive, as a conceptual artefact for colonial legitimation. It allowed Mill and others to justify and advocate despotic rule for India by marshalling the concept of tradition and locating it as India's cultural essence. It is through this device that India was judged as fundamentally unsuited to democracy, and positively responsive to authoritarianism. This same sentiment was expressed by James Mill in his *Essay on Government*, while his son John Stuart Mill (1972/1859) in *On Liberty* justified a despotic, though enlightening rule of India on the same grounds.[13] Later Indian demands for a constitutional rule could be thus dismissed on this very ground. Marx's essays on colonialism and India, along with the thesis of lack of history, contains the same credo of Asiatic despotism.

Developing further the colonial project of ethnicization, Mill constructed Hindus and Muslims into separate and self-enclosed cultural categories and organized Indian history into three periods of rule, namely Hindu, Muslim, and British, with particular social ethos ascribed to the rulers. This process of fragmentation and categorization, started in the eighteenth century, became a developed historiography in *The History of British India*. It lent itself to a periodization pattern of European cultural and social history. The 'golden age of the Aryans' thus declined into the 'dark middle ages' of Muslim conquests and rule, followed by the enlightened rule of Britain. Contrary to all evidence, Muslims were projected as foreigners or outsiders, and the composite or hybrid culture of North and East India were ignored. All this provided a distortion of Indian history, while providing the bases for a colonialist strategy of divide and rule. While the British presence was legitimated by trade permissions and land grants given by the Muslim emperors and lesser Muslim rulers, the Muslims themselves were portrayed as usurpers. Indeed the fear that they were seen by Indians as invaders and usurpers was never allayed for the English even by their massive military might. The equation therefore of themselves with the Mughals as equally and a better type of outsider, as well as the negative depiction of the Muslims, gave the English a moral prerogative to rule. It is not surprising therefore that Mill's claim of Europeans as better rulers rests upon negative stereotypes of Muslims as warlike and full of 'Saracenic' fanaticism, with an inbuilt tendency towards sensuality, cruelty, and luxury. The fact that the Muslims made a self-conscious historical effort by writing biographies and descriptions or keeping state records, or produced great art, architecture, mathematics, and philosophy, did not redeem them in Mill's eyes. Nor was he able to see Indian Islam as a specifically Indian and syncretic formation, or Muslims as Indians in diverse groups in their regional cultural varieties.

By reinforcing the Orientalist notion of the Hindus as the (ab)original sons of the soil, Mill 'Hinduized' India in a highly effective way, while taking away from 'Hindu India' the attributes of a progressive or significant civilization. Thus, the Hindus were greatly in need of being civilized, which the Muslim rulers, who were themselves barbaric, and unlike the English, succumbed to the Hindu culture instead, could not provide. Distancing himself from the seduced Orientalists, Mill had no project for restoring India to its pristine ancient glory. The ancient venerable India of the Orientalists is for Mill mainly a moment of civilizational immaturity, 'the dawn of childhood of human kind.' As a patriarchal and patrician stern ruler and judge, rather than an indological scholar, Mill (1968: 123, n. 1) advocates discipline and punishment for the good of this 'wild, barbaric, savage and rude' people. As far as he was concerned, Indians were 'a people over whom the love of repose exerts the greatest sway, and in whose character aversion to danger forms a principal ingredient' (ibid.: 153).

It is interesting to note how Mill slides between binary notions, such as age and childhood, order and chaos, nature and culture, barbarism and tradition, in his ideological construction of India. He resolves the contradiction between tradition and savagery or barbarism by positing that their traditionality is itself an indication of savagery. It is this elision between tradition and savagery, or culture and nature, or better still, culture as nature (see Dirks 1992: 1–3) that allows Mill the maximum leverage to accommodate diverse cultural features without himself suffering from any sense of contradiction (Niranjana 1990: 776). It also allows him to systematically introject inferiority into the difference between Europeans and their Indian colonized subjects. This silences the Indian prerogative of self-representation and justifies colonial rule as an expression of progress or improvement.

Mill completed his project in 1817, but his historiographical method, which produces ideology, separating forms of knowing from ways of being, both in history and in present-day social organization, continues. The project of inventing cultural categories to accomplish the task of ruling continues unabated. The attribution of tradition to any society is still a legitimation for domination, and an excuse to modernize, that is, to re-colonize.

NOTES

1 This essay is part of a long study I have undertaken to grasp the concept of ideology and find its workings in colonial texts. It is also related to a book I am working on about 'Reform, Hegemony, and Women in Nineteenth-Century Bengal' forthcoming from Kali for Women (India). Another article, on William Jones, applying the same method of critique of ideology sensitized by the work of D.E. Smith, appears in *Left History* (1994).

2 See Edward Said (1978) regarding cultural–colonial construction of 'the Orient' or 'the East' as a knowledge and power category and the implication of 'the West's' cultural–political identity and politics.

3 See Raymond Williams (1983: 318–20) for an evolution and application of this concept.

4 See the discussion of modernization theorists of the MIT school in the context of 'development,' such as Rostow and Kuznet, for an overall grasp of this position.

5 See Ronald Inden (1990) for an extended discussion of this colonial cultural–political construction of India, which attempts a project partially similar to Said's *Orientalism*.

6 See also Smith (1987a: 181–5) on the notion of 'standpoint' of knowledge and

Smith (1990a: 31–57) on the ideological (that is, ruling) role of intellectuals (sociologists and others) in the construction and maintenance of the ruling apparatus.

7 See also Smith (1987a: 49–69) on the implications of knower's location in the production of knowledge.

8 See Mill's 'Preface' to vol. 1 for the full exposition of his method of history writing and his conception of what properly constitutes 'history.'

9 Throughout volume 1, Book 2, Mill disputes with the Orientalist historians and translators just as much as he disputes the fact of India having a history.

10 For Hastings and personal law, see Sangari and Vaid (1990).

11 See also R. Hyam (1992) for a reworked version of masculinity and personality of colonized males.

12 See Wilson's footnotes on issues of caste and other social practices in Chapter 2, and on government laws in Chapter 3, esp. pp. 126–40.

13 'Despotism is a legitimate mode of government in dealings with barbarians, provided the end be their improvement, and the means justified by actually effecting that end' (John Stuart Mill 1972: 73).

Violence and the Relations of Ruling: Lessons from the Battered Women's Movement[1]

GILLIAN WALKER

In Vancouver in the late 1970s I worked on a multi-agency task force aimed at providing information, coordinating services, and pressuring government to recognize and respond to the emerging problem of 'family violence.' On this task force, as elsewhere, women's movement groups working with battered women often found themselves in opposition to the generalized approach to 'family violence' put forward by professionals from institutions and agencies. As the issue was made more visible by community level organizing all over the country, feminists within the federal government organized a national consultation of women's groups working in the area of wife battering to pressure the government for a coordinated response at the national level. These and later events such as federal and provincial (Ontario) public hearings before standing committees of both legislative bodies, provide the context in which I examine the process of conceptual coordination of the issue of wife battering in relation to notions of 'family violence' that took place in subsequent years.

This essay examines five reports that span a seven-year period early in the feminist struggle to address the situation of women beaten and otherwise abused by the men with whom they had intimate relationships. The struggle focused on the need to name what was happening to women in ways that would articulate experiences and needs to institutional resources and solutions. The reports are treated here as moments in a conceptual process bringing into being a 'social problem.' This theoretical approach is a reading of documents as textual practices forming a basis for the exercise of power in advanced capitalist societies (Smith 1990a). An examination of each of the five reports provides access to a series of events, revealing the discursive features of the relations between local sites of struggle and the general terrain of ruling. These particular documents are not chosen to draw direct causal connections, though some might be made. Rather I use them to show how the work of each report shapes the issue and sets the conceptual groundwork for the next. This captures a moment in a generalizing relation mediated by texts.[2]

The reports both shaped a generalized way of understanding what was happening to women and what should be done about it and at the same time reorganized the work of feminists away from their initial political undertaking and towards a role as marginalized providers of crisis shelter services. In particular, my examination of these reports identifies the distinctively different concerns put forward by activists engaged in organizing against the subordination of women and by professional service providers challenged to respond to a new 'population at risk.' The analysis of the reports shows how the struggle moved from the local level to a centralized and generalized milieu which, in turn, provided a conceptual framework that could be reapplied to regulate and coordinate local responses to the issue thus defined. The generalizing relation accomplished by the process of conceptual coordination that I will trace in the documents is one which appropriates and absorbs both women's experience and the political struggle itself.

GENERALIZING THE PARTICULAR: REPORTS ONE AND TWO

By the mid-1970s the work of the women's movement across North America and Europe had begun to identify the hitherto unacknowledged extent of brutality that women experienced at the hands of men. Academic research, books, and newspaper and magazine articles had begun to draw public attention to actions variously described as wife battering, beating, or abuse. In 1976 the United Way of Greater Vancouver, an institution charged with the coordination of fund-raising and support for community agencies, sponsored a study of police approaches to 'domestic crisis intervention.' This study prompted a further enquiry into the extent of the 'battered wife problem' and 'a still larger concern with family centred violence in general, embracing a concomitant study of the incidence of child abuse' (Downey and Howel 1976: Foreword).

With funding from the United Way and the National Department of Health and Welfare, researchers set out to 'assist in developing adequate programs for wives who are subjected to physical abuse and assault through a review of programs, treatment modes and needs and an estimation of the degree and severity of the battered wife problem' (Downey and Howel 1976: Appendix A, i). They did this by asking a number of social service agencies to count how often in the past six months they had encountered the 'battered wife syndrome,' a term coined from the academic discourse in Britain and the United States. They also surveyed legal, medical, and educational organizations across the country, including several research clearing houses, and produced an annotated bibliography drawing together both popular and academic articles and books on the subject.

The study resulted in a report titled *Wife Battering: A Review and Preliminary Enquiry into Local Incidence, Needs, and Resources*. The authors began by reviewing the range of academic discourse on violence, homicide, and aggression. These features were found to be taken up differently in such disciplines as sociology, sociobiology, criminology, psychology, and psychoanalysis. The report set out to examine violence in a particular setting, 'the family,' characterized in the social science discourse as being the place where patterns of violent interaction were practised and passed on from generation to generation.

Having developed a framework for understanding that wife battering was to be regarded as an aspect of violence in the family, the authors presented the findings from their survey of local agencies. It was clear that with the notable exception of the local Transition House and the Status of Women Office, little usable data existed. Many agencies simply did not regularly collect statistics on wife battering as a distinct problem. Although some agencies participated in data-gathering projects for the study and identified a higher incidence of violence than anticipated, 'the battered wife' was not, at this point, formulated as a recognized syndrome in the work of agencies and professionals in the Lower Mainland of Vancouver.

Given the dearth of response to the survey, and the authors' judgment that research relying 'upon the information provided almost exclusively by wives' was too narrow and biased to be considered reliable (Downey and Howel 1976: 88), studies from other communities and even other countries were used to interpret local interviews and to shape recommendations for action. Within an analytic framework provided by American sociological studies of 'family violence' these recommendations formed a 'logical' response to a carefully researched and written exploration of 'the problem.' The report recommended a network of family crisis centres in urban areas across British Columbia. These centres were to be under the auspices of existing family agencies and would provide emergency service to wives, husbands, and children while also coordinating access to a range of professional services. This would potentially remedy the fragmentary and inadequate nature of existing services that were 'not oriented to the violent family' (ibid.: Conclusions and Recommendations, 1).

Though the recommendations addressed the need for more support for transition houses as the best form of temporary relief and shelter for women, this concern about women was qualified by an emphasis on the needs of children, especially in transition houses. Children were seen to be coping not only with disrupted lives but also with 'crowded conditions in a totally female environment and an atmosphere of hostility towards their fathers and men generally' (ibid.: 2). In contrast, Family Crisis Centres were seen as providing a long-term treatment alternative geared to the needs of the family as a whole. The report in general served as an indict-ment of professional practice, drawing the attention of local agencies to deficiencies in their services and making recommendations concerning the need for proper training for police, justice officials, and other professionals. It urged more studies, public education, and the considerate treatment of violent men who seek help.

Though locally produced and not widely distributed, this report pro-vides a point of access to the generalizing relation that I am tracing in this essay. It introduced the social science discourse to organize an understand-ing of women's experience of being beaten and abused as an aspect of the larger issue of violence in the family, setting up academics as experts, and dismissing as partisan the voices of women who had been beaten. At the same time it marginalized the political work of feminists at the community level, discounting the valuable work of Transition House by interpreting it as hostile to men and harmful to children. The report also served as the basis for the next set of activities and for the second report analysed here. The recommendations for public and professional education became the basis for organizing a symposium, not on wife battering but on 'family vio-lence.' Women's groups were again marginalized. Their representatives were invited by the United Way to take part in the planning process, but only after the decisions about terms of reference and expert guest speakers had been made. During the symposium feminists angrily disputed the approach taken by academics and professionals and carried on the dispute as members of the multi-agency task force set up by the United Way to implement the symposium recommendations. The struggle continued over two years and can be recovered in the report of the task force's activities.[3]

This second United Way sponsored report, produced in 1978, was titled *Family Violence* (MacLeod 1979). Its introductory section detailed the con-nections between wife battering and child abuse and the reasons for taking them up together, thus instructing readers in a particular understanding of 'the issue of family violence.' These theoretical connections constructed an account based on the work and opinions of fieldworkers, professionals, and knowledgeable laypeople (ibid.: 1). Recommendations for action were made to the organizations that these workers represented, returning the issue to them to be acted upon as such – as 'family violence.'

The problem with this process of constructing knowledge is that it refers us back, not to the lived world where women are being beaten, but to an abstracted version of events that can then be entered, as objectified knowledge, into theories that represent the relevancies of those whose job it is to manage social problems.[4] The things that people do and the contexts in which they do them, which are the connectives that make up social relations, are stripped away and dropped out of the conceptual form to be replaced by connectives which account for experiences in terms of theory and discourse. The circular process that produces such 'expert' knowledge thus excludes both what is known by those who live the experience and the structures that effect their lives. It is these conceptual processes that are relied on in the creation and administration of social programs and policies.

The theoretical connections set up in the introduction to the *Family Violence* report served to obscure all the different ways and situations in which men ill-treat the women around them and all the different and possible ways in which children are mistreated by those who have charge of them. These are taken out of context and collapsed into 'instances of family violence.' It is impossible to tell who is hurting whom: all that we can tell, from the introduction, is that 'the Family is a violent place.' In his keynote address to the symposium, Murray Strauss, a renowned sociologist from the United States, further added that the family 'is the most violent group or setting that a typical citizen is likely to encounter' (ibid.: 2). These statements, quoted in the introduction, were seen as describing families of all 'cultural and social backgrounds, ages or income levels' (ibid.: 2). 'Family violence' thus defined can only be explained in terms provided by the discourse, such as deviance, aggression, stress, breakdown, or pathology in the individuals concerned. Such discourse categories provide a way of seeing every instance of 'family violence' as equivalent to every other, a conflation of generalized and universalized theories of 'the family' and 'violence.' The fact that over 70 per cent of so-called instances of family violence are attacks by men on women is not visible. The pain and suffering that women experience as a result of these attacks disappears; the circumstances of their lives are obscured. Women who are punched and kicked during pregnancy by their male partners, for example, become, through the 'work of researchers,' instances of 'intrauterine child abuse' (ibid.: 2). This disassociation from context and consequences was evident in studies by Strauss and others that 'proved' women to be as violent as, if not more violent than men. These studies not only gave undue prominence to notions that there were equal numbers of battered husbands, but also provided the justification for an antifeminist and misogynist backlash that blamed women for the breakdown of the family unit.[5]

The introduction to the report set up the theoretical connections for future action in this emerging policy field. Since it also set up directions for a reading of the report that included references to the contribution of women's groups and took institutions and agencies roundly to task, it appeared to strike a balance and represent all viewpoints as accepting the 'family violence' framework for action. The content of the rest of the document, however, showed that there were other readings to be made and that a struggle was in progress. Fierce dissent over the report's production had resulted in the accounts of the grass-roots women's groups being included in the final document, in the form of reports from the task force's different working groups. In the accounts of the work of the education group and in the report of groups concerned with wife battering, for example, which was where I did my work on the task force, there was clearly a different understanding of the issue. This came from starting, not in the social science discourse of 'family violence' but with the experiences of women who had been beaten and abused. From this standpoint it was evident that there were other ways of accounting for the commonality of women's experience, in the structural bases of their subordination, rather than as 'instances of family violence.'

I am not in any way suggesting that the method of proceeding adopted in the report's introduction is intentionally misleading. It was a way of thinking and acting that those of us trained as professionals and social scientists have learned to see as appropriate: the objective, scientific production of facts, upon which to build a theoretical basis for understanding and action. In opposing the objectified knowledge claimed by academics and professionals such as Strauss, the outrage expressed by feminists at the symposium and on the task force in relation to what we knew from experience appeared biased, subjective, naive, inappropriate, and sometimes strident and divisive. Ours were not valid voices and what we knew could not be easily accommodated within the knowledge-making circle. The introduction gave us, as activists, our allotted place as the identifiers of wife battering, and also as potential evaluators of the system's response to victims of 'family violence.' But we were relegated to the category of 'knowledgeable laypeople' with the power to monitor only from the sidelines.

Activists in other places shared similar experiences to those of us working with the United Way in Vancouver. We found that linking wife battering and child abuse focused the issue in such a way that women's experience came to be subsumed by an emphasis on child abuse and services to men who battered their wives. We discovered that we had to be vigilant, vigorous, and persistent in putting forward battered women's situation. This was necessary in order to counteract the way that the concept of 'family violence' implicated women and failed to protect them from the actions of men even when these endangered their lives. Such actions, and the suffering they produced, disappeared in an objectified professional language.

This language arose out of and fed back into the work of professional agencies and institutions whose mandate it was to maintain the existing organization and power relations of the family and its place in the relations of ruling (D. Smith 1979). This inclined them towards clinical interventions designed to fix up the 'the family' and help 'it' deal with 'its violence.' In response, the political objective around which many of us focused our work was to force a recognition of wife battering and abuse as an issue in its own right, representing the overwhelming preponderance of 'instances of family violence.' This involved us in a structural critique of 'the family' as an institution which embodied the subordination of women at its most personal, a critique that was not accepted readily by the professionals with whom we struggled. We wanted to maintain control of the definition of the issue against attempts to remove it from its context in a political movement. The struggle became more intense and more complex as it moved on to the national stage.

MALE VIOLENCE AGAINST WOMEN: NEW SITES OF STRUGGLE

In 1980 the Canadian Advisory Council on the Status of Women[6] organized a national consultation to 'examine ... the problems experienced both by those women working in services to battered women and by those working to improve the response to wife battering in the criminal justice system, medical and health professions, and other social agencies' (MacLeod 1980a: 2).

Several representatives of Vancouver women's groups presented our experience on the United Way task force as the basis of a critique of the way that the 'family violence' framework worked against the interests of women. While all of us present had no difficulty in agreeing that men's violence towards women had to be addressed in any strategy for change, some participants concentrated on the structural features of women's dependence in relation to the family and the workforce, emphasizing the trap that this creates, especially for women with children. Others saw the organization of the family and the workforce as a manifestation of the overriding issue of male domination and the control of women's sexuality by force or threat of force in a patriarchal system. For them, male violence was the primary target for action.

The deliberations of the women at the consultation were drawn together to emphasize this latter position in the report of the proceedings. In it the council worked hard to develop a position that would unite professional concerns for the proper management of the problem and the conflicting accounts of the roots of the issue put forward by activists. By extending the definition of wife battering to include many of women's experiences of discrimination, harassment, and sexual abuse, the document packaged the various positions into one which could be seen to stand for all. 'We women,' the document declared, 'must unite to oppose male violence'; 'we women' must also maintain control of the issue. This approach attempted to link concepts that operated at a bureaucratic and professional level, such as 'family violence,' to those with a political mobilizing intent such as 'wife battering' or 'abuse,' 'wife assault,' and 'male violence.' Adopting the theme of one presentation, 'Wife Battering is Everywoman's Issue,' as its title, the report organized an account of the event that appeared to bring women together as women and dissolve differences in location between professionals, service providers, activists, and women who are beaten, all of whom became 'women vulnerable to male violence' (ibid.: 2).

Although the consultation was set up by feminists on the council and in the federal government as an opportunity to use federal funds to bring together grass-roots women's groups, the council had other agendas that included the release of the first Canadian book and film on the topic.[7] The consultation provided for and signalled a shift in levels of management of an emerging 'social problem.' As such it was part of the council's strategy of pressuring the federal government to take action on the issue of violence against women. The conceptual formulation developed in the report allowed the various positions identified in it to be absorbed into this generalizing strategy.

Linking a male violence framework with that of a family violence framework was accomplished by focusing on violence itself as the problem uniting both. This allowed the issue to be reformulated in terms of the laws on assault, with pressure to extend the application of the law to those women whose status as wives or intimates was seen as having left them unprotected within the private realm of the family. This reformulation, proposed as one of several during the consultation, began to gain popularity. It provided a focus for mobilizing the mounting anger of many women's groups faced with the need to turn away from the few existing shelters numbers of women in danger of being beaten or killed. It also allowed women's groups to compete for newly available research funding from various justice departments at both the provincial and federal levels. In the process of adopting this formulation, however, the analysis of women's oppression in the broader structures of society was in danger of being subsumed by the strategy of invoking women's rights as individuals under the law.

ASSAULT UNDER THE LAW

In 1981 a private member's motion to the House of Commons, asking that the subject of 'intra-family violence' be addressed, was carried unanimously and referred to the Standing Committee on Health, Welfare, and Social Affairs. The committee held public hearings, focused on 'battered wives and dependents,' at which a surprisingly concerted approach to the issue of wife battering as criminal assault was evident in the presentations and briefs. A range of submissions, from women's groups (including some who had been part of the task force in Vancouver and the federal consultation), academics, professional agencies, and individuals, defined battered women as the victims of male violence. The focus had thus shifted so that apparently competing analyses coincided to emphasize the criminal nature of wife battering as a category of assault under the law.

The Standing Committee's report to the House of Commons, *Report on Violence in the Family: Wife Battering (Canada 1982)*, included a number of 'case histories' focusing on women's experiences of assault and the inadequate responses of the criminal justice system to their attempts to free themselves from their assailants. It acknowledged the seriousness and complexity of 'the problem' and the jurisdictional difficulties that arise in attempting to 'manage' it. While upholding the privacy of the family, the Standing Committee justified the need to intervene in family relations in the case of wife assault. 'To ignore the problem,' the report stated, 'is to ignore society's fundamental obligation to preserve the life and health of its members. Our institutions must occupy themselves with the problem more actively than they have done in the past' (Canada 1982: 15). The report first took up the needs of the battered wife, concluding, on the basis of the presentations put before it, that the first priority was protection from assault as well as the opportunity to gain financial and emotional independence from her violent partner. It further concluded that the battering husband had to be treated as a criminal and processed through the criminal justice system and that measures had to be taken to lay assault charges on the woman's behalf and to encourage her to cooperate in the prosecution. The committee favoured criminal sentences that would refer the batterer to treatment programs where available, arguing that research was also needed to uncover the causes of wife battering, in order to understand what it is a symptom of, how it is produced, and how it might be prevented. In particular the report argued that the learned and interactive aspects of violence within the family unit, and the lessons of aggression and passivity that society teaches men and women respectively, must be unlearned. The text of the report concluded: 'We must educate ourselves ... to identify violence and to control its consequences, for the sake of battered women, and for the sake of us all' (Canada 1982: 17).

The standing committee addressed issues under federal jurisdiction in relation to the RCMP, the appointment of federal judges, certain housing and immigration policies, and the Departments of Health and Welfare and Justice research funding. It also addressed issues under provincial and private jurisdiction, commenting on the need for shelter funding, emergency income provision, advocacy services, and education for professionals. The report formulated wife battering as assault that takes place within the family unit and as a national and societal problem that was not being addressed adequately by the appropriate institutions. It suggested ways in which the government might act to control violence at the federal level and reapportioned other aspects of the generalized problem to local sites of regulation controlled by the provinces.

RELOCATING THE GENERAL

The final phase of my analysis shows how the federal hearings and report provided the impetus for renewed struggles across the country as activists attempted to influence governments to act on aspects of the issue that could only be addressed at the provincial and municipal levels. In Ontario, for example, the Standing Committee on Social Development of the Ontario Legislature was induced, by various energetic pressure tactics, to take up 'the issue of abuse' in the wake of the federal report. Some of the federal briefs and research reports were made available to the provincial committee; a representative of the federal committee was present at the provincial hearings, and the federal report itself was frequently referred to. This provided a correlation of information on policies and practices while at the same time contributing to the negotiation and shaping up of the issue for action at the provincial level.

In December 1982 the Ontario committee produced its *First Report on Family Violence: Wife Battering* (Ontario 1982). Acceptance of 'violence' as the underlying issue to be addressed resulted in recommendations that would allow for the laying of criminal charges, in matters between husband and wife, on the one hand, and ameliorate the legal framework to allow for clinical responses to criminal charges, on the other. The 'violence' framework provided the necessary conceptual coordination to link justice and social service jurisdictions at the local level and to organize the relations of all parties to the problem, to the action to be taken, and to each other. The committee was convinced of the inadequacy of existing institutional responses to wife battering and the resulting recommendations had the potential to provide a range of mechanisms that would standardize measures and make them more equitable and effective.

The conceptual framework also operated as an 'ordering procedure' for assembling both the body of the text and the recommendations in the Ontario committee's report. An examination of the full range of all recommendations put before the committee in close to a hundred presentations, letters, and briefs, compared with the actual recommendations in the report itself, provides an example of how the position taken by women's groups was transformed and absorbed into the text. The sequence of the material placed the police and justice system sections and recommendations ahead of the discussion of transition houses and funding needs, thus reinforcing the importance of addressing the assault aspects of the issue. And indeed this conceptual ordering provided for the ordering of action. Women's groups, almost unanimously, had asked the government for control of the issue through proper funding and consultative procedures that would acknowledge and make use of their expertise and experience. This might involve, where necessary, back-up from police and the court system and support from social services and other government departments. The report, however, reversed this, proposing a major emphasis on the criminal justice system, allied with the social service system to sponsor legislation on funding, and coordinated with other departmental, professional, and community groups. Interval and transition houses (and the women's groups connected to them) were to become part of the back-up support and crisis service network, integrated into the social service system at the community level.

The framework also excluded many recommendations that addressed the needs for structural changes relating to the generally oppressive conditions of women's lives, particularly those of immigrant, native, francophone, and rural women. Requests for a range of social changes were transformed in the report into recommendations addressing the need for special services such as language training, interpreters, special facilities, transportation, and so on. These were designed to address the individual difficulties of particular populations of women in a social service context but did not involve making changes in the structures that create these difficulties in the first place. The need for such structural change was transformed into need for social services and absorbed into those institutions designed to manage social problems on behalf of the state.

RECLAIMING VIOLENCE

The Ontario report is the last link in the particular chain of documents that form my analysis of the conceptual ordering of official attention to the abuse of women by those men with whom they have intimate relationships. Each text has been mined, not, to cite Dorothy Smith (1990b: 4), 'as a specimen or sample, but as a means of access, a direct line to the relations it organizes.' The first United Way report from Vancouver shows that wife battering was not visible as a fully formed social problem for either local or national agencies and institutions. The social science concepts of 'violence' and 'family violence' suggested directions for professional intervention, while work done by shelters and other feminist services was marginalized as not addressing the needs of 'the family.' The second United Way report attempted to use the discursive framework of 'family violence' to draw attention to a social problem to be addressed by coordinated professional and institutional responses. It also, however, revealed the dimensions of the struggle between grass-roots feminist groups and professional service providers over the definition of wife battering and appropriate ways to address the issue.

In the third document a different phase of the process can be identified. Women involved in a consultation at the national level, under the auspices of the federal government, put forward their own theoretical construction of the issue as one aspect of 'male violence against women.' This paved the way for a concerted strategy between feminists and other interested parties to convince the federal government that wife battering was assault and must be treated as such under the criminal law. Document four shows that the federal standing committee accepted this approach, yet by maintaining 'wife assault' within the conceptual framework of 'family violence' attempted to bridge the justice and welfare systems. The division of powers between federal and provincial governments, however, meant that the report could only recommend limited federal action and make suggestions for a more fully coordinated response from the provinces. My brief review of document five, the Ontario report, shows an attempt to make the bridge between assault strategies that offered battered women protection under the law but could not address their need for financial support and welfare strategies that provided support but not safety. Organizing the issue as a criminal matter with clinical correlates provided the bridge by allowing for intervention into 'the family' that would provide treatment options for batterers, but this maintained the issue in the realm of individual rights under the law.

This essay is not a simply theoretical enterprise but an attempt to discover what documents can show us about how feminist work is caught up, through our participation in their formation, into processes of absorption and transformation. As we were increasingly drawn into relationship with the state, feminists' work was entered into the liberal democratic representational process. In order to be heard women served on committees and task forces; shaped funding proposals to fit governmental imperatives; and scrambled to prepare briefs for professional bodies and for various government hearings and conferences. Working in this way reorganized our work into a more professional mode as pressure and lobbying groups or as service providers. We had to break the arena of struggle into various issues or components that would fit with state funding and administrative priorities. The wife assault strategy came in part from the combining of feminist and state interests in the management of violence through the justice system.

Throughout the process described here, feminists struggled to break the connectives of theory and to maintain the connectives of our experience of women's everyday lives. We attempted to do this by setting wife battering in the context of male violence towards women. But 'violence' was already more than a description of acts of cruelty and coercion. It had been taken up into a range of discourses to form the basis for theories and courses of action that are part of the way in which power is exercised and regulated in the process of ruling. We are caught up in this ruling discourse when we confront the state with demands that violence be controlled. The law has not proved to be a deterrent to men determined to attack women or an adequate champion of women's right to protection. Furthermore most men actually convicted of wife assault have proved to come from the working class or they are of indigenous or racial minorities. Women from these groups are often placed in invidious positions when criminal action is taken against their men. Treatment programs have yet to prove their effectiveness and still reach a tiny minority of men who beat their female partners. On the broader level, linking 'male violence' and 'family violence' by defining wife battering as assault, while it did expand the circle of knowledge created by the 'family violence' framework to allow wife battering visibility as an issue in its own right, shifted the attention of activists and government alike to the global and undifferentiated problem of 'violence' and 'its' management and away from the structural features of women's subordination with all its interrelated facets of gender, race, and class. Generalizing conceptual practices obscure not only the diverse lived experience of women but also the relations of ruling that such practices constitute. Women who are beaten become a welfare problem; their batterers a problem for the criminal justice system.

The dilemma being raised, as the struggle continues on the terrain established by the conceptual practices identified here, is that of maintaining the grounding of feminism in the everyday features of women's subordination, while finding ways to stop the abuse that we have identified as 'violence' in our lives, on our own terms. This study attempts to move our efforts forward by uncovering for our understanding a feature of how our work comes to be organized against us by the textually mediated processes in which we engage.

NOTES

1 Parts of this essay have appeared in other versions in *Family Violence and the Women's Movement: The Conceptual Politics of Struggle* (Toronto 1990a) and *Studies in Political Economy* 33 (1990b) and are reproduced here with permission. The data from which I drew my account and analysis were provided by specific events, some of which I took part in, and by a number of documents such as reports, transcripts, and academic texts that were a feature of the process of generalization and absorption. A more detailed account of some of the events described here can be found in Chapters 3, 7, and 11 of *Family Violence and the Women's Movement*. I am grateful to Sue Findlay, Alison Griffith, Adele Mueller, George Smith, and Susan Turner for their comments on various drafts of this essay, and to Marie Campbell and Ann Manicom for the intense and helpful editorial attention paid to producing this version.

2 Here I invoke the notion of the 'relations of ruling' as identified by Dorothy Smith. These relations are exercised in social forms: in the talk, reporting, and accounting procedures, documents, and categories of professional and bureaucratic practices; in the ideological forms in which objective knowledge is constructed by intellectuals; and ultimately when necessary by the use of force to maintain power. See Dorothy Smith, *The Conceptual Practices of Power* (1990a).

3 For a more detailed description of this series of events see J. Barnsley, *Feminist*

Action, Institutional Reaction: Responses to Wife Assault (1985) and G.A. Walker, 'Doing It the United Way' (1981).

4 Smith uses the term 'ideology' to analyse this way of constructing knowledge from a ruling perspective. She develops this use of the term from the works of Marx and Engels, particularly from *The German Ideology* (1970). See also Chapters 2 and 6 in Smith's *The Conceptual Practices of Power* (1990a) for an elaboration of the method

5 The first crucial study in this regard was M.A. Strauss, R. Gelles, and S.K. Steinmetz, *Behind Closed Doors: Violence in the American Family* (1974). See also R.L. Neely and G. Robinson-Simpson, 'The Truth about Domestic Violence: A Falsely Framed Issue,' (1987) for an essay that refutes every feminist tenet and uses the sociological studies on 'family violence' to argue that women are more violent than men, despite the many critiques of these data.

6 The Canadian Advisory Council on the Status of Women is a body appointed by the federal government in 1973 in the wake of the Royal Commission on the Status of Women, with a mandate of public education and advice to the government on policy issues pertaining to women.

7 The consultation followed closely upon the publication by the council of the first Canadian book on the topic, L. MacLeod's *Wife Battering in Canada* (1980b) and was the occasion used to release the National Film Board's 1979 production of 'Loved, Honoured and Bruised.'

The Textual Practices of Sexual Rule: Sexual Policing and Gay Men

GARY KINSMAN

To construct the standpoint taken up in this essay I begin with a few experiences by gay men of official discourse and regulation in Canadian history that will be returned to later. When Axel Otto Olson, a gay man, gave testimony to the Royal Commission on Criminal Sexual Psychopaths in 1956 about his experiences of blackmail and police harassment, he was consistently interrupted and reference to his testimony was left out of the commission's report. In 1966 Everett Klippert, who had been convicted of a series of charges of 'gross indecency' for sex with other males, was 'stunned' when he received a notice for a hearing to have him declared a 'dangerous sexual offender.' A series of police and legal relations were constructed outside his immediate world as his life was entered into a course of action that would lead to indefinite detention. Doug Sanders, a gay rights activist in the 1960s, described the 1969 Canadian reform which partially decriminalized some homosexual acts in private as 'an issue [that] had been stolen from us.' Law reform was addressed solely within the confines of the public/private distinction and there was no increased acceptance of homosexuality after the reform. This essay is written to be on the side of Olson, Klippert, and Sanders. As a gay activist in the 1990s I am producing knowledge to account for their experiences in the past and for our experiences of oppressive regulation in the present.

INTRODUCTION

Ruling social frames of consciousness regarding homosexuality as a 'social danger' or as 'sickness' are not simply backward ideas in some people's heads. Rather, these are actively organized within the worlds of official discourse and ruling relations. Our contemporary experiences assume and rest upon specific social and historical processes, mediated through the use of texts. These relations continue to constrain our activities in the present and to stand over and against our lives. The past lives on in the present, as resilient conceptual frameworks continue to be actively used in organizing sexual rule.

This essay[1] traces the resiliency of textual strategies held in place through the criminal code: while the discourse and regulatory practices shift, the criminalization and medicalization remain. The essay shows that in the production of regulatory texts, the standpoint is that of those who rule: the everyday/everynight experiences of gay men are transformed in the production of the regulatory practices. The essay also sketches how regulatory practices serve to police the lives of gay men, catching them up in courses of action in differing regulatory sites, including psychiatry and the criminal system.

This essay outlines how certain official texts from the 1950s and 1960s have participated in organizing sexual regulation. During this period two contending strategies of sexual regulation were struggled over as part of the transformation of a range of social relations in postwar capitalism, including changes in class, gender, sexual, and state relations. The first strategy is what I call the extending criminalization of homosexuality as social danger frame, which includes the criminal sexual psychopath (CSP) and dangerous sexual offender (DSO) sections of the Criminal Code. Put in place in the 1950s, this frame shifted over the next two decades to a second strategy, the public/private partial decriminalization frame of regulation identified with the 1957 British Wolfenden Report. The shift in focus included active contention and the subordination of one strategy to the other in the construction of hegemony.

DISJUNCTURES AND STANDPOINTS

There is a continuing and shifting disjuncture[2] between the experiences of men engaging in sexual activities with each other and the organization of such regulatory practices as the 'criminal-justice system.' This rupture between the bodily eroticism of gay men and the social organization of heterosexual hegemony[3] is organized through social relations of oppression rooted in sexual policing and regulation.[4] From the standpoints of gay men, however, it is not our sexual activities that are the problem; instead, the problem is sexual policing and oppressive sexual regulation.

Sexual regulation occurs within a zone of broader ruling relations. The focus in this essay is on the conceptual organization of this sexual regulation especially as it mandates sexual policing of gay men. The essay identifies the relations established historically between gay men, police, courts, and the Criminal Code – including linkages of psychiatric discourse with legal procedures.

Inspired by Dorothy Smith's work on a sociology *for* women and the social organization of knowledge, this essay develops a historical sociology *for* gay men. A sociology starting from the experiences of gay men and exploring how these are organized through extended social relations over time brings into view the textually mediated character of sexual rule. This historical sociology explores how ruling relations organize problems in the everyday/everynight worlds of gay men.[5]

Textual Practices and Ruling

As many other essays in this volume show, regulatory work is textually mediated. Texts are actively used within ruling relations to organize and coordinate social relations.[6] Textual mediation is a crucial aspect of the contemporary social organization of ruling. Police work, as one form of regulatory work, is textually mediated through the conceptual organization of the Criminal Code.

Critical analysis of official texts is crucial to explicating how sexual regulation is conceptually held together. Sexual regulation (like other social regulations) is ruled by concepts (see D.E. Smith 1990a and Walker 1990a and this volume). For example, the concepts of 'dangerous sexual offender,' 'gross indecency,' and 'acts of indecency' have ruled the experiences of gay men charged under such designations and the procedures thus mandated. These 'offences' are terms of sexual rule.

Two terms, *cogency* and *resiliency*, are used in this essay's exploration of textual practices and social regulation and how sexual rule changes over time. 'Cogency' (for those who rule) pertains to how effectively conceptual frameworks coordinate ruling relations to manage and deal with social changes (see D. Smith and· G. Smith 1990). 'Resiliency' refers to the continuing cogency of conceptual frameworks, where textual practices developed in previous historical periods continue to be activated as attempted regulatory strategies.

Since textual practices help to shape our 'historical present,'[7] analysis of textual practices is vital for historical sociology. Conceptual regulatory strategies formed in the past continue to be remobilized in the coordination of social relations through the activation of their perspectives and the social relations they carry with them. Even if they are technically off the books, regulatory strategies can still be very actively used to shape our present, for example, by those arguing that homosexuality is a social danger.

Given their capacity to hold relations in place across space and time, texts can be used by actors within ruling relations to manage social changes and struggles. In this essay we see how the mobilization of textual strategies can both hold in place and also shift the oppression gay men face.

A Historical Sociology for Gay Men

Through the following historical sociological sketch I stress the importance of examining how textual strategies gain official cogency, superseding earlier regulatory strategies which still remain available as 'active texts' to be used against gays. For example, in the context of the AIDS crisis and the continuing conceptualization of gays as 'child sex abusers,' one can see the social resiliency over time of conceptualizations of gays as 'sick' or dangerous. Investigations of these textual practices allow us to trace this continuing social resiliency. This allows us to grasp how such conceptualizations can continue to be re-mobilized against us. If we can understand where these dangerous conceptualizations arise and how they maintain their resiliency we are in a much better position to transform them.

HOMOSEXUALITY AS A CRIMINAL SOCIAL DANGER

As part of an early 1950s conservative political project related to the Cold war, 'national security,' McCarthyism, and the reconstruction of patriarchal heterosexual hegemonies following the 'disruptions' of the war mobilization, homosexuality was constructed as a national, social, and sexual danger in Canada (see Kinsman 1987, 1989, 1993b; and for the experience in the United States, D'Emilio 1983, 1992). Homosexuals were defined as 'national security risks.' There were purges in the military and civil service as well as government and RCMP investigations (Kinsman 1995). In 1952, legislation excluding homosexuals from immigrating into Canada was passed.[8] These purges and policies of exclusion were mandated by regulations and laws.

In examining how the conceptual frame of homosexuality as criminal social danger was put in place in Canada, I want to focus on two textually mediated procedures: the conceptualizing of the homosexual as criminal sexual psychopath (CSP) through legislation initially passed in 1948 and extended to cover homosexual acts in 1953; and the resiliency of this framework as it is reworked into dangerous sexual offender (DSO) in the

McRuer Royal Commission on the Criminal Law relating to Criminal Sexual Psychopaths, established in 1954. In both instances we can see the construction (and reconstruction) of linkages between psychological discourse and criminal discourse, which put in place the connective and coordinating work of different state agents and professionals through the CSP/DSO section of the Criminal Code. The psychological discourse on homosexuality as illness becomes articulated to criminal procedures.

Both the legislation and the royal commission were, of course, built on earlier developments. A particular psychological discourse was already in place. During the Second World War homosexuals could be classified in Canadian military organization as 'psychopaths' with 'abnormal sexuality' and on this basis purged from the military. Psychological sciences, incorporating an earlier history from forensic psychiatry and its hostility to homosexuality, were articulated to practices within the military. 'Psychopath' became an active coordinating concept, targeting a kind of dangerous or uncontrollable personality which could include homosexuals (Freedman 1987; Kinsman 1989). This helped to create some of the basis for the cogency of criminal sexual psychopath legislation in postwar Canada.

In this postwar context, earlier discourses associating homosexuals with national degeneration and danger to young people were mobilized and transformed, linking criminal and psychological discourses and practices in a particular way. Notions of homosexual mental illness were successfully articulated to the criminalization strategy: homosexuals became coded as 'criminal sexual psychopaths.'

Criminal Sexual Psychopath Legislation

Criminal sexual psychopath (CSP) legislation was enacted in Canada in 1948 (Criminal Code 1988). A criminal sexual psychopath was defined as a 'person who by a course of misconduct has evidenced a lack of power to control his sexual impulses and who as a result is likely to attack or otherwise inflict injury, loss, pain or other evil on any person' (Royal Commission on Criminal Law Relating to Criminal Sexual Psychopaths 1958: 15). The legislation mandated a course of action linking several state and professional sites. The course of action required first a police arrest and conviction on certain specified 'triggering' sex offences. Triggering offences were sexual offences that could be committed in the public, extra-familial realm, not the private realm. In 1953, as part of defining the *public ream* of 'sexual danger,' all homosexual-related offences (including 'buggery' and 'gross indecency')[9] became triggering offences. Following conviction on these offences a sentencing procedure to declare a person a CSP could then be initiated with the approval of the attorney general. Sentencing as a CSP amounted to indefinite detention. Homosexual sexual activity discovered by the police and resulting in conviction on one of the triggering offences could make one liable to a CSP procedure. As part of this procedure, the provision of psychiatric evidence was crucial. In establishing whether the person fit the CSP definition, this procedure was organized at two different 'levels' of inscription: first, through the 'triggering' sex offence of the Criminal Code, and second, through the definitions of CSP (and later, dangerous sexual offender) at sentencing.

The CSP process of 'inscription' is therefore more complex than just transforming behaviour into sexual offence categories. The procedure is coordinated and organized at a number of sites through concepts and definitions produced in differing discourses. The CSP process laid out a course of action with each 'stage' intending the next and the next accomplishing the previous. There is vital connective and coordinating work of the activities of different state agents and professionals through the CSP/DSO section of the Criminal Code. Psychological and criminal discourses and practices intersect to regulate the lives of gay men.

The cogency of the frame of criminalizing homosexuality for the work of ruling and the resiliency of the frame over time is visible in the work of the McRuer Royal Commission.

McRuer Commission

Royal commissions are textually mediated processes. No matter what their topic, royal commissions coordinate a series of ruling relations through their work processes.[10]

Motivated by a 'public' concern that not enough men were being sentenced under the CSP provision, the Royal Commission on the Criminal Law Relating to Criminal Sexual Psychopaths (McRuer Commission) was established in 1954 (Report 1958: 32; Girard 1985: 86). Through this commission the coordination of ruling relations included police work, psychiatric knowledge, the media organization of 'public opinion,' and Canadian legal history.

The terms of reference given to a royal commission are central in guiding how it accomplishes its work. The mandate given to the McRuer Commission did not question the 'triggering' sex offences in the Criminal Code or the indefinite detention provision. The commission was not asked to study sexuality or sexual danger as it was experienced in all its diversities. For instance, incest was not a triggering offence, and rape within a marriage was not even in the Criminal Code. Rather, its mandate focused on sexual danger in the 'public' realm to which the 'triggering' offences referred. The work and terms of reference of the commission thus presupposed the basic features of the CSP section of the Criminal Code and related triggering offences; it presupposed the criminalization of homosexual activities.

While the McRuer Commission did rework some of the problems and contradictions in the CSP procedure, it nonetheless held constant the criminalization of homosexuality. Basically, the commission took up the standpoint of the police against gay men. In the commission's report, homosexuality is associated with danger to young people, and there is a reliance on police testimony, especially that of Chief John Chisholm of the Toronto Police Force, to define its position against homosexuality.[11] Taking the standpoint of the police excluded the experiences of men such as Axel Otto Olson, who told the commission in a private session in 1956 that 'I don't believe the sex deviate, so to speak, is the main problem. I think the most serious problem is the problem of the blackmailers' (Canada 1956: 143).[12] Justice McRuer responded that blackmail was 'not one of the things within the compass of our terms of reference' (ibid.: 146). Invoking its terms of reference in this way enabled the commission to exclude experiences of gay men, in this instance to rule that blackmail and violence against gays was not relevant to its task. This analysis makes it clear whose standpoint matters here.

The conceptual framework of the commission's report was defined by an argument for changing the definition from CSP to dangerous sexual offender (DSO). It was an argument for strengthening the cogency of the concept for the work of ruling. It argued that DSO could be less psychiatrically defined, and therefore would be an easier category under which people could be sentenced. At the same time psychiatric testimony was still to be crucial in this reformed procedure, to establish whether the person being sentenced fit the definition. When the recommendations of the commission were implemented by Parliament in 1961, a further change was made to ease successful sentencing under this procedure. A clause was added as an alternative definition or 'test': the phrase 'or who is likely to commit a further sexual offence' (Girard 1985: 94–5). The strategy of criminalizing homosexuality, while shifting in a limited way from CSP to DSO, was fundamentally held in place.

Examining the experiences of Everett Klippert clarifies how the DSO section worked. Klippert, arrested on a series of 'gross indecency' charges in 1965, was 'stunned' when he was informed following his conviction on these offences that a DSO procedure had been initiated against him.[13] His life was entered into a web of legal and psychiatric relations he had no familiarity with.

The first moment of transformation in Klippert's experiences was from the consensual sexual activities he engaged in into 'gross indecency.' 'Gross indecency' is a term located not in the everyday/everynight worlds of men who have sex with men but in the Criminal Code and sexual policing. When Klippert was convicted the Crown proceeded with an application under the DSO procedure. This allowed Klippert to be entered into a sentencing process that determined him to be a DSO, a conceptualization produced through the Criminal Code. All of the moments of this course of action are textual practices mediated through the Criminal Code.

The two psychiatrists' testimony, especially their statements that he would continue to engage in homosexual activities, allowed Klippert to be entered into this indefinite detention procedure by the judge at sentencing. Klippert was 'captured' by the 'likely to commit a further sexual offence' and also by the 'failure to control' his sexual impulses part of the DSO definition. This established a history of homosexual sex *per se* as itself a social threat.

The frameworks of criminal sexual psychopath, and then dangerous sexual offender, and the textually mediated courses of action they were implicated in, were crucial in extending the criminalization of homosexuality. But at the same time a contradictory course of action, the public/private reform strategy, was also being developed, first in Britain and then in Canada. This reform strategy became a limited resource for homophile activists while it nonetheless continued to maintain heterosexual hegemony.

PUBLIC/PRIVATE REGULATION

In the late 1950s in Britain and in the 1960s in Canada, a new strategy of sexual and moral regulation focused on a public/private distinction as distinct from the criminalization of all sex between men. The basis for this liberal reform strategy developed in the 1950s. Internal professional struggles against the usefulness of 'psychopath' in the psychological professions emerged. More 'liberal' tendencies in sexological research, including the Kinsey reports, and discussions in some church groups, began to oppose total criminalization of homosexuality.

Transformations of class, familial, and sexual relations within corporate capitalism began to lessen dependence on 'traditional' heterosexual familial relations. This created new contexts for the development of sexual experiences and relationships and for the limited expansion of gay networks which in turn undermined the effectiveness of previous regulatory strategies. In this context, the cogency of the CSP and DSO (their efficiency as concepts for the work of ruling) began to be undermined. The criminalization of homosexuality strategy began to lose its cogency and was seen by some to be generating growing problems.

The cogency of a reformulated strategy for regulating gay sexuality in Canada, the partial decriminalization of homosexuality perspective, was socially organized through processes located both within ruling relations and within gay community formation. The resulting partial decriminalization (through what I call here the Wolfenden perspective, which conceptualized the public/private regulatory strategy in Britain in the late 1950s) enabled the cogency of the regulatory work to be reasserted. In Canada, the official cogency of the new conceptual framework was fully established with the passage of the 1969 Criminal Code reform which implemented the Wolfenden strategy for regulating homosexuality in the Canadian state.

This sketch provides an overview of events and the general social context. To examine the details of the work of producing this new regulatory strategy, I now turn my attention to exploring how the public/private Wolfenden strategy came to have an active impact in Canadian state formation. How was its cogency organized?

The Wolfenden Approach

The partial decriminalization reform approach crystallized in the British Wolfenden Report (1957). The Wolfenden Committee was set up in 1954 in the broader context of postwar social change and in the particular context of British 'spy' scandals and 'security' scares involving men identified as homosexuals and concerns over London street prostitutes. The committee dealt with both prostitution and homosexuality, and aside from bottom-line assumptions of homosexuality and prostitution as social problems, the terms of reference were more open than those of the McRuer Commission in Canada.

While embodying the general standpoints of heterosexual hegemony and sexual rule, the Wolfenden Committee was given a wide latitude to work over and shift these regulations. This provided space for the work of reforming while simultaneously maintaining ruling strategies. The Wolfenden Committee developed a perspective which could conceptually regulate both homosexuality and prostitution, for reforming the law as it relates to sexual regulation in a more general sense to handle social and sexual changes within postwar capitalism.

The articulation of a conceptual framework for regulating both homosexuality and prostitution required a crucial conceptual distinction between 'private' and 'public' sex. For the Wolfenden Committee, the public/private distinction was fixed and defined territorially. It was not based in what people do in their everyday/everynight worlds to construct privacy and intimacy (G. Smith 1983). Rather, the committee argued that the purpose of the criminal law regarding sexuality and morality was to preserve and defend 'public decency' (Wolfenden Committee 1957). This public/private conceptual frame allowed for the holding together of the report's more restrictive proposals regarding 'public' prostitution and its more 'liberal' proposals regarding 'private' adult homosexuality.[14]

Nonetheless, as pointed out above, there is a social resiliency over time of conceptualizations of gays as 'sick' or as dangerous. The resiliency of this notion can be seen in how the Wolfenden perspective linked the public/private distinction to an adult/youth distinction in the regulation of sex between males. The report embodied particular fears over male adolescents being led astray by homosexual advances. Male homosexuals, it was suggested, presented a higher 'social danger' to youths. The age of consent for 'private' acts of 'buggery' and 'gross indecency' was therefore set at twenty-one.[15] One of the implications of this regulatory strategy was to transfer jurisdiction over 'private' adult homosexual activity from the criminal law to the professions of medicine, therapy, psychology, sociology, and social work.

This strategy was thus both a relaxation of and an intensification of oppressive sexual regulation. The concepts the Wolfenden strategy provided were used to write a certain coherence into sexual and social regulation in many different sites and terrains. The abstract character of the public/private conceptualization meant that this classification could be taken up more easily in extra-local strategies of regulation establishing a particular form of cogency. This approach was taken up in many different countries and contexts.

In North America readings of the Wolfenden Report were articulated with the sickness frame of homosexuality. It was argued that if homosexuals were 'sick' or 'ill' they should be in a doctor's or therapist's care and homosexuality should not be addressed as simply a criminal matter. This partial decriminalization strategy re-articulated the medicalization of homosexuality away from the criminalization strategy towards this new approach. The resiliency of conceptualizations of homosexuality as illness was maintained while its deployment was shifted.

Law Reform in the Canadian Context

The Wolfenden approach had an important impact in Canada because it argued for reform of the same offences (buggery, gross indecency) that existed in the Canadian Criminal Code. Social changes and struggles were also making reform measures more cogent in the Canadian context.

Homophile reformers were able to use this report and the conceptual frame it developed in Britain (where the Homosexual Law Reform Society was formed in 1958) and later in Canada. The approach helped to open up a limited social space for homophile lobbying, educational efforts, and activism. The expansion of gay networks and cultures during the 1960s in Canada created the basis for more extended homophile activism, including the formation in 1964 of the Association for Social Knowledge (ASK) in Vancouver, involved in popular education and law reform lobbying. There was pressure for change from the expansion and growing visibility of gay networks.

By the mid-1960s the Wolfenden perspective began to be seen as a cogent way of organizing and responding to these and other pressures for social reform in Canada and other countries. The Wolfenden approach became a valuable conceptualization for managing, reorganizing, and handling these social changes through allowing for a limited 'private' adult space for homosexuals while intensifying policing in 'public.' The Wolfenden strategy was actively used in organizing and reorganizing social regulations. It was used to provide frames to inform media coverage and church and professional discussions, and it came to influence lawyers and parliamentary lawmakers.

Earlier, I described the case of Everett Klippert. Sentenced to indefinite detention under the DSO provisions in 1965, he appealed the decision. In the 1967 appeal a Supreme Court of Canada majority decided that Klippert had been sentenced properly. This appeal decision, and the publicity surrounding it, played a crucial part in facilitating law reform in Canada in the context of broader social changes and the growing organization of cogency for the Wolfenden strategy. The decision of the Supreme Court in this case was a literal reading of the section that found that Klippert was a DSO because he was likely to continue to engage in homosexual activities. There was a direct clash in this legal decision between the extended criminalization strategy (which was then the law in Canada) and the public/private reform strategy. This textually mediated clash of different strategies was organized through different conceptual frames and based in different texts and legal provisions. Ten years after the release of the Wolfenden Report and just after the British government had adopted its recommendations on homosexuality in England and Wales, the Supreme Court of Canada, in the Klippert appeal decision, affirmed a judgment which virtually deemed all sexually active homosexuals as dangerous sexual offenders subject to indefinite detention.

But it was a clash that ultimately facilitated the reformulation of sexual regulatory strategies, since Wolfenden-based textual practices were key in the 1969 Criminal Code reform debates in the Canadian Parliament. The conceptual frame and often the specific remarks used in the Canadian debates by the 'reform' camp were lifted from the Wolfenden text. A key part of this debate was the successful articulation of 'sickness' to the public/private regulatory strategy by reform supporters. For example, MP Steven Otto argued that 'members of the medical profession tell us that homosexuality is a sickness ... These people should not be treated as criminals' (Hansard 1969: 7666).

As in the formulation of previous regulatory strategies, the real experiences of gay men were transformed into terms that reflected the standpoint of the state. Doug Sanders's response to Trudeau's remark about the state having no place in the bedrooms of the nation is useful to remember. He stated that Trudeau's remark 'takes the gay issue and describes it in non-homosexual terms ... And so homosexuals are no more real after the reform than before ... I felt that an issue had been stolen from us'.[16] As the local concerns of gay reformers for more popular acceptance and education regarding homosexuality entered into the official discourses of ruling relations, their concerns were transformed. In official discourse lesbian and gay concerns and our sexualities became questions of whether it was sex in public or in private and whether it was with adults or youths. Certainly it was not a matter of establishing the social right to be lesbian/gay. Thus, heterosexual hegemony was not so much challenged as shifted in form. The 'sickness' model was firmly established as the hegemonic explanation of homosexuality.

Again, however, as in the earlier regulatory strategies, the contradictions of the public/private strategy would soon become visible. By the 1970s this new conceptual framework began to become less cogent in ruling circles, through challenges from subordinated groups. Lesbians and gays used the 1969 Criminal Code reform as an opening to seize more visible social space for networks and community formation. In response to this 'public' visibility there was an intensification of sexual policing against gays such as in the bath raids across the country in the late 1970s and early 1980s.

Thus, in examining the Wolfenden perspective over time, three moments can be seen. First, the loss of cogency for the earlier framework and the organization of support for this reform strategy; then the full establishment of the new partial decriminalization strategy in the 1969 Criminal Code reform; and finally the expansion of gay community formation and the intensification of gay rights activism, leading to a loss of cogency of the strategy for its work of ruling.

RELEVANCE FOR HISTORICAL SOCIOLOGY

In tracing the cogency and resiliency of strategies for regulating sexuality, we can see how texts of sexual rule have been activated to hold in place different strategies of regulation over decades. Those actors located in ruling institutions have attempted to grapple with and manage historical social changes through reformulating regulatory strategies. At the same time those outside the ruling institutions, through gay community formation and activism, have reshaped the grounds for regulatory strategies. Textual practices help to create different conditions of struggle for social movements. The McRuer Commission Report created virtually no space for homophile reformers, especially as it actively silenced gay concerns. The Wolfenden strategy, along with the growth of gay and lesbian networks, opened up some spaces that homophile reformers could use to their advantage.

This study makes visible the difference in active capacities and resiliency between different textual strategies. The more wide-open terms of reference and the innovative conceptual framework developed in the Wolfenden Report produced a greater long-term cogency for this approach.

The approach to texts in this essay has implications for social and political strategies of resistance and transformation. We need to engage much more clearly in the contestation of the textually mediated regulations we face. Knowing how sexual regulation has been put in place is not this transformation itself. We need to transform not only how we investigate the social organization of sexual regulation but sexual rule itself. As Marx wrote 'The philosophers [and I would add others here] have only interpreted the world, in various ways; the point, however, is to change it' (Marx 1975: 30). If sexual regulation is put together in social activities it can be socially transformed. An important part of this is the transformation of the conceptual practices of sexual rule.

TOWARDS SOCIAL TRANSFORMATION

The critical historical sociology sketched here explicates the roots of the current contradictions of sexual regulation in Canada, showing where present strategies of sexual regulation have come from and the terrains upon which current struggles are taking place. Regulatory strategies put in place in the past still shape our present; there is, for example, a continuing resiliency of the framing of gays as 'child sex abusers' such as I encountered in examining the social organization of the Newfoundland Royal Commission Inquiry (1989–91) into the 'cover-up' of the physical and sexual assaults that took place at Mount Cashel Orphanage in the mid-1970s. I have explored how this commission and associated mass media coverage has again produced homosexuals as 'child sexual abusers' in part through the reactivation of discourses formed in the 1950s and through the legacy of police criminalization of homosexuality (see Kinsman 1992a, 1993a).

There is also the 'remedicalization' of homosexuality in the association of homosexuality with AIDS in dominant discourses. Homosexuality continues to be defined in many circles as sickness and contagion. Notions of 'sickness' were partially dislodged through gay and lesbian activism in the 1970s. However, at the same time, the character of the 1969 reform and the ways in which the law reform was interpreted buttressed notions of homosexual sickness. Discourses of homosexual illness and danger continue to be very much alive in the social organization of the AIDS crisis.[17]

Our sexualities can still be labelled 'indecent' and criminal. This continues to be organized through the Criminal Code, despite the abolition of 'gross indecency' as an offence in Canada in 1988.[18] There is a continuing resiliency of 'indecency,' 'obscenity,' and criminality applied to gays. There remains a need to dislodge conceptualizations of criminality, sickness, and danger which are associated with our sexualities and the courses of action these concepts mandate.

NOTES

1 This essay had its beginning in research done for my doctoral dissertation (Kinsman 1989). I again thank my thesis supervisor Dorothy E. Smith, and Ruth Pierson and Philip Corrigan. Special thanks also go to Gillian Walker, George Smith, Adele Mueller, Roxana Ng, Ann Manicom, Marie Campbell, and Patrick Barnholden for their comments and assistance on this essay. Responsibilities for mistakes or errors of interpretation are, of course, mine alone. For more detailed analysis, see Kinsman 1987, 1989, and 1991a.
2 On the social organization of disjuncture see Dorothy E. Smith *The Conceptual Practices of Power* (1990a) and *The Everyday World as Problematic* (1987a: 49–60).
3 Heterosexual hegemony is my attempt to name the generalized social tension

between the lived experiences of lesbians and gay men and ruling relations that organize heterosexuality as 'normal,' 'natural,' and 'healthy,' while at the same time constructing same-gender eroticism as 'unnatural,' 'deviant,' 'sick,' or 'dangerous'; see Kinsman (1987).

4 See a number of articles written by George Smith (1983 and 1988: 163–83); see also his essay in this volume.

5 I will not address lesbian experience in any direct way here since it is socially organized and regulated in different ways. See Didi Khayatt (1992 and in this volume).

6 See D.E. Smith, 'The Active Text: A Textual Analysis of the Social Relations of Public Textual Discourse,' in her book *Texts, Facts, and Femininity* (1990b: 120–58).

7 The inspiration for the use of 'historical present' comes from Jeffrey Weeks (1985). My use of 'historical present' differs, however, from that of Weeks in that my usage is not that of a history of relatively ungrounded discourses of sexuality.

8 The exclusion of homosexuals from immigration was in place in Canada until 1977 in a very active legacy of the 1950s. It was repealed as part of a broader package of immigration reforms following gay liberation agitation for its removal.

9 On the history of 'gross indecency,' see Kinsman (1987: 92–4, and 1989: 154–5).

10 In English/British and Canadian history the royal commission can be seen as a way for the government to manage and repair official discourse and practice. The McRuer Commission was an attempt to 'repair' ruling relations and deal with the problems that had become apparent in the operation of the CSP section from a standpoint within ruling relations. On royal commissions, see Kinsman (1989: 195–6, and 1992a).

11 See the *Report of the Royal Commission on the Criminal Law Relating to Criminal Sexual Psychopaths* (Ottawa: Queen's Printer 1958: 27). Jim Egan, Canada's first gay activist, did a wonderful deconstruction of Chisholm's testimony after he read the commission report. See Egan (1959).

12 Olson's submission to the Private Sessions of the Royal Commission was on 13 February 1956 at Osgoode Hall.

13 Doug Sanders interviewed Everett Klippert in the Prince Albert Penitentiary. See two accounts of the interview in Sanders (1968a and 1968b).

14 The recommendations of the report carried rather different implications for female prostitutes and male homosexuals. Regarding female prostitutes this included the social construction of gender relations confining women to the 'private' realm and how 'streetwalkers' were defined as the main problem because they offended 'public' decency.

15 This was changed in Canada only in 1988; the age of consent for male homosexual acts was lowered to eighteen years in Britain only in 1994, according to Smith and Richardson (1994).

16 Gary Kinsman interview with Doug Sanders, 14 June 1986, Vancouver.

17 See two of my articles on AIDS: 'Their Silence, Our Deaths' (Kinsman 1991b) and 'Managing AIDS Organizing' (Kinsman 1992b: 215–31).

18 The offence of 'gross indecency' was abolished on 1 January 1988, although it still can be used for offences prior to this date. The use of 'gross indecency' charges against some of the priests and Brothers in Newfoundland helped to construct the 'homosexual' character of this problem. See my article, 'Restoring Confidence in the Criminal Justice System' (Kinsman 1992a).

Beginning in the Standpoint of Women: An Investigation of the Gap between *Cholas* and 'Women in Peru'

ADELE MUELLER

This essay[1] demonstrates the distinctive shift in feminist sociology from a focus on women as a research topic to a methodology which begins where women are socially located and explores how their worlds come into being for them. The standpoint of women centres an inquiry in the lives of actual women and moves out from there to the forces which shape women's experiences and consciousness, yet spiral beyond any one moment in their lives. As developed by Dorothy Smith, it is a powerful methodological tool with which to investigate the extended relations of gender, race, and class as they converge in ways which women experience as local and specific. The standpoint of women breaks through the formidable discursive barrier which separates the practices of sociology from the everyday world in which people make, and make sense of, their lives. This use of 'standpoint of women' as a methodological tool is distinguished from its more common treatment as an abstracted epistemological point (Harding 1991) which is taken as the basis for a restrictive focus on women or conflated with a feminist perspective.

The subordination of the everyday world to ruling relations comprises the central problematic in this feminist sociology. But this is not to posit a 'real' world prior to a socially constituted one, nor to claim that women occupy a distinctive sphere. The standpoint of women is the essential pivot in a methodology to explicate the everyday world problematic. It positions the researcher at precisely that moment at which people's ordinary, everyday lives are touched by the discourses and disciplines of domination which powerfully shape (but do not determine) them. The research project begins in the standpoint of actual women, in their particular interests, from their specific perspectives; its purpose is to display the ruling relations which order contemporary society as they take significance in those women's lives; its goal is to contribute to the store of knowledge in the struggles for liberation in the women's movement.

This methodological pivot is illustrated with a group of women who are subordinated to the powerful international Development[2] regime,[3] which participates in bringing the poorest nation-states into economic and political domination by the richest. This beginning place is particularly significant, for 'it is from the perspective of the most oppressed – i.e., women who suffer on account of class, race, and nationality – that we can most clearly grasp the nature of the links of the chain of oppression and explore the kinds of actions that we must now take' (Sen and Grown 1987: 20). The Development regime is the network comprising state and international agencies, state regulated 'non-governmental organizations,' universities and academic disciplines such as sociology, agricultural economics and other technical fields, independent consulting enterprises, and the work practices of professionals, scholars, bureaucrats, technicians, and experts of all kinds. This essay is addressed to professionals who work in this network. These issues are relevant in other social policy fields, as shown in a number of essays in this volume. What follows presents the shift from research about women to research which explicates ruling relations.

In the town of Juliaca in the Andean highlands of Peru, cholas, wearing the many layers of full skirts, hair braids, and distinctive hats which are associated with indigenous women, set up their stalls piled high with hand-knitted alpaca wool sweaters around the perimeter of the town square next to the train station. All day the women are there. They take care of small children and talk with each other, but most of all they knit more sweaters to sell to the foreign tourists who arrive on the train.

One way a sociologist might bring these women's lives into her research is to live for some period in the community, learn Quechua so that she might talk with them, learn their daily round of work, listen to them talk about their problems, their interests, and so on. This is the time-honoured participant observation methodology on which anthropology is based. The monograph the sociologist writes might include extensive quotations from the women, and so she might title it 'Cholas Speak for Themselves.' If she were a Development expert, she might deploy the method of Rapid Rural Appraisal, which is much what the name suggests, to document the suitability of the cholas to be clients in a Development agency project. In either methodology, the researcher's task is to make cholas her research topic and to write accounts which will represent them to other scholars and professionals in the First World who will read the reports and thereby know about cholas in Peru.

These are ways of doing research that do focus on women to produce knowledge about women, but then continue along the accustomed route through university and state networks which knit together knowledge and power. These methods take the social organization of knowledge in the Development regime as it is given, its intentions pre-eminent and unexplored. This knowledge circuit zips through academic, professional, and bureaucratic hands, transforming the subjectivities of the women in the square into the objectified format which is deemed knowledge. The knowers are made the known and are thereby entered into the Development regime, which becomes the principal actor within the field of action it creates. The standpoint of women, however, works differently; it turns the Women in Development problematic on its head. Instead of making women its topic, the Development regime itself is brought under investigation.

Visualize us – author and reader – there in Juliaca, standing side-by-side with the women already present. In the standpoint of the cholas. Look around. We see the women who are there each day, of course, and the town around us. We also see the researcher – ourselves – for there is no methodological sleight of hand which will allow her head to go where her body does not. But for the moment, nothing further out of the ordinary catches our eye. Then the train announces its noisy arrival and all attention turns to the train station.

For the European and North American tourists who get off the train, the cholas and Juliaca are exotic, and they try to capture that strangeness in a few snapshots and souvenir sweaters. But in the cholas' standpoint, the train itself comes powerfully into view as it plays an important function in their living strategies. They depend on this resource for the livelihood of their families and community.

The routine appearance of the train in Juliaca is made possible by a complex coordination of the work of many people comprising the social relations of the global order. It is part of the international information, communication, and transportation systems which link the economic periphery to the metropoles of advanced capitalism. The British built the rail system in the last century to carry wool to the port of Lima, from where it was shipped to feed Britain's great industrializing machine. The train was an instrument in the colonialism which drew political and economic boundaries still demarcating First World and Third World.

Today the train plays a different but still significant role in the lives of the women at the square. Without the train there would be no tourists and no market for alpaca sweaters. The women are at the town square, they knit and sell sweaters, they are cholas, a term commonly translated as indigenous women who make small goods to sell at local informal markets, as a consequence of the train's passing through Juliaca on its route connecting the highlands of Peru to markets in the First World. The train's significance in the women's lives cannot be fully explained through their immediate experiences and talk of it or from its mere presence in Juliaca, for the train originates and travels far beyond what can be directly known in that setting. My research project is an explication of the connections between the local, where things are known as they are experienced, and the extra-local, which organizes the local setting.

The train is only one constituent in the social, economic, political, and cultural relations which position Juliaca and the women there in the hierarchical global order. The imagery of the train tracks is useful here to alert us to the extended character of ruling relations which connect distant sites and the people who occupy them, and also to the material and practical accomplishment of First World – Third World relations. That is, the lives of marginalized peoples in Peru and throughout the Third World are greatly affected by the work practices of professionals in Washington and Ottawa, and by the work of intellectuals in university towns such as Guelph, Ontario, and Columbia, Missouri. My research traces these relations to numerous sites in North America to problematize the model of research about 'Women in Peru.' We see in the most practical manner how professionals compose the intellectual information systems that overlap to normalize and make rational the domination of North over South.

The international Development regime plays a prominent role in these normalizing processes. Development was invented and the whole apparatus established in the West after the Second World War, expressly to contain the Soviet Union and communism, to reconnect newly independent nation-states to advanced capitalist powers, and to lock the economic periphery into globalizing capitalism; and in these purposes it has been hugely successful. In its contradicting goal to improve the lives of the masses of poor in the Third World, Development's record is spotty at best. It is into this latter goal that the Women in Development field has been positioned, but it now carries within it the contradictions between Development as bureaucratic imperialism and Development as social change.

Many feminist professionals experience these contradictions and conflicts in their work to mediate between marginalized women and state bureaucracies (Mueller 1991), the implicit mandates of which may not work in the interests of those women, and, paradoxically, may contribute further to their subordination. As the field of Women in Development has come to be institutionalised in First World organizations like the International Development Research Centre in Canada and the United States Agency for International Development, many feminists in the Third World (Mbilinyi 1984) and in the First (Mohanty 1991) oppose its goal to 'integrate women into Development,' that is, into the Development regime. They question the political wisdom of staking feminist claims in the already occupied territory of the First World state. To do so necessarily involves transposing the actualities of people's living into policy categories which activate further bureaucratic procedures. This is the ideological move detailed in the next section. Those women living in Juliaca disappear, and in their place the concept 'Women in Peru' articulates the conceptualizing and policy procedures of the Development regime.

THE IDEOLOGICAL MOVE[4]

Bringing Development attention to women seemed at first to be merely a matter of justice; once the absence of women as subjects in Development processes was seen, a significant if not radical rethinking of Development would ensue. It was only a matter of presenting the facts of the case. But it has quickly become clear to feminists working in the Development regime that getting attention to women means less arguing well the justice issue than it does producing data in the specific format that articulates agency information systems. To make the women in Juliaca visible to agency procedures, they must be made invisible in the format of abstracted policy categories to which the scientific epithets, 'facticity,' 'objectivity,' and 'political neutrality' may be attached.

But as is now argued widely in the social sciences, facticity is a social construction and not a direct relation to any 'real' phenomenon (Foucault 1980). The Development regime itself intervenes between an actuality and the account which transposes it to fit the policy frame, between the women in Juliaca and 'Women in Peru.' This is the ideological move. The social organization for the production of Development knowledge is not a neutral filter through which information is gently sifted, to reappear in purified form in empirical texts. Conceptualizing practices borrowed from sociology create a virtual reality which exists only in texts circulating inside the Development regime.

'Women in Peru' is not imaginary, however, for it is on this basis that Development agencies design the programs and projects which greatly affect women's lives, though not always in the planned manner. The ideological gap between the women in Juliaca and 'Women in Peru' insures that the women's experiences and knowing are subordinated to, and not just ignored by, the warranted procedures of the Development regime.

The following analysis recontextualizes 'Women in Peru' in the circumstances of its production and circulation, through conceptual and administrative procedures and into the Development information systems. The policy category will tell us a great deal about the Development regime; but the lives, experiences, actions, interests, subjectivities of any actual women disappear from accounts which describe 'Women in Peru' in bureaucratic and academic hallways distant from Juliaca and Peru.

How Do We Know about 'Women in Peru'?

The brief presentation here of the policy category 'Women in Peru' is taken from two databases, one produced in the United Nations (1985) and the other produced for the United States Agency for International Development by the Bureau of the Census (1984). Both structure statistical data in the form of indicators of women's 'status' as regards commonly accepted elements of development: literacy and education, economic activity, marital and household status, fertility, and health. The format facilitates comparison of women to men and among countries. Both databases were designed to meet information needs in planning, program development, and project design. They are part of the documentation necessary to position 'Third World Women' as a properly constituted 'beneficiary' category in further bureaucratic and policy procedures.

What Do We Know about 'Women in Peru'?

In 1980 there were 8,581,000 females in Peru, 16 per cent of whom lived in rural areas. There were more men, 8,715,000, but the percentage of women and men living in rural areas was the same. In 1970 20 per cent of females ages fifteen to twenty-four and 42 per cent of females ages twenty-five to forty-four were illiterate. Men had much lower illiteracy rates, 7 per cent and 16 per cent in the two age groups, respectively. The literacy rate for women was higher in Taiwan, the Republic of Korea, Sri Lanka, Thailand, Columbia, and Costa Rica. It was lower in Cameroon, Ghana, Morocco,

Tanzania, Bangladesh, India, Nepal, Pakistan, and Guatemala. In 1981 women trailed men at all levels of school enrolment: 1,518,000 to 1,660,000 at the primary level; 574,000 to 641,000 at the secondary level; 101,000 to 195,000 at the postsecondary level.

Fourteen per cent of all females were in the labour force, compared with 45 per cent of males. For the year 2000 it is predicted that male labour force participation will rise only slightly to 46 per cent, while female participation will go up to 19 per cent. Peru is in the group of countries with low labour force participation rates for females over ten years old. Ghana, Tanzania, and Jamaica had rates over 60 per cent, while Peru, Morocco, Bangladesh, India, Pakistan, Brazil, Chile, Columbia, Costa Rica, Guatemala, Honduras, and Mexico had rates at or below 20 per cent. In all the Latin American and Central American countries about 80 per cent or more of the female labour force was in the non-agricultural sector, while in most countries in Asia and Africa more than 50 per cent was in the agricultural sector.

The fertility rate, the approximate total number of children an average woman will bear in her lifetime, was 6.56 in 1970 and 5.37 in 1980. It is predicted to be 3.5 in the year 2000. Forty-one per cent of married women were using contraceptives in 1981. The fertility rate was higher, between about seven and eight in Kenya, Bangladesh, Pakistan, and Honduras. It was lower, about three, in Taiwan, the Republic of Korea, and Chile. Women's life expectancy at birth was higher than that of men: 58.8 years compared with 55.2. Life expectancy for women was about the same as in Kenya, higher than that in Senegal (41.6 years), and lower than that in Costa Rica (70 years).

What Does 'Women in Peru' Make Unknowable?

This depiction, dense with statistical data, has a certain verisimilitude for many professionals. They might question the accuracy of a figure like the low percentage of females in the labour force, or the adequacy of the definition of a census category like 'labour force' for including women. But this depiction of the 'facts' constituting 'Women in Peru' is a way of knowing which is at the same time a way of not knowing. It makes irrelevant several features of the systematic subordination of women's ordinary lives to the operations of the Development regime itself.

Further analytical procedures are limited by the format of the categories. For instance, aggregate school participation or literacy rates may be correlated to aggregate rates of parental education, family wealth, and rural or urban residence. Explanations or causes are sought within and bounded by the available data. These categories stand in for, and conceal from our view, the historical and particular circumstances of how schools come to be set up, teachers placed, curricula written, and students present or not.

If we think of 'Women in Peru,' we are likely to see the cholas selling hand-knitted goods, with too many children, little education, and no qualifications for jobs in the modern labour force. Some women living in Peru will not be seen as 'Women in Peru' – doctors, for instance, or wives of doctors. In its official formulation, 'Women in Peru' is an aggregate category which masks, for example, class relations that exist between women professionals in Lima and the marginalized women in the highlands to whom they provide social services.

In this aggregate categorizing process, women are differentiated from men in a profoundly essentialized manner. Of course there are differences in women's and men's lives, but there are also many practical interconnections that bind them together. 'Women in Peru' is an abstraction isolated out of the multiple connections and complexities of women's lives. The statistical indicators stand in for the realities of living, sometimes in a most peculiar way, as when fertility rates are attached exclusively to women in total disregard of the 'facts of life.'

Peru, too, disappears. It is reduced to specific indicators which, in that form only, can be compared with the indicators for other countries. 'Women in Peru' is cut off from the historical, economic, political, and social relations out of which the nation-state of Peru has been carved. Development activities transpose matters such as hunger into technological problems, concealing the history of European colonialism, World Bank regulation of the Third World debt to the international finance system, the whole set of social relations which locate Peru in the periphery of the capitalist world order and place women in a class society; in short, all the details which give Peru its contemporary character disappear.

What Do the Databases Tell Us about the Development Regime?

The ideological gap between the women in Juliaca and 'Women in Peru' cannot be closed. It does not represent a research lacuna, for knowledge and power cannot be disentangled in an intellectual exercise alone. The descriptions are not merely partial or incomplete; their significance lies in the relationship of such categories to the organization of Development policies. This is a political terrain on which the official apparatus claims power as the principal actor and subordinates women to its interests and intentions.

It must be emphasized that 'Women in Peru' does not conceal or justify power; it accomplishes it. 'Labelling as part of the bureaucratic, compartmentalized management of services is not just evidence of power; it is a relationship of power, asymmetrical and one-sided' (Wood 1985a: 353). Such categories are integral elements in how bureaucratic procedures go forward, how state apparatuses operate, and thus how the governing of societies is carried out.

What the statistical indicators indicate are the types of information which state and international agencies need to mobilize bureaucratic work processes. 'What such statistics tend to monitor,' writes the Government Statisticians' Collective, 'is not so much social conditions of wealth, unemployment or homelessness, but rather the operations of state agencies responsible for dealing with the matter' (Government Statisticians' Collective, 1979: 140). Conceptualizations of social problems based on official statistics extend governing power over new subject populations, reconstituted in the form of beneficiary, client, or recipient categories. The same agencies are warranted to provide services which they determine to 'clients' whom they conceptualize in order to remediate problems which they define: a neat ideological circuit which reinforces ruling relations.

Institutional databases are composed and operated to further agency procedures to enumerate, regulate, manage, and govern the lives of subordinated women. Government and international agencies need key types of information to act as measures of Development, defined programmatically as growth in the market economy. Policy makers need labour force information in the areas of women's reproductive rates, the size of the economically inactive female labour force, and the educational level of the current and future female labour force. The practical and political restrictiveness of such data leads the Government Statisticians' Collective to conclude that 'it is extremely difficult, if not impossible, to make a really radical criticism of society using available statistical sources, which imprison us in the concepts and concerns that dominate official political and economic life' (ibid.: 138).

Policy language moves in two directions. In one direction it isolates and names some part of a population as suffering an 'underdevelopment problem.' In the other it authorizes governing bureaucracies to be holders of 'Development solutions.' Through policy vocabulary people are 'reorganized as fragmented objects of a policy of partial interventions – the recipients of skill training, credit and services, ghettoed into small scale, income generating activities, an entrepreneurial model in which significant success could only possibly be enjoyed by a few and thereby absorbed without overall structural change' (Wood 1985b: 470). It is this closed circuit which connects the professionals who are the active subjects in policy language and the 'clients' who are its acted upon objects.

THE DEVELOPMENT CONNECTION

This analysis has moved some distance from its beginning in the standpoint of certain women, but that is the point: policy categories are real only within institutional information systems. However, they do transform realities in women's everyday lives. What does 'Women in Peru' have to do with the cholas? Conceptually, very little, as I have shown; but politically, a great deal.

Abstracting a policy category from women's ongoing lives effectively reorganizes the political bases for social action. Policy procedures disconnect people from knowledge of the ruling relations in which the features of their lives – such as the coalescing of class and gender relations – are made available to them and from which locations they might resist or oppose subordinating power. The connections and flow of happenings and situations in people's lives are transposed into organizational courses of action. A proposal for a project to get more protein to poor rural children, for example, enters the complex situations of people's access to food into Development agency mandates to make intergovernmental loans and set terms for repayment, to identify and hire technical experts, to conduct research, to purchase technological goods, to call professional conferences, to establish intertextual links throughout the Development regime institution, and to be accountable to funding sources for millions of dollars.

This process – and not any putative biological or social commonality qua women – is what connects the women in Juliaca and feminist professionals. While the Development regime has in fact given little attention to women, it has been effective in circumscribing the legitimate arena for social change within its language and intentions, and it has absorbed a considerable amount of feminist energy in the First World. The troubling character of the goal to incorporate women – as 'clients' and as professionals – into any of the great policy regimes like Development or welfare lies in the tremendous capacity of these regimes to organize relationships among women across class, race, and national contradictions, along tracks like those passing through Juliaca which have already been laid by powerful global forces.

The methodological strategy to begin in the standpoint of women, coupled with the feminist commitment to advance the struggles of those women who are most at risk from the forces of subordination, brings into focus a research protocol which turns a policy regime inside out, like a shirt, so we can inspect the seams of construction. This project is particularly urgent as more feminists find ourselves working as professionals and intellectuals in policy disciplines, producing knowledge *about* women to bring them under bureaucratic domination. Often we find ourselves in an 'in and against' stance (Mueller 1991), making places to work in the interests of marginalized women in institutional settings which we know have contradicting intentions.

We thus have the possibility and the responsibility to investigate the ways that our own professional work practices may participate in reproducing other women's marginalization, particularly our facility with the information systems which are ubiquitous in the governing apparatus and the policy institutions which organize them. The research focus of this essay has been on the location of professionals in Development relations. But ruling relations like those connecting Peru and Ottawa or Washington are extended and complex. Many different research projects are necessary to explicate them, some closer to the women in Juliaca and aimed specifically at extending their knowledge to enable them to act more powerfully in their own interests. Feminist professionals in Peru might want to know how First World funding of Women in Development projects shapes local agendas so that they may begin to claim more control over these processes. Accumulations of feminist knowledge about ruling relations make possible a multiplicity of local struggles and their coordination along tracks which we make our own in opposition to ruling relations. It is only in making visible the social relations already connecting women in ways which bring us into contradictions and divisions that we can begin to go about resisting, opposing, and dismantling them, and forging new connections and alliances among women and with other subordinated populations.

NOTES

1 The original research on which this essay is based was conducted for my dissertation (1987). While I conducted fieldwork in Peru, my research, as I explain here, was on the workings of the Development regime both there and in the United States and Canada.
2 I use capital letters to distinguish terms such as Development, Third World, and 'Women in Peru' from their everyday meanings so as to specify their creation in the operations of the Development regime. See, for instance, Pletsch (1981) on the invention of the 'Third World.'
3 The notion of regime is developed from Krasner (1983) and Strange (1983) on

international regimes. Escobar (1984–5), Keeley (1990), and Dubois (1991) problematize Development by means of a Foucauldian approach.

4 Dorothy Smith (1975) demonstrates that statistics are statements embedded in an institutional discourse which express its warranted procedures and intentions. This essay uses that analytical method to show what statistics can tell us about the operations of institutions.

Mothering, Schooling, and Children's Development[1]

ALISON I. GRIFFITH

When my children were in school, I was often called to meet with their teachers. Sometimes I asked about their reading or printing. Other times I was asked if I read to my children at night, if they were given responsibility for household chores, if they watched too much television. Usually, the answer was yes, even though the definition of 'too much' was unexplored. Sometimes I understood the relationship between the teachers' questions or my questions and my children's progression through schooling. Other times, I resented the intrusion and wondered what their questions had to do with caring for my sons. Other mothers describe similar experiences – talking with teachers about their child's school experience and learning to see their child through the eyes of the school. For example, one mother described to me how she learned to see her daughter's progress through school 'Her printing was not the greatest and I was kind of worried because she wasn't enthralled with printing either. The teacher said that that's all interrelated with them sitting still in their desk – small muscle movement' (fieldnotes, D.E. Smith and A.I. Griffith, Winter 1985)

As I learned about schools and schooling, I came to see those interactions as an experiential moment in the social relation constructed between the personal and historical relationships of families and the organizational individuation of students through mass compulsory schooling. These social interactions are part of a discursive[2] or textually organized social relation shaped by the 'child development discourse.' The 'child development discourse,' as I talk about it in this essay, is the basis of expert knowledge about children and their maturation; it is scientific rather than experiential knowledge.

The normative and prescriptive concept of child development that this scientific discourse establishes is ideologically organized (Smith 1990a).

This essay traces the child development discourse, showing it to organize the related discourses of mothering and child-centred education which, in turn, have come to coordinate mothers' work in the family with that of the school. In these coordinated discourses, the actual conditions under which mothering is done are rarely attended to as serious constraints on mothers' actions. Women's mothering work often falls short of the discursive ideal and, in my research, mothers' talk is replete with anecdotes of their inability to organize their mothering in the way they 'should.' The actual conditions under which mothering is done stays outside the seamless (ideological) conceptual framework of child development.

The analysis developed here shifts our focus from the conceptual frame of the child development discourse to the actual conditions under which mothering is done. When we do we see, as Manicom (1988) has argued, that children's achievement in school is a co-production of a mother's and teachers' work. Here I explore the ideological conceptions about children's maturation that underpin schooling – normative conceptions that limit educational understanding of the increasing cultural and social diversity of children and their families.

RESEARCH BACKGROUND

Over the past decade Dorothy Smith and I have been researching the relation between the family and the educational process[3] (Griffith 1984, 1986; Griffith and Smith 1987, 1990; Smith 1987a; Smith and Griffith 1990). In three ethnographic research projects, we interviewed parents, teachers, school administrators, social workers, school psychologists, and central office administrators in three boards of education in two mid-sized cities and one large metropolis in southern Ontario. In each board of education, we chose two local school neighbourhoods that could be differentiated by social class. We met our informants through schools and community centres, using a snowball sampling technique or selecting families from school records. Our informants were white Canadians from diverse ethnic backgrounds, an artefact of demography, the vagaries of school access in Ontario, and language constraints.

In our institutional ethnography, in contrast to any other research on the relation between families and schools (for example, Coleman et al. 1966; Bourdieu and Passeron 1977; Connell et al. 1982; David 1980; Lareau 1989), we *began* with mothers and interviewed them about their everyday work of constructing the family–school relation. We explored with mothers how the extensive family work process provides for the child's participation in schooling. Only then did we develop the research questions for our interviews at the school and central administrative levels. Thus, our research in the schools held to the interests and concerns of the mothers we had interviewed, deliberately structuring our research of schooling to illuminate the social relations that had come into view through our focus on mothers' standpoint.

Interest in the 'standpoint of women' reflects a particular methodology and our interviews with mothers were the ethnographic point of entry for our inquiry (Smith 1987a). Our research and analysis moved from this experiential base to explore the family–school relation constructed by families, educators, administrators, the media, the scientific knowledge of psychologists and sociologists, and so on. This fundamental link between the particularity of women's life experiences and the social relations of the society in which they/we live is our ground of inquiry.

DEVELOPING CHILDREN, DEVELOPING MOTHERS:
THE DISCURSIVE ORGANIZATION OF CHILDREN'S DEVELOPMENT

Foucault (1979) has described discourse as a conversation organized through a variety of textual forms. Smith's (1990a) work shows how discursive or textually organized social relations are structured to coordinate institutional action. One discourse is often conceptually linked to others providing for coordination and articulation of institutional activities. Smith's unique contribution to understanding everyday life has been to discover how ideas, legitimated through coordinated discourses, organize knowledge and action. Discourses have particular ideological force, shaping our knowledge of the everyday world to conform to interests outside our own. Smith's work illuminates how 'discourse' is an active relation of power between textually organized knowledge and the actions in everyday life it organizes.

The child development discourse is an historically developed conception of children's maturation. It stands as the scientific ground of knowledge about children's development and therefore the knowledge base for strategies and activities to facilitate children's maturation in many settings. While it underpins the conception of childhood in many disciplines, it is the philosophical framework that links psychology and education (Walkerdine 1984, 1988). As with all discursively organized social relations, this textual conversation is also a debate that constantly revises the particularities of our knowledge about children while leaving unquestioned the underlying normative assumptions about children and the families of which they are a part.

Child development, as discourse, is a set of claims about children's maturational processes based in biological processes, understood to be facilitated or hindered by the child's environment. It asserts that all children have their own developmental pace which is normal for them and that they proceed through sequential stages in the developmental process. Children are conceptualized as naturally spontaneous, inquiring, purposeful, requiring direction, not force, and so on. Their development moves from self-interest to interest in others; from a simple to a complex morality; from obvious connections between phenomena to the subtleties of logic. Because the child's development is environmentally situated, children's 'natural' social, emotional, cognitive, and physical development is directly tied to their social and psychological relationships: their interactions with particular environments and adults – such as parents, teachers, child care workers – shaping the development of children's potential (see, for examples, Gruber and Voneche 1977; Phillips 1969; Snow and Ferguson 1977).

These ideas about childhood are the conceptual ground of child psychology and the basis of curricular, pedagogical, and educational assessment practices in the schooling process - child-centred education (Griffith 1984; Walkerdine 1984).

The texts of the child development discourse are interdependent: one set of texts (for example, developmental psychology) is the empirical and theoretical basis for another related but distinct set of texts (for example, primary level curriculum, or advice to mothers in popular magazines). The discursive regulation of our knowledge about children produces 'the possibility of certain behaviours and then read[s] them back as "true," creating a normalizing vision of the "natural" child' (Walkerdine 1988: 5). This is an ideological process made possible by the articulation of one discourse with another. As a conceptual framework for understanding and managing children and their maturation, the child development discourse provides for the coordination of such disparate institutional sites as the school system, the social service system, the communications media, and the branches of government responsible for family policy development and administration.

Both through their education and through state-sponsored programs, the child development discourse coordinates the work of professionals – child psychologists and psychiatrists, social workers, child care workers, educators, and authors in the popular press and television. Through the work of these professionals, it normatively structures the limits and possibilities of our knowledge about children's maturation. As such, this discourse forms the lens through which educators and social service professionals evaluate the work of mothering in the family. It also informs mothering work, subordinating mothers' experiential understanding of their children to the generalities constructed within the ruling relations of the child development discourse. The dual emphases on individual development and environmental influence linked to empirically derived, normative developmental rules brings the family and the school into the equation in unprecedented ways.

The Discourse on Mothering

The particular organization of mothering we recognize today has, like the child development discourse, developed historically (Davin 1978, 1982). A mothering discourse, now taken for granted, is the textual presentation of the dyadic mother–child interaction in terms that have been structured by the child development discourse. It includes (but is not limited to) the advice literature to mothers in magazines and newspapers, portrayals of 'good' and 'bad' mothers on television and radio, the academic discourse on families and the educational literature telling mothers how to improve their child's success at school. The mothering discourse links the scientific discourse on the development of children to particular mothering activities in families. The mothering discourse provides systematically developed knowledge, recommendations, systems of categories, and concepts coordinating the division of labour between a universalized public educational system and the family (Smith 1988; Richardson 1989). Of particular relevance here is the way the mothering discourse recommends mothering practices that facilitate a particular version of children's psychological and social maturation, some examples of which are discussed below. A circularity is constructed in which the mothering discourse reaffirms the precepts of the child development discourse (Griffith and Smith 1987).

A major site for the textual organization of the mothering discourse is the literature that advises mothers on their children's development (Ehrenreich and English 1978). The twentieth-century advice literature translates the findings of child psychology into magazine columns, tracts on child rearing, and popular books read by many first-time mothers – for example, Spock's *Baby and Child Care*, Bettleheim's column during the early 1960s in *Redbook* magazine, as well as child-rearing articles often carried in the daily newspaper. There is an extensive largely feminist-inspired literature reviewing the advice literature (see, for example, Mechling 1975; Strong-Boag 1982).

Several authors have addressed the particular coordination of discourse and mothering which is of interest here. Weiss (1978) traces the historically developed connection between the advice of experts on child rearing and the structuring of mothering work. She states that the literature, nominally on child rearing, could just as appropriately be called 'mother-rearing tracts ... [because they] have as much to say about the lives of women as about the children for whom they are caring.' (ibid.: 29) The psychological literature on children's development was well established by the 1930s (Richardson 1989). Weiss notes a shift in emphasis in the advice literature in the post-Second World War period when authors of child-rearing manuals 'began to incorporate scientific information from the field of psychology' into their advice tracts (Weiss 1978: 39). Weiss's analysis shows the mothering discourse moving from a physiological and medical focus to a developmental one in which mothering work made the difference between the possibilities of reaching the individual's full potential and the social waste of unrealized development.

As the scientific knowledge about children and their development prescribed a particular version of child-rearing, so too it organized a particular version of mothering. Women's work in the family-household became more focused on children. Children required *more* than physical care. They also required social, emotional, and cognitive care – developmentally organized activities which would facilitate their maturation. Mothering work intensified in response to the developmental conceptualizations of children's maturation discovered within the psychological and psychiatric discourse.

Chamboredon and Prevot (1975) describe the historical links that developed in France between the normative child development paradigm and home- and school-based pedagogy. The conception of childhood as developmentally distinct stages stipulates stage-specific educational practices. The designation of the years between two and five as 'early childhood,' a crucial period in the child's development, constructed the child as the focus of mothering and teaching practices making the child the pedagogical subject of her mother's educational work in the French bourgeois home. Chamboredon and Prevot's analysis illustrates the relationship between the conceptions of children's maturation held within the child development discourse and the complementary but invisible mothering work on which it depends.

In the United States and Canada, the links between the mothering discourse and education were organized through a number of social sites. One was the 'mental hygiene' movement of the early twentieth century that coordinated public health and educational policy and, of course, mothering work. Public health nurses working in the school and educational staff checked students' personal hygiene. Students whose personal hygiene did not meet public health standards were refused permission to attend school (Richardson 1989). During that same era, another coordinative process was the parent education movement. It was 'aggressively nurtured' and coordinated through philanthropic funding. 'The status of the parent education movement was heavily dependent on its purported foundation in scientifically controlled observations of children in laboratory and nursery school settings' (Schlossman 1981: 276). The mental hygiene movement and the parent education movement coordinated children's health, education, and mothering through the scientific discourse on children's development (see Manicom, this volume).

These accounts bring into view a discursively organized historical shift in educational and familial understandings about children. Children came to be viewed less through lenses based in tradition and local experience and more through a scientific standard of maturation developed extra-locally. The mothering discourse and the child development discourse are parallel discourses, one informing the other through shared normative conceptions of children's maturation.

My argument, thus far, is that the transformation of childhood is also a transformation of the social definition of mothering work. A particular organization of mothering work is required in order to develop the child. In the mothering discourse, the work of mothering is tightly tied to the conceptions of the child development discourse and, as we will see below, child-centred education.

Mothering Practices in Ontario: Discourse and Social Class

When we bring this view of discourse to bear on the contemporary practices of mothers in Ontario, we discover that mothers engage in discursive relations in a variety of ways. While discourses are organized extra-locally, mothers participate in them, regardless of intent, in the context of their everyday lives and experience. Each mother embodies the discourse differently depending on her individual biography and current family circumstances. This diversity of practice coalesces around divisions of social class as I shall demonstrate from my research data. In discussing 'class' in relation to mothers in my study, I begin with common-sense notions such as 'what their neighbourhoods looked like.' However, the analysis I make builds towards a different understanding of class and class effects, one which shows how class is constituted in daily practices of ideologically organized mothering and schooling.

I selected two mothers, Ms Daly and Ms Evans, as embodying vivid and contrasting relationships between discourse and social class. Most of the mothers we interviewed described their relation to discourse in ways similar to that of Ms Daly and Ms Evans. Ms Evans[4] lives in a middle-class neighbourhood with her husband, a secondary school teacher, and her two children. She works full-time in the home. Her children are in Junior Kindergarten (age four) and Grade 1 (age six). She has read much of the popular literature on child-rearing. When her daughter was small, a neighbour, a Montessori teacher, brought Ms Evans a number of child-rearing books to read. At the time of the interview (1987), she noted that she still paid attention to the advice columns and articles in the newspaper and to the various courses offered in the community, although with less interest than when her children were smaller. She had enrolled her son in several classes at the community centre as a way of teaching him skills that would not be available at the school and as a way of preparing him for his school experience.

In contrast, Ms Daly lives in a working-class neighbourhood with her husband, a driver for the city's mobile library, and her four sons ages six months to ten years. She works full-time in her home and volunteers at the school library one morning a week. When asked if she read the literature or watched television programs on child rearing, she answered that she had in the past but now she did not have time and, after four children, she sort of knew what she was doing. She also noted that her husband did not enjoy educational programs and so they rarely watched them together. When asked about buying educational toys for her children, she said she paid attention to the Fischer-Price labels for age-appropriate toys.

These two women describe their mothering work very differently. Ms Evans described her activities and family interaction in terms which oriented us to the child development discourse – developing her children for school and as individuals. Ms Evans's everyday work of mothering was embedded in the organization of knowledge about children constructed within the child development discourse. She organized her mothering for schooling based, in large part, on a knowledge of children that was congruent with the mothering discourse. For example, Ms Evans described how she had encouraged her children to select their favourite Shakespearian play as part of their Christmas present.

In contrast, Ms Daly's talk included few referents to developing her children and many to their individual personalities and how that shaped their school experiences. For example, one son was having serious difficulties in Grade 3 (age eight). Ms Daly attributed some of these difficulties to his 'shyness' as well as to a teacher she characterized as 'horrible.' Although to a limited extent, Ms Daly used concepts drawn from the mothering discourse, Ms Daly described her mothering in terms of her own experience and that of her family and neighbours. For example, her son's difficulties were said to be partially the result of heredity (with shyness as a family trait).

This account supports other studies that show family classing practices to be central to the child's school participation (for example, Lareau 1989; Bourdieu and Passeron 1977). It also shows the role of discourse in social class. For many middle-class mothers and some working-class mothers, mothering work is organized in discursive terms. In these families, the ordinary work of mothering teaches the child discursively informed skills, attitudes, and behaviours. For example, Ms Evans is aware of and can construct an account of her mothering work in discursive terms. Thus, Ms Evans's mothering links her family to the local school within a conceptual framework that appears to benefit the children – her daughter has received excellent report cards. Ms Daly may be aware of this discursive organization of knowledge, but she does not describe her work in the home nor her children in those terms. Her mothering work and her children's participation in schooling are not organized in terms which fit with the conceptual framework of child development that informs the work of the local school – Ms Daly's sons are having difficulty maintaining their grade levels. As we will see below, this lack of coordination between home and school means that educators cannot rely on the family to do the work on which the school depends. Several studies (Coleman et al. 1966; Connell et al. 1982; David 1980; Griffith 1984; Manicom 1988; Walkerdine 1984) have argued that social class is produced through schooling. The coordination of the family–school relation through mothering work that is discursively organized is one aspect of this intergenerational production of social class.

CHILD-CENTRED EDUCATION: CONNECTING
MOTHERING AND SCHOOLING

Child-centred education is the dominant paradigm in educational theory in Canada and Great Britain (Walkerdine 1988). The term 'child-centred education' is used to describe the philosophy of a school as well as to describe particular classroom practices. Child-centred education is part of a liberal–democratic educational tradition which includes Rousseau, Froebel, Montessori, Pestalozzi, Dewey, and Piaget (Sharp and Green 1975: 40). Development, and therefore learning, is viewed as an integrated and interdependent process, extending the pedagogical and evaluational concerns of the school past curricular activity in the classroom, into the interconnected social, emotional, and cognitive development of the child.

David notes that child-centred education both organizes the work of mothers in families in relation to schooling and attributes individual student difficulties to their family background (1980: 177–8). Walkerdine describes the discursive links between education and psychology as the 'child psychology/child centred pedagogy couple' noting the distinctive consequences for educational practice: 'the very lynchpin of developmental psychology, the "developing child," is an object premised on the location of certain capacities within "the child" and therefore within the domain of psychology. Other features are thereby externalized as aspects of a social domain, which influence or affect the pattern of development and, consequently, the conditions of educability' (Walkerdine 1984: 154).

The child development discourse in general, but particularly child-centred education, facilitates an increasingly complementary relation between mothering and the mass public education system, providing for a coordinated division of labour between the family and the school. The boundaries between home and school are maintained by a socially constructed division of responsibility for the child's development: the school is primarily responsible for the child's cognitive development while the family (typically the mother) has responsibility for maintaining the child's emotional and social development. The conception of the developing child blurs those boundaries, generating tension between parents and teachers as it provides a basis for attribution of blame for difficulties (Lareau 1989; Lightfoot 1978; Manicom 1988; Sharp and Green 1975).

Child-Centred Educational Policy and Practice in Ontario

The same division that Walkerdine (1984) noted between the child's capacities and conditions of educability of the child's environment appears in Ontario's child-centred education policy: the curricular process is built on the basis of individual variation in the children's personalities and family backgrounds – a stage-appropriate curriculum (Government of Ontario, Ministry of Education [MOE] 1975: 10). The policy recognizes two factors as key to the child's educability: 'stages of the individual child's emotional, physical, cognitive and moral development' and 'extrinsic factors such as the child's pre-school environment' (ibid.: 9).

Child-centred education constructs the family and the school as 'partners' in the educational project focused on the child. The family's educational practices come under scrutiny and assessment, however indirectly, through evaluations of the child in the schooling process. Even though the child provides the common focus of interest for the two physically separate work processes of mothers and teachers (Manicom, this volume), this does not mean that the mother and the teacher interact with the child in the same way. The child may be the pedagogical subject of educational practices in the home and the school, but those educational practices are given different shapes by the social relations of the two sites. In practical terms this means that the educational work of the school requires a complementary, but not identical work process within the family. Where this complementarity is lacking, the 'problems' which arise are viewed by educators as located outside the school, in the neighbourhood or in the family (Griffith 1984).

Schools can and do assume that most, although certainly not all, families would ensure that the issues and concerns of the school would be shared by the family, a complementarity which we have shown to exist in most *middle-class* families (Smith and Griffith 1990; see also Lareau 1989). Indeed, middle-class parents may be as familiar, perhaps even more familiar than teachers, with the child development literature and its applications to education. As Ueda (1986, and this volume) has noted, well-educated bourgeois mothers will often press the school to educate their children in ways that are congruent with the family's education level and social opportunities. In the working-class schools of our research, it was a different story.

In 1987, Dorothy Smith and I interviewed the administration, and primary and kindergarten teachers in a working-class school. They described the families of their students as everything from 'perfect' to those families who cannot or will not orient themselves to the discursively organized aims of the school: 'single parents,' 'couples who are working,' 'single fathers,' 'children who have been through the courts,' 'broken homes,' children from 'substandard housing,' and so on. According to the school staff, it is not the family structure that makes a difference for the school, but rather the kind of attention the parents (typically the mother) pay to the work of the school – the 'parent's attitude to schooling.' In our interviews, however, it became clear that the 'parent's attitude' is more than an attitude to school. It must translate into a concrete work organization within the home that 'fits' with the child-centred education discourse of the school.

The school relies on a teaching process which has gone on in the home prior to the child's entry into the schooling process. Teachers recognize and approve of mothering work that includes the 'stimulation' of the child through creative play with scissors and glue. A kindergarten teacher described junior kindergarten as a strategy to help 'those children who are not stimulated at home, who are not allowed to use the glue, the scissors, the crayons because it's going to make a mess.' Classroom teachers also rely on mothers to teach the child in ways that match the work routines of the school. As one teacher stated: 'If the home situation is rather untidy, then you will find it [tidiness in the classroom] has got to be taught right from the beginning and they've got to be reminded and reminded to gather up their belongings and keep their clothing tidy and so on in the cloakroom.' Schooling requires mothering which takes up the relevances of the school, for example, 'stimulation' activities which are congruent with the skills being evaluated in the school and personal habits that match the work routines of the classroom.

Many of the families in this school catchment area did not construct their mothering work in ways that were congruent with the discursive organization of the school. Many children were not skilled in the ordinary tasks on which schooling depends. So, in the terms popularized by child-centred education, the problem becomes one of developing the child's 'capacities' when the 'conditions of educability,' particularly the child's family background, militate against the discursive agenda. The problem appears to be situated in the neighbourhood and the family – in the external factors which limit the educator's ability to reach the goals of child-centred education.

We can begin to see neighbourhood and family as integral to the work organization of child-centred education. As we saw above, most middle-class mothers know how to organize their children's participation in school in terms recognizable within the child-centred education discourse. In working-class schools, however, most mothers do not construct their mothering work in these terms. With all the good 'attitudes' in the world, they do not fully participate in a family–school relation organized discursively.

CONCLUSION

The three discursive textually interdependent organizations of knowledge I have sketched are the child development discourse, the mothering discourse and the child-centred educational discourse. They have in common their reliance on particular kinds of caring and educative work, approaches which give substantial emphasis to child psychology and development. Typically, that work is done by women, both as mothers and as elementary school teachers whose everyday experience is subordinated within this generalizing discourse.

But all mothers do not participate in discourse in the same way. The mothering practices recommended in the mothering discourse depend upon the availability of personal, social, economic, and educational resources within the family – resources on which the mother can draw for her discursively organized work. Some mothers, typically those of the middle class, appear to engage relatively easily with the mothering discourse in their child care and pedagogical work in the home. Others, particularly working-class mothers, do not describe their family work organization in discursive terms. And it makes a difference, according to the teachers interviewed.

Child-centred education relies on an understanding of children constructed in the child development discourse. Moving from the precepts of the child development discourse, educators and administrators orient to an ideal family–school relation – home and school working together to develop the child. In families where the family-household resources cannot be appropriated by the school to the extent required to accomplish the discursive family–school relation (for example, where the mother is working outside the home full-time, where the parent's education has not provided an understanding of the precepts of child development, where parents do not agree with the developmental aims of the school, where ethnicity or language do not facilitate the goals of the school), the family's relation to the school deviates from the normative conceptions of child-centred education. The findings of my study suggest that this occurs most often in the relation between mass compulsory education and working-class families. It is this disjuncture which allows us to see how child-centred education, in coordinating mothering work with the interests of mass compulsory schooling, contributes to the social organization and reproduction of class.

Class and class inequality have long since been understood to be intergenerationally reproduced. Education has been treated both as 'the problem' and, alternatively, as 'the solution.' As Lareau (1989) notes there is an extensive literature showing that children's school success is increased when families (read working-class mothers) are taught how to link their home work to that of the school (see, for example, Epstein 1987). It is my contention that while this may be a necessary step, it is simply inadequate as a solution to the ongoing production of inequality through schooling. While teaching mothers how to participate more effectively in their children's education will increase their knowledge about schools, it does not increase the school's knowledge of mothering. Mothers who cannot or do not (for whatever reason) construct their mothering in discursive terms will continue to organize their mothering outside the normative work organization on which schools depend. The focus on educating mothers leaves intact the discursive organization of mothering and schooling, with its built-in inequities. Dismantling it requires a radical rethinking of how the social sciences and professional disciplines structure our knowledge of chil-

dren and, thus, of our work as mothers. Awareness of how we all participate in such everyday discursively organized practices will expand women's
capacity to act 'politically' and effectively.

NOTES

1 This work was originally presented as a paper at the Society for the Study of
  Social Problems Meetings, Chicago, 1987.
2 'Discourse' refers to an organization of relations among people participating in a
  conversation mediated by written, filmed/videoed, and printed materials. The
  term is adapted from Michel Foucault *The Archeology of Knowledge* (1972). As
  we use it, the term does not refer just to the 'texts' of this conversation and their
  production alone, but to the ways in which people organize their activities in
  relation to them.
3 The research projects were funded by the Social Science and Humanities
  Research Council as a Doctoral Fellowship (1980–3), a three-year General
  Research Grant, Dorothy E. Smith principal investigator (#410–84–0450, 1984–
  7), and through Transfer Grant Research Funding at the Ontario Institute for
  Studies in Education, Dorothy E. Smith and Alison Griffith, co-principal inves-
  tigators (1988–9).
4 Throughout our research and subsequent writing, we use pseudonyms when
  referring to those we interviewed.

Corporate Wives: Gendered Education of Their Children

YOKO UEDA[1]

Japanese major corporations recruit young people fresh from universities as future managerial and professional staff, but do so in a distinctive manner. These recruits must follow a standard Japanese educational pattern *culminating in a degree from a 'good' Japanese university*. Without this very specific educational basis, there is little chance of entering the labour force with a good corporate job. This presents a serious problem for children of corporate employees who live and work abroad. Many studies indicate that one of the major causes of the increased reluctance towards overseas assignment among corporate employees is the education of their children (see Inui and Sono 1977; Y. Sakamoto 1976; U. Sakamoto 1974; Wallach and Metcalf 1980, 1981). Besides differing educational standards, politics, and ideologies in foreign countries, there are also cultural and linguistic differences to deal with. Beyond these differences, outside of Japan the urgency that drives parents and children in the preparation for educational success may be missing. Addressing the potential flaws in their children's preparation to compete for good schools becomes the work of expatriate Japanese corporate wives. As this essay will argue, this work also accomplishes the reproduction of gender.

Data for this essay come from two studies. The first is of the Japanese expatriate community in Metropolitan Toronto conducted in mid-1980 (Ueda 1986). Drawing on Smith's procedure of institutional ethnography (1987a), that study begins from the actual experience of Japanese corporate wives and looks at their work oriented to their children's education. These women participate in complex relations of ruling (Smith 1990a) which set for them an externally organized normative pattern of activities that organizes their actual lived experience. The second study drawn on here is an ethnographic study I conducted at Nippon Telegraph and Telephone Corporation in Japan during 1989.[2]

This essay explicates the social processes at work organizing and coordinating aspects of Japanese family life with larger institutional and organizational forms. I argue that the activities that Japanese expatriates perform as wives and mothers become part of the relations of ruling whereby corporate capitalism penetrates family life, organizing children's schooling to sustain and reproduce the (Japanese) corporate and patriarchal order.

Smith, writing of the stable form of North American family which emerged prior to the recent women's movement, argues that 'the modern family in the dominant class is organized as a service unit vis-à-vis the development and appropriate educational achievement of children' (Smith 1973: 23). Thus, what a woman does for the individual members of the family becomes 'a service to the institutional and organizational form' in which the middle class is organized and sustained. Smith calls this relation of middle-class family to the external system 'subcontractual': 'the corporation 'subcontracts' to the family the work which must be done to and for the members of the corporation to keep it going, but which is not provided for within the corporation itself' (Smith 1973: 20). More recently, Smith's (1988, 1993) research on schooling has drawn her attention to how mothers, as well as people in the educational system, researchers, etc., orientate themselves and their goals in relation to 'ideological codes' that are socially organized and pervasive in the culture. (See also Smith and Griffith 1990, and Griffith in this volume.)

My research brings Smith's ideas into the context of the Japanese middle-class family. I found in my Toronto study that these women's activities become directed towards the realization of an external moral order that operates in the interests of the corporate capitalist enterprise. Specifically of interest here are the processes through which the education of middle-class children fulfils corporate hiring requirements. The realization of the corporate requirements in her children, in concert with a Japanese educational system that accomplishes and credentials it, is accepted as being a middle-class mother's responsibility. I shall argue that these women attend to a discourse on 'educational success' which shapes their child-raising practices in gender-specific ways, particularly in relation to schooling. The attitude to schooling, career, and work that aligns the behaviour of Japanese children to corporate needs may well be the result of an 'ideological code'[3] carried in educational materials as well as in other aspects in Japanese schooling and cultural life.

Doing this work is more demanding for expatriate mothers. In a foreign culture, the ideological codes expressing Japanese corporate policy that reinforce the 'proper' relation of children to the educational project are missing from everyday life. Expatriate Japanese mothers must take the necessary steps to reproduce in Canada the conditions that legitimate the required Japanese approach to learning and competition. I shall argue that what is required is distinctly different for girls and boys.

JAPANESE EDUCATIONAL PRACTICES AND THE CORPORATION

In the past quarter of a century, growing numbers of multinational corporate employees have been assigned to overseas work. These are the people who Toffler (1971) referred to as the 'new nomads' who move around globally throughout their career as their company requires them to do so. These employees are usually accompanied by their families, although an increasing number of employees routinely decide to make a special arrangement in which a wife stays in the home country with the children while her husband is working overseas.

The Japanese call this situation *tanshin-funin*[4] which has become a part of the lifestyle for these 'new nomads.' Sometimes a Japanese wife takes her children back home, leaving her husband in the overseas post before the completion of his assignment, or the couple may send their children back home and place them under the care of relatives. Whichever arrangement is made, it is the wife who takes direct responsibility for raising and schooling children.

Tanshin-funin, or temporary separation, typically found among Japanese corporate employees, is not a contingent phenomenon. It has roots in the Japanese educational system and employment practices in which mothers take an active part, as this essay argues. Japanese mothers find themselves responsible for ensuring their children's success in a Japanese university and high school entrance examination system often referred to as 'examination hell.' This examination process is part of the Japanese educational system that has become known for its competitive character.

Every spring in Japan, millions of children and students write entrance examinations for admission to desired high schools and universities. Japanese employment practices have been largely responsible for the development of this competitive educational system. Once a year Japan's major corporations and government bureaux recruit a large number of new graduates from high schools and universities. Other than their intake of new graduates, the organizations rarely hire a person for a managerial or professional position from outside. Most organizations recruit university graduates on a long-term basis and train them as future managers. In general, major corporations do not even consider hiring the graduates from less prestigious universities. Because 'lifetime employment' is still commonly practised by larger corporations, an individual's first job is overwhelmingly important in his/her future career. To be admitted to a large and successful firm, one must have graduated from the 'right' university in the eyes of the firm; and to be admitted to the 'right' university, one must have attended a 'right' high school to prepare for the entrance examination, and so on. In Japan, as in most Western nations, university degrees are prerequisites for most professions. Major employers generally consider the degree the basic requirement, even when it is from the preferred university, and they further evaluate applicants upon hiring. Getting into a first-rate university through years of hard work is, however, regarded as evidence of an individual's 'natural talents,' potentials, and stability.

Once a company hires such workers, they are likely to place them in pro-longed training. The research I recently conducted on Japanese corporate training shows the link between educational requirements for recruits and strategic corporate policy. Corporations want recruits prepared with a high standard of 'basic skills' (an educated mass), but 'unfinished,' making it possible for the corporation to train and flexibly deploy them. In 1989, for instance, Nippon Telegraph and Telephone Corporation (NTT), the world's largest corporation, put more than 2,800 newly employed workers, mainly university graduated males, into long-term training programs.

Japanese high technology and economic success is often attributed to a cooperative government–business relationship and to Japan's active state intervention in industry through industrial policies. Yet, as I have argued elsewhere (Ueda 1991), another important feature of Japanese competitive success is a highly developed system of human resources. Rather than training employees to perform a job properly on a short-term basis to accommodate the immediate needs of an office or company, the training emphasis is on being responsive to the expansionary needs of the corporation and the industry. One telecommunications executive I interviewed put it this way:

Technologically there is no limitation on us in the development of highly sophisti-cated telecommunications technology and in leading the world just as we are doing in INS [the Information Network System, a comprehensive information infrastruc-ture for Japan] development. The problem is the application and diffusion of the technology. At present we don't have enough specialists who can effectively deploy the very technology we develop. To make matters worse, there aren't enough cus-tomers who have skilled people to take advantage of the new technology we offer. (Ueda 1991: 18)

Industries must look into the future and prepare workers to meet the needs arising throughout their whole industry and productive cycle, as they develop their human resources strategy. At NTT and other major corporations, the training of new recruits attempts to familiarize them with every aspect of the company's operation and help them find their aptitude in the company. There is a need for a broadly educated and company-committed worker, according to a NTT personnel manager: 'Once [the trainees] acquire enough knowledge and skills in the telecommunications industry, which, by the way, must be reinforced by daily learning through work as well as *jiko-keihatsu* [self-edification], we think that they are capable of taking up any kind of work in the future with minimum additional training.' Corporations such as NTT expect recruits to accept unquestioningly that they may be moved around, even into different occupations within the company, for example, an engineer into customer relations or accounting. Given the magnitude of technological advancement and the increasing competitive pressures in the market, workers learn to see that such changes are inevitable and that they had better be prepared.

It is for these kinds of careers that young Japanese boys are being prepared, through their parents' careful attention to choosing the right schools and cultivating in the children the right attitudes to the whole preparatory process. During the years of preparation, the mother takes the major responsibility for managing her children's schooling. Expatriate women must deal with this educational system from outside of Japan. As we shall see in the rest of the essay, in Canada, mothers have the extra task of guarding and replicating a moral order aimed at making their children 'successful' in terms that all Japanese middle-class parents, whether located in Japan or abroad, understand.

The Discourse Surrounding 'Educational Success'

The Japanese mother does most of the groundwork in deciding to which school or university her child should be sent. Providing for mothers' competent participation in their children's preparation for universities is an 'educational success' discourse, produced in a Japanese industry which involves publishers, communication companies, various types of cram schools (preparatory schools), and nationwide mock-test agencies.

A mother's involvement in the whole educational process, including the feverish ritual around 'examination hell' is often caricatured in popular newspapers and magazines in which mothers are portrayed as *Kyoiku-mama*[5] who sacrifice their lives for their children's success. A mother must manage everything, not the least of which is to bring the child to the best condition physically and mentally on the very day of examination. As each entrance examination requires a couple of days to complete, the period of writing examinations sometimes stretches to more than a month. Therefore, in the pre-examination period, a mother makes sure that her child is fed well and sleeps enough without cutting study hours. The fever of entrance examinations is repeated year after year, and its images are reinforced through media as they publish not only names of individuals who are accepted by major universities, but also examination questions and model answers such as those of Tokyo University.

To help their children to secure a place in the best possible school, mothers not only read publications and pass around the information pertaining to entrance examinations among peers with teenaged children, but they also attend workshops and consultation meetings held by schools for parents. Mothers' knowledge of better schools and universities is acquired through the discourse organized by the schools, the specialized 'educational success' industry, and by regular newspapers and magazines which supply statistical data listed by individual corporations on university graduates gaining an employment position.

Many publishers devote entire publications to discussion of university entrance examinations. One particular company, which is the most popular and trusted among students, for example, publishes every year a series of guidebooks, called in translation *Trend and Strategy*; it offers students analysis of the trends in examinations by university and subject and gives them advice and forecasts for what to expect in the coming year.

The same publisher also puts out a monthly magazine in which there are articles concerned with lifestyle of high school students, experts' advice to prospective candidates for examination, and general counselling as well as current social issues, sports, and entertainment. The targeted readership of these books and magazines are high school students who are preparing for entrance examinations. Through reading these publications the students enter the examination discourse mediated by the texts which organize and shape the ways in which they 'see' themselves and their opportunities and, of course, how they prepare for examinations. The discourse is also gendered in subtle ways. One of many possible examples is of advertisements for private colleges and universities carried in these magazines that routinely carry photos such as of boys gathered in a science lab in stained uniforms, while the girls, dressed fashionably, are assembled in a language lab. These magazines are persuasive. Students study subjects following the publisher's advice, review their strengths and weaknesses according to the given forecast, consult with teachers, and work out a strategy to meet the requirements.

Mothers' Education-Oriented Work, at Home and Abroad

As most children in Japan share their concerns with their mother and seek help such as getting extra books and/or sometimes getting a tutor and changing cram schools, mothers are drawn into the text-mediated examination discourse. For example, an article in a magazine gives advice to students not to eat heavy night snacks two hours before bedtime, as that is considered to interfere with the most mentally alert and effective learning period of the evening and also it disturbs sleep. Mother may know best what and when to serve her particular child for night snack, however, the way she takes care of her child's health and well-being is ordered and determined by the discourse.

Placed in a foreign environment, what expatriate women do in relation to children's schooling begins to look as though they were operating a business enterprise. They deal both with the children's local schools and the (Saturday) Japanese school for overseas children, as well as corresponding with the high schools and universities in Japan. They also manage the personnel such as Japanese tutors hired to supplement their children's studies and, in the case where the children are sent back home, the guardian.

My informants in Toronto held what they called 'strategy meetings' on a regular basis. At these meetings, they would circulate the materials they had each discovered – newspaper clippings, photocopied magazine and journal articles, verbal reports about what they had heard on radio and TV news and on videotapes from Japan. They kept up-to-date with Japanese popular culture and fashion. They also gossiped about what they had heard from other groups of mothers and their children. The mothers did not necessarily read all the materials they collected for their children, yet they managed to acquire enough knowledge, for instance, to determine what university was moving in what direction on a particular subject. This would be a matter of strategic concern in preparing their children to take entrance examinations.

Mothers use the meetings to check with other mothers the implications of information that their children are bringing to them from their reading. I heard, for instance, a discussion of a shift in exam questions, away from organic to inorganic chemistry, as reported in the *Trend and Strategy* magazine. The discussion went on in this manner: are the other mothers getting the same information? What does this mean about that university? Mothers would compare other publications, check the rate of competition for desired universities, and determine the weight of examination scores against each subject in order to decide whether individual children should pursue what they had originally planned. Or, alternatively, they might decide that their children should be given some extra support to adjust themselves to the new trend.

A Japanese middle-class woman's efforts and thought in her daily practices as a wife and mother are not a mere personal service to her family members, but a service to the corporation. My analysis of the *coordination* of corporate recruitment strategy and mothers' work shows how mothers are producing the next generation of managers with the prerequisite character, oriented to a competitive stance, and yet also trained to be compliant to the expectations of an external authority. How well the mother performs her work affects not only the children's future success but the success of the corporate strategy. It should not be forgotten that her work also relieves her husband so that he is free to concentrate on his corporate responsibilities. In this particular relation, her everyday practices are directed towards sustenance and reproduction of her class. But these practices are not only about class. They are reproducing gender as well.

CONSTITUTING 'SUCCESS' FROM ABROAD FOR BOYS AND GIRLS

Although the Japanese use the terms 'education' and 'schooling' interchangeably, when the child's gender is concerned, the boundary of meaning between the two becomes clear. The two terms are gender differentiated and hierarchically ordered. That is, schooling is something that has to be given to male children at the right time in the right place, and has priority over female children's education. *Tanshin-funin*, or sending children back home would be rare if the couple's children were all girls. For girls, overseas experience is considered good for their education, while it is considered a disadvantage for the schooling of boys. The practice of gender-specific educational choices has been noted in other studies of Japanese corporate expatriate couples (Lee 1981; White, 1979, cited in Lee). Lee's study shows that all of the children sent back home were boys, and no daughters were returned for educational reasons. Japanese corporate couples routinely take daughters along wherever they are assigned. Thus, the girls are constantly on the move with parents, which reduces their chance of being admitted to one of the prestigious universities and ultimately reduces their career opportunities.

Most Japanese corporate couples still hope that their daughters will marry and have a family. Particularly the wives want their daughters to be so-called professional housewives who can handle any kind of situation which a middle-class woman might confront. To raise a daughter to be a good and educated wife and mother, Japanese corporate couples think that they should take the daughter along wherever they are assigned, show her the world outside, and encourage her to gain a broad experience. At a party for a woman who was to take her son back to Tokyo, in order for him to prepare for university, Keiko, an informant, happily said: 'Well, I am fortunate. Mine are all girls. I planned this before I married [laughs]. I have never worried about their schooling. Of course, next year I have to send one to university, but I am telling her to go to a Canadian university. A woman can fit in anywhere if she speaks English, I suppose.'

Corporate couples do encourage their daughters to have university education but do not necessarily expect them to pursue a professional career. Mothers may give this as direct verbal advice to the daughter. The mother tells her daughter that a university degree or college diploma is one of the 'musts' for girls to obtain in order to find an intelligent and educated husband with a stable occupation. She often reminds her daughter that a highly educated and professional man is also interested in meeting a bright and educated young woman. In the meantime she encourages the daughter to take various kinds of private lessons in music, art, crafts, and sports.

Given their geographical location, the intensity of entrance examinations in Japan, and the extreme difficulty for children living overseas to enter the university of their choice, mothers must be in charge of all aspects of their children's lives, particularly their best use of limited time for study. This explains the enthusiasm for the 'strategy meetings' discussed previously. Women with no male child are, however, often left out of the discussions even though a girl wishing to pursue a career in the future has to go through the same competition as a boy does. A girl's future career is, however, hardly in question in such strategy meetings. Women with no sons nonetheless attend these meetings to give moral support to the mothers with sons.

I found that many women who brought their teenaged sons overseas expressed their regrets. Not only did they consider this a setback for their children's schooling, but also they sometimes met with rebellion on the part of the children. Another informant, Kikuko, talked about such an incident:

I have to take Tsutomu back to Japan. He is 11 years old. Saturday Japanese school is not enough [for him to prepare for high school]. Last night he begged us to let him stay in Toronto until at least his father's term is over. My husband got upset and said, 'Okay. You can stay here and end up selling peanuts at the corner of Yonge and Bloor. I don't care what you do!' That was his [my husband's] mistake. Tsutomu took him at his word and said, 'What's wrong with selling peanuts at the street corner?' I tried hard to calm them down. It was awful to see them argue. My son only thinks I am pulling him apart from his friends. My husband blames me for having spoiled Tsutomu. They can never understand me ... what I am doing is all for them.

Generally speaking, however, the children of corporate couples tolerate the situation they are in. This may be partly because they do not stay long enough to develop a strong attachment to one place or country. Since their parents are rotated at approximately three- to five-year intervals via a Japanese posting, they become more Japanese-oriented rather than having a cosmopolitan outlook. Also, their frequent uprooting and the absentee father create an enormous dependency upon the mother. To cope with a new environment and secure their future schooling, they generally cooperate with the parents, especially with the mother. The problem of delinquency is hardly heard of among the children in the Japanese expatriate community. The teenaged children perceive themselves as too 'square' and 'dead earnest' compared with their Canadian counterparts. In fact, they do not have enough time to associate with Canadian children of their age outside of the regular school hours.

Students must work diligently on all the subjects they are taking, while their mothers work out a 'strategy' for them and push them hard towards the goal. The goal, however, is not set by the children themselves. It is set by the parents who participate in the middle-class moral order. By learning to be personally invested in a goal imposed upon them from outside, the children aiming for a corporate career learn and embody the prerequisite character of the Japanese corporate employee. However, the parents generally feel that girls should not go through the 'hell' as boys do. They try to lay an easy path for their daughters so that they can protect them from any kind of hardship. One mother, Atsuko, said:

I am going to send my 17-year-old daughter, Rika, to the University of Toronto next year ... Now that we have been here for several years, it is very hard for Rika to get into a Japanese university. She speaks Japanese all right, I suppose. But her reading and writing ability is not good enough to pass an essay test of S University in Tokyo, to which my husband and I wish to send her. My son, who is in the second year at K University, spent two years as a *ronin*[6] to get in there. I hate to see Rika go through the same ordeal.

A man with a 13-year-old daughter said: 'I would like to see my daughter happily married and have children. But that is up to her ... If she wishes to have her own career, I will let her do it and give as much support as I can. Nowadays, a girl has a choice. She can be a housewife or a 'career woman,' can't she? [smiles].'

Like this man, most my informants indicated their willingness to give support if their daughters wanted to pursue a career. Both men and their wives seem to believe that girls are free to make a choice. Although they no longer think that girls must only marry and raise children, they never call into question the assumption that a girl 'must choose' between career and marriage. For them, it is taken for granted that if a girl wishes to make a career, she would give up having a family. Unlike girls, boys have no 'choice' other than pursuing a career. A career, however, does not prevent them from having a family. On the contrary, for a man, the family is often an essential element in his career advancement.

Compared with boys whose education is narrowly defined as 'schooling' and highly structured, girls seem to have more opportunities. They spend more time enriching their education by travelling to many countries, attending various kinds of social functions, and receiving a variety of private lessons. However, their everyday life is tightly controlled by parents. One of the reasons that parents take female children along wherever they are assigned is so that they can 'protect their daughters within eyeshot.'

Daughters are allowed to enrol in a foreign university if they wish. However, most parents I interviewed do not believe that their daughters would be interested in pursuing a career. The mothers who encourage their daughters to go to a Canadian university usually think that getting into a Canadian university is easier for them than seeking admission to a prestigious university in Japan. For instance, Atsuko, an informant who wanted her daughter to attend the University of Toronto said: 'If we are not choosy, there are a lot of universities available to her. But I don't like to send her to an unknown university. Instead, I think I should send her to the U of T ... I've heard that although it is hard to get into S University from a high school in Japan, it is a lot easier for a foreign university student to transfer credits.' S University has a reputation as one of the most prestigious women's private universities in Japan which offers liberal arts, language, and social science courses. The wives of public figures are often found to be the graduates of the university. Since Atsuko does not think that her daughter will pursue a career, she is not concerned about where and in what program her daughter studies, so long as the university is well known and the credits are transferable to her preferred Japanese university.

Although the number of career-oriented girls is still small, those who wish to pursue a professional career are very much aware that they face extra difficulties in preparing for the entrance examination to the desired university. Some of the difficulties result from the string of choices their parents have made for them, in their own 'best interests.' Girls who are committed to a career early in their lives usually ask their parents to send them back to Japan before reaching high school age. In fact, the parents who are concerned with a daughter's career do not initially bring her overseas. A woman who left one of her daughters in Japan under her parents' care said:

Fukiko has just become sixteen years old. Next year she has to write the entrance examination of T University and several others. She is trying to get into medicine ... Her grandfather, my father-in-law, is a physician and is placing his hopes on her. My husband is his only son, but he disappointed his father by becoming a salary-man [*sic*]. Now Fukiko thinks she could fulfil her grandpa's wish ... I wish her to marry after graduation from university and live an ordinary life. But I can't do anything about it, because it's her choice. People are accusing me of leaving a daughter in Japan. I know they are saying behind my back that I am a *kyoiku-mama*.

Gender differentiation is clearly expressed by the Japanese corporate couples especially when the heir of the family is concerned. Although the traditional family form has changed since the last world war (Vogel 1963; Ishida 1971; Fukutake 1974), it is still considered very important for the eldest son to succeed symbolically to the family name and tradition. Therefore, gendered education practised among Japanese middle-class couples is sometimes in conflict with this traditional family order. When the corporate couple does not have a male child, one of the daughters, usually the eldest one, is expected to fill a son's place. If this is the case, a couple may not take all their daughters with them to an overseas post, so that at least one daughter might receive adequate training at the 'right' school, preparing for a desired university and a future career.

The girls who pursue a future career are therefore given an opportunity in a different way than boys. Girls learn that their future careers are important to their families but their careers are organized with a view to sustaining the patriarchal moral order. Boys' future careers, on the other hand, are to provide for them to become active members of a corporation and for their own advancement within Japanese society.

CONCLUSION: CONTINUITY OF CLASS AND GENDER

We have seen how the overarching requirements of corporate recruitment and training policies are carried abroad. There, supported by the 'educational success' discourse, women's work in the family is the heart and soul of the reproduction of a gendered moral order. A Japanese woman's labour is available to her sons as a service to them in the same manner as it is available to her husband. Thus, from mothers' work, male children learn the lessons of their own gender (Smith 1983b), which allows them to pursue a career for future participation in the corporation, while daughters are directed towards the replication of the mother's role as middle-class woman. In fact, the world to which girls are exposed by accompanying their parents abroad is a gendered one in which women participate in the relations of ruling on behalf of their sons.

The middle-class woman's access to class privilege is through the family's relation to the Japanese corporation. These women are active in the interests of the ruling apparatus which determines, organizes, and coordinates their everyday practices. By subordinating their lives to their children's socialization, schooling, and education, Japanese women serve to sustain and reproduce the social organization of class and gender.

NOTES

1 I am deeply indebted to Marie Campbell who helped me put my fragmented thoughts into shape. Without her generous help, I could not have produced this essay.

2 The study was funded by the Social Sciences and Humanities Research Council of Canada Grant #484-88-0027.

3 Dorothy Smith has identified the workings of an 'ideological code' as a 'schema that replicates its organization in multiple and various sites ... [and that] can generate the same order in widely different settings of talk, or writing – legislative, social scientific, popular writing, administrative, television advertising, and whatever' (1993: 51–2).

4 *Tanshin-funin*: going away from home alone for an assignment while leaving the family at home for a long period of time.

5 *Kyoiku-mama*: roughly translated into 'education mother.' The term refers to the intense nurturing control a particular mother will exercise over her children in direct competition with other mothers in her neighbourhood or social circle to see to it that her own children do better in the educational system' (De Vos and Wagatsuma 1970: 356).

6 *Ronin*: used to mean the lordless warrior in feudal Japan. Today it is used for the students who are not attached to any school or university. Many of these students previously failed the entrance examination and are waiting for the next chance, in the meantime attending special preparatory schools.

What's Health Got to Do with It? Class, Gender, and Teachers' Work

ANN MANICOM

The formal role of schools is to foster the social and intellectual development of children. Its formal curriculum comprises a range of subject areas, including health. However, although schools are mandated to *teach* health, on the surface at least they are not organizationally warranted or structured to *do* health. The official elementary school curriculum is not meant to address tired children, undernourished children, children with abscessed teeth, children with colds or chapped hands, or children living under conditions of stress caused by poverty and deprivation. Yet the real life of teaching young children *is* about such matters. In the course of the school year, a teacher of young children copes with outbreaks of chicken pox and flu. She bandages scraped knees and puts cold cloths on bleeding noses. She finds herself handing out tissues for runny noses, sending feverish children home, and cleaning up when someone has thrown up. She finds herself concerned about children who seem not to be getting enough sleep or who seem to be eating junk food. Elementary teachers talk about watching over and acting upon such aspects of children's health.[1] This talk signals a set of practices distinct from the official Health Education curriculum: I call these instances 'doing health.' Of interest in this essay is what is revealed through an analysis of 'doing health' in elementary schools.

This essay examines what teachers of early elementary grades do about children's health and how this 'doing' shapes their work. Drawing on Smith's (1986) institutional ethnography, the analytical procedure entails three interwoven steps. The first is to display teachers' everyday experiences of attending to the health and welfare needs of children. Then, the social organization of these aspects of teachers' work is investigated by examining the ways teachers' work processes intersect with the work processes of the family, other school personnel, and other professionals such as social workers. Finally, there is an investigation of the ways intersecting work processes are structured through documentary practices, which link and regulate work processes in particular ways, drawing the local and particular into extra-local social relations. This movement beyond the entry point of the local and particular reveals aspects of the social organization of teachers' work and how it is constituent of and constituted by the relations of class and gender. While these three procedures entailed in institutional ethnography underpin the larger study, what is available in this essay is only a glimpse of what can be revealed through this method.

What has been so important about my engagement with the work of Dorothy Smith has been the way it enables teachers, engaged in addressing their difficulties teaching in inner city schools (particularly in discussing poverty and class as the source of these difficulties), to shift away from a theorizing that locates the blame for the problems in either inadequate parenting or teachers' middle-class attitudes and expectations. Thus, the politics of this essay connect to a long-term project of working with teachers to analyse their locatedness in the relations of class and gender, a project which has implications for their individual decisions as teachers as well as for their collective work within teachers' movements and in alliances with other progressive social movements.

The research[2] reported in this essay was carried out in an urban centre using interviews with teachers of early elementary grades, located in two clusters of schools, whose catchment areas could be described as either inner city or middle class/affluent. Of the two inner city schools, one was in the downtown core, the other in the suburbs; 90 per cent of the housing was rental housing, much of it subsidized, with people experiencing high rates of social assistance and unemployment. The five schools were all within the same school system, governed by the same regulations, curriculum guidelines, and resources from the central office.

TEACHERS' WORK: RESOURCE CONDITIONS

'We can examine the classroom as an actual work organization in which problems of time and other resources in the performance of tasks for which the teacher is held responsible must be solved' (Smith 1986: 9). Resource conditions of teaching are often thought of in terms of pupil–teacher ratios, texts, supplies, and availability of specialists. In analysing teachers' work, a generally neglected resource feature is *time*, even though it governs the daily, weekly, and yearly teaching activities (Ball et al. 1984; Corrigan 1987;

Hilsum and Cane 1971). Its central structuring effects are enormously taken for granted.

Time with students is a finite resource. Teachers see students for about 190 days a year, for a specific period each day, and while they may see some students briefly for extra work at noon hours, in general the school day (the formal time with students) has a clear beginning and end. What does not, however, have clear beginning and end is the definition of what counts as teachers' work.

Pertinent to this essay are two features of teachers' work in elementary grades: its elasticity and its central ideological frame (the 'whole child'). 'Elasticity' refers to the fact that teachers' work is without clear definition or boundaries; teachers of early elementary grades routinely respond to a multitude of anticipated and unanticipated events. Teaching tasks expand to include extra demands, explicit or implicit, from principals, other teachers, parents, children; there are clerical tasks, nursing tasks, domestic tasks, parenting tasks, as well as instructional tasks.[3]

Behind this elasticity is the ideology of the 'whole child,' the psychological discourse that underpins much of teachers' talk and professional texts (curriculum guidelines, curriculum materials, policy statements, and teacher education texts). (See Griffith in this volume for detailed discussion of this discourse.) Pedagogical discourse is firmly rooted in the discourse of developmental psychology which has provided normative accounts of stages of cognitive, physical, social, emotional, and moral development, all of which are assumed to intertwine. The pedagogical implication of this theorizing is that the ethos of early elementary schooling is 'child-centred'; all aspects of development are pertinent to the practice of teaching. Some of the elasticity mentioned above can be accounted for by this broad ideological framework of teachers' work. We will return to both of these features at the end of the essay.

DOING HEALTH: TEACHERS' WORK

In general, when elementary teachers talk about 'children's health,' they mean both physical and emotional health.[4] These two aspects of health are linked both in discourse and in practice, and (consistent with the ideology of the whole child) physical care is taken to be both necessary to, and evidence of, proper emotional care.

In the interviews undertaken for this study, teachers' talk about children's physical health included proper food (nutritious snacks and regular breakfasts), sufficient sleep, adequate supervision (evening babysitters of a suitable age, supervision during lunch hour and after school), clean and seasonally appropriate clothing, access to medical care when sick, and proper dental care. Their talk about emotional health included provision by care-givers of love, security, consistency, self-esteem, 'togetherness,' and trust. It included the consequences on the family of alcoholism, wife battering and family breakup.

In some respects, all the early elementary teachers in this study, whether in inner city or mixed/affluent schools, shared similar concerns about health. They all commented, for example, on nutrition and sleep or on parents being 'over-permissive' or not spending much time with the child. However, although many of the same topics arose in the accounts of both groups of teachers, there was both a qualitative and a quantitative difference in their experiences.

In part this difference was one of degree: health matters seemed more in the forefront of inner city teachers' concerns. It was only quite late in the interviews that health matters arose, if at all, with the teachers in the mixed/affluent schools. In contrast, in the interviews with the inner city teachers, in every instance, matters of health arose in the first fifteen minutes. Overall, health matters seemed to be of less urgency for teachers in the mixed/affluent schools; children's emotional and physical health problems were not events of daily significance, did not constitute problems *for the teacher*. For the inner city teachers, however, what was visible in the interviews was an intensification of these concerns. Their talk was full of accounts of late nights, no breakfasts, listlessness, neglect, and abuse. The inner city teachers perceived themselves to be faced with an assemblage of such problems, in many children rather than in just one or two. What is crucial to note here (and which we will revisit later in this essay) is the cumulative effect on inner city teachers' work. A multiplicity of occurrences has an effect on a teacher's work processes, an effect that cannot be readily absorbed. It has consequences for the allocation of *time* in schooling, and, as will be argued, makes visible how school provisioning is in fact unequal given that time is finite. This can help us understand schools as sites for the transgenerational production of class relations.

From the interview data, it is possible to identify the consequences for inner city teachers of the 'health' demands on their time, both in class and out of class.

In-Class Time

One consequence for the utilization of time appeared in the inner city teachers' descriptions of what they did during in-class time to handle children's emotional and physical health problems. The teachers, as best they could, responded in a number of ways: they 'watched for problems,' they 'took time to talk' about such things as nutrition and sleep, they described themselves as 'compensating' for what they saw as emotional deprivation, and they sometimes shifted their classroom routines in response to certain events, such as children not having breakfasted. (For example, they might give the students their free milk and cookies first thing in the morning; most Primary and Grade 1 teachers do this after recess.)

In-class time is instructional time; it is time when official curriculum is taught, which in early elementary grades consists primarily of basic literacy and numeracy development. Exploring relationships concerning in-class instructional time and health problems brings into view features of the social organization of teachers' work.

First, people who are overtired, undernourished, or stressed work and learn less efficiently. Children who are tired and hungry have less energy for any kind of task; they have less capacity to deal with dissent, with waiting, with sitting still, with concentration. This affects their learning in in-class time. Second, the teacher's allocation of in-class time to health problems affects the instructional pace and time. As teachers pay additional attention to emotional and physical health, they reduce the time allocated to mandated curriculum.

Teachers' work embodies a clear contradiction here: children cannot learn if they do not have the energy or if they are stressed. But taking time to deal with their physical and emotional welfare reduces time available for 'official' learning, because, as noted earlier, time with students ('actual teaching time') is a finite resource condition of teachers' work.

One might note here that 'taking time' is one of those phrases which glosses differences in teachers' work. In some instances, taking 'extra time' has a pay-off; 'taking time' at one moment can ease problems later. For example, if a teacher takes time in September to systematically help her students learn to work in groups, this will save her considerable 'management time' in future months of the school year. But the constant recurrence of health and welfare problems means that time *continually* is taken, week after week, year after year. Time taken *now* does not mean more time available tomorrow; time taken from instructional work *now* to attend to health does not mean more instructional time tomorrow. The cumulative effects of such processes distinguish teaching in inner city schools, and are an instance of how schooling practices can be seen as classing practices, that is, as constituent of class relations and inequitable schooling.

Overall, in the talk of inner city teachers interviewed for this study, there was a sense that allocating time to children's physical and emotional welfare meant accomplishing less, academically: 'Well, I think you get less work done. Doing more administering to needs that aren't met in the home. You know, you are doing more mothering and you are doing more peacemaking, and you are doing more – just general living types of things with them rather than the academic. I mean, you have to do the academics too, but the children don't have some of the other things, and those things have to be met somehow' (Teacher K, inner city, Grade 2). The cumulative effect of this 'taking time' on one classroom, and over time, multiplied throughout a school, is a classing practice. It produces class-based inequities in schooling.

Out-of-Class Time

Hilsum and Cane (1971), in an early study of the work of primary teachers, indicate that only 58 per cent of teachers' work is time spent in the actual classroom. Thus, it is significant to attend to what teachers' work looks like outside the classroom. The above description is of how time is used differently in those hours when children are actually in the classroom. But many of the activities pertaining to health-related matters occur in out-of-class time: recesses, lunch times, before and after school, sometimes evenings and weekends.

Normally, teachers use out-of-class times for the short- and long-term preparatory work of teaching, for filing materials, for mounting displays of children's work, and the like. Such time can be used for developing special projects or for professional development and reflection. Activities such as these were what the mixed/affluent school teachers in this study talked about doing in their after-school time. Teachers in mixed/affluent schools did, of course, use some after-school time for health matters, but not to the extent described by the inner city teachers.

The inner city teachers used considerable portions of out-of-school time to attend to health concerns. They had conversations with parents or wrote notes to parents, particularly when the mother either did not come to the school or did not have a phone (see Griffith in this volume for a discussion of the allocation to *mothers* of this and other school-related work). One teacher described how that very morning a child had come with a swollen mouth, after having stayed at home the previous day because she had a toothache. The teacher was concerned about the swelling and wanted to get the mother to do something about it: 'She doesn't have a phone, so I wrote a note home and said I was really sorry to hear that she [the child] had a toothache, and I knew that can be quite painful, and that it can also be quite serious, if it's left unattended ... And I just said that if she didn't have a dentist then I was sure the school could make arrangements' (Teacher E, inner city, Grade 1). Note here that the teacher not only decides she must bring the seriousness of the matter to the mother's attention, but also offers advice on what medical action to take, to the extent of offering the school's services.[5]

In addition to times taken to talk to (mostly) mothers about the children's health problems, inner city teachers used out-of-class time to have meetings with other related professionals (for example, a social worker or public health nurse) concerning a child's needs. In intersecting with the work of such professionals as social workers or public health nurses, teachers' work processes become articulated to work processes within another jurisdiction. Like teachers, people employed in health and welfare fields work under particular resource conditions, and their work is managed through certain textually mediated organizational practices (see, for example, de Montigny, in this volume). In terms of structuring teachers' work, the most immediate point here is that with many health issues, teachers have to insert their work and their knowledge into a whole set of practices outside of what is taken to be 'normal teaching work'; they spend time filling out forms, monitoring behaviours for referral purposes, attending case team meetings, and so on.

The use of out-of-class time affects the work process, although a teacher cannot say precisely what she would have done otherwise if she had not made that phone call, had that discussion, written that note. However, one can assume that *something* is not done; only a certain number of things *can* be done within a finite time period, and choices have to be made. We know, from general accounts of teachers' work, what activities teachers often do in their out-of-class time: marking, preparing next day's lessons, or working on special materials for children with particular needs. Since it is into this time that 'doing health' impinges, it must be that some of these preparatory activities are reallocated, simplified, or abandoned.

Consider this in terms of literacy instruction alone, in inner city schools. Reading series – the textbooks used in teaching reading in early elementary grades – (whether the old basal series or the newer whole language series) are used by most teachers, but many of the stories and specified activities are inappropriate to the interests, knowledge, culture, and experiences of many children who live in inner city areas. Developing alternatives to, or even extensions of, a reading series program takes time. The pressures on out-of-class time make it less likely that inner city teachers will have time to develop alternative strategies, despite the fact that one could argue that alternatives are even more needed in their situations. This is true not only for literacy instruction, but for all the other educational work for which an early elementary teacher is responsible.

If there is only one child in a classroom with the sorts of health problems that worry teachers, the teacher absorbs it readily into her daily work process. But if attention to the health needs of many children is a prevalent and constant feature of a teacher's work, it alters the work process, particularly in the allocation of time. It is the intensifications and the multiple occurrences of children's health problems among many children that help construct inner city teaching as a class relation.

MAKING SENSE OF DATA: DIFFERENT WAYS TO DO IT

We have begun to see how time as a resource condition for teaching (and therefore for learning) can be shaped by how much 'health' the teachers have had to 'do' with the children. Time in inner city schools is doubly truncated: in actual in-class instructional time and in out-of-class curriculum development time. The key theme that emerges here is this: the provision of actual education for children in inner city schools is thus *unequal*, at least as concerns the resource condition of *time* allocated to developing those skills valued and rewarded in academic settings.

Typically, such differences in teachers' work (and the concomitant differences in students' school experiences) would be 'explained' by a causal connection linking families, poverty, class, and schooling. As many educational critics have demonstrated, these are often 'explanations' that locate the problem in the family's lack of resources, its 'inadequate parenting,' its culture of poverty. Following this line of thinking, the experiences of teachers in my study would be seen as the result of 'external' class factors having an 'impact' on classrooms. However, I am not satisfied with such an account, which most often blames the family (the mother) for the children's health-related needs.

But how else can we understand what is going on? One step in understanding the embeddedness of schooling practices in class relations is to examine how teachers' work processes link with the work processes of others, beyond the immediate school setting. An institutional ethnography offers a feminist materialist method which examines linkages among work processes, in this case, displaying how the resource conditions of teachers' work are intertwined with the resource conditions of others who work with children: the mothers (or other female caregivers like older sisters, grandmothers, or neighbours).

The analysis changes shape if a feminist perspective is brought to women's work within the family, in the labour market and in relation to the state. Instead of locating the 'problem' in 'the family,' what comes into view are the resource conditions under which different women accomplish their work as mothers.

Health as Mother's Work

Children's health, in most prescriptive accounts, is the responsibility of the mother (Helterline 1980; Weiss 1978; see also Griffith, in this volume). This ascription of responsibility to mothers is central to the understandings about class developed in this essay. That is, once the gendered character of the theories and practices concerning child and maternal health are rendered visible, one can see that understanding class necessitates understanding gender.

Central to an institutional ethnography that examines teachers' experiences and actions in 'doing health' is to conceptualize children's health as a product of the family work process *and the resource conditions* within which that work is accomplished. Feminist analyses have made clear how the work processes of families (and in particular the lives of women) are structured by processes such as the domestic division of labour, gendered segregation of the labour market, and gender differentiation in state and social service provisioning. Of particular interest for this essay are the resource conditions under which women, mothers[6], carry out their mothering work in school catchment areas characterized by poverty, reliance on foodbanks, high levels of unemployment or sporadic employment, high levels of social assistance, and not enough affordable quality child care. Clearly, how individual women's lives are articulated to these processes will differ.[7] But for all the differences in the particulars of individual lives, there remain the general resource conditions within which all the women clean their living spaces, feed and clothe their children, attend to their children's health, pay their rent, find employment – in general accomplish their daily work processes. Each woman has differing personal resources, history and experiences, but each operates within the basic resource conditions of her neighbourhood. It is this overall set of resource conditions in a school catchment area which become part of the resource conditions of teachers' work.

Further health-specific resource conditions in a school catchment area include the availability of medical clinics and doctors' or dentists' offices in the vicinity; a family's access to transportation to these sites, as well as to the hospital; a family's access to medical coverage through such things as dental plans or extended medical insurance. It is within this set of resource conditions of families that children's health is accomplished. So when teachers 'do' children's health, their work intersects with the work processes of the family (mother). But given the above sketch of family resource conditions, teachers who 'do health' are linking not only with a particular family/mother but also with the way her work processes are materially structured (and textually mediated; see Griffith and Smith, 1990). Thus, the teacher's work processes are woven into broader sets of social relations – relations of class, gender, race. But even if a grasp of these broader structural processes helps teachers begin to understand the complexity of their work in relation to the daily lives of families, it still does not illuminate how the teaching work process *itself* is organized in ways that interact with family work processes to continue to produce (constitute) these social relations.

How can the teaching work process be seen, not as merely responding to, but as *part of*, classing practices? For this, we need to return to the points made at the beginning of this essay about the two features of teachers' work: its elasticity and the ideology of the whole child.

SCHOOLS AS PART OF THE PROBLEM

Attending to matters of health is *routine*; it is a normal part of a work process characterized by elasticity of boundaries. The teacher adapts constantly to expected and unexpected events. Teachers' work is routinely adaptable, routinely flexible.

Matters pertaining to children's health are absorbed in this process. It is a routine matter to adapt and respond to the health and welfare events that surface in a given day's work. All the notes home, the conversations with mothers, the shifting of milk and cookie time, the 'keeping an eye open for teeth,' the discussions with children about bedtimes and breakfasts and healthy recesses, trying to find donations of mittens and scarves, the meetings with social workers – all of these become part of getting the work done. They are routine.

No job description of teaching in early elementary grades includes talking to a parent about a welfare cheque, about budgeting, about being a single parent.[8] Yet the daily work process of many inner city teachers includes such events. The task of being a teacher expands to absorb such courses of action. The elasticity means that the limits can stretch to include attention to such matters.

Thus, attention to health and welfare is both a form of disruption and intensification of teachers' work *and* an instance of the routine flexibility of teachers' work. The point being developed here is that classing practices lie in the rendering of certain intensifications as routine. The intensification in the area of health, and the consequent re-allocation of time by inner city teachers is masked, or rendered matter of fact, in this routine adaptability that is so fundamental a characteristic of teachers' work.

But attending to matters of health is more than a routine course of action in a job whose limits are vague. It is also a matter of *good practice*. A central assumption of teachers of young children is that they are teaching the 'whole child.' The psychological and pedagogical 'whole child' discourses provide the rationale, the legitimation, and even the necessity for teachers to attend to matters of physical and emotional health of children. But attending to the 'whole child' is more than discourse driven 'good practice.' It also seems to be a matter of elementary teachers' self-image. For early elementary teachers, the notion that they do deal with the 'whole child' is a source of their sense of who they are (McPherson 1972; Nias 1988). Attending to the health and welfare needs of a child is what any 'decent and caring' teacher would do. A major source of pride therefore is precisely this sense of craft and attention to a multiplicity of events which teachers bring to their work. Attending to physical and emotional welfare is evidence of the competencies required of, and the complexities of the work of, teachers of young children.

CLASSING PRACTICES

The ethos of concern for the 'whole child' meshes with the routine elasticity of a teacher's job. Taken together with the finite resource of time, one can begin to see how the very structuring of teachers' work produces class relations. Classing practices, the social relations of class, are daily brought into being as teaching work processes intersect with family work processes and the work processes of other professionals within the education and social service sectors, all of which are governed by particular resource conditions. That this classing remains invisible to teachers except as an *effect* on their work has to do with the structure of their own work which masks the classing practices under particular ideologies and ever-expanding work tasks.

The argument is that attending to children's health is not to be understood as class simply 'impacting' on teachers' work; rather, classing practices are produced partly *in the structure* of the teacher's work processes as these intersect with other work processes, in this instance those that produce children's health problems. The resource conditions of women's work (as both teachers and mothers) are structured by both class and gender relations.

Examining how teachers attend to health provides only a partial mapping of the classed character of teachers' work, and this should be understood in relation to what can be said about other aspects of the curriculum, including processes of literacy instruction, curriculum content, and streaming processes. The analysis in this essay shows how teachers actively participate in producing class relations and yet their teaching practices render invisible part of the school's role in the transgenerational production of class. The interest here has been to understand the local and particularized experiences of teachers as these are organized by social relations that extend beyond the immediate setting. Social relations are *immanent in* teachers' talk about their work *because their work is embedded in these relations.* The social relations are *in* their work, organizing it, and are brought continually into being as teachers' work coordinates with the work of others. It is this substructing of the work process that has been displayed here. The beginning is in the everyday experience of teachers, followed by an explication of how this is socially organized. What is displayed are the ways class relations are made and remade in teaching work processes.

NOTES

1 Aspects of 'children's health' are named in these pages as though 'health' had a simple facticity. However, the very terms people use to talk about health, particularly emotional health, are social constructions. Historical and contemporary social practices have produced, and continue to rework, prevailing assumptions about 'proper care' and the terms used to speak of it: neglect, abuse, malnourishment, emotional deprivation, and the like. Much of this talk is situated in the intertwining of psychological discourse and administrative practices (Ehrenreich and English 1978; Henriques et al. 1984; Levine and Estable 1981; Riley 1983; Smith 1974c, 1983a). Teachers, in their talk, enter unproblematically into this discourse. Thus, readers should think of the health-related words in this essay as bracketed, as a reminder of their character as social constructions.

2 This analysis is part of a study of how elementary teachers' work is both constituted by and constitutive of class and gender relations (see Manicom 1988). The teachers involved had taught in their schools for several years at the same grade level, had six to sixteen years experience, and had completed either a bachelor's or master's degree in education at local universities. The analysis draws princi-

pally on interviews with twelve teachers of Grades Primary to 2, from five inner city and affluent/mixed schools. As well, use was made of informal classroom observations throughout the school system and background census data on the catchment areas of the schools. The original research was supported by a doctoral fellowship from the Social Sciences and Humanities Council of Canada.

3 Lortie (1975) claims that teaching is fraught with endemic uncertainties; Rosenholtz (1989) argues that 'uncertainty' is a key category in analysing teachers' work. Ashton and Webb (1986) have also pointed to this characteristic of teachers' work. They say: 'The demand for service from teachers is infinitely elastic and will always stretch beyond whatever is supplied. In a sense then, no act a teacher may perform remains beyond the call of duty for very long' (ibid.: 39). See Manicom (1988) plus other accounts of the character of elementary teachers' work: Boyd 1984; Delamont 1987; Hartley 1985; King 1978; Lieberman and Miller 1984; Nias 1988 and 1989; Sharp and Green 1975; Walkerdine 1984.

4 The physical and mental-emotional health couple has been forged in this century through processes which link psychological discourse, legislative provisioning, and activities accomplished in the health and social services sectors. The emotional-physical health couple initially developed through philanthropic activity; was consolidated and institutionalized through federal, provincial, and municipal legislation; was legitimated through discourse practice, particularly psychological discourse; continuously was transformed into popular child-rearing advice (Beekman 1979; Brim 1959; Helterline 1980; Weiss 1978); and entered into professional training literature, particularly for teachers and social workers. See Smith (1974c, 1983a, 1984) for a discussion of the processes by which discourses develop and circulate within the ruling apparatus. Also see Smith's *Conceptual Practices of Power* (1990a).

5 One might note here a point about the social construction of health problems as faced by teachers of young children: children's health problems only become classroom problems in particular instances. In some early elementary classrooms, a sore tooth might mean that a teacher would suggest that a child put her head on the desk until it was time to go home for lunch, and then her mum and dad would make sure it got fixed. So there would be a momentary attending in the work process, a brief expression of concern. But in this instance, the abscessed tooth means a discussion with the mother about the importance of attending to the tooth, a concern about whether the mother has a dentist, and a suggestion that if she does not, the school could make arrangements to find her one. In both instances the child has a toothache. But in one instance this becomes a problem for the teacher, becomes something to which she allocates time in her work process. It is processes such as these that are important throughout the analysis being developed here: the instances where social courses

of action enter into the teacher's work process, and structure her decisions about the allocation of her time.

6 'Mothers' here should be understood, for many of these families, to sometimes mean a grandmother, or perhaps an aunt, or an older sister.

7 See Armstrong and Armstrong (1984), Levine and Estable (1981), Luxton (1980), Rubin (1976), Sidel (1986), and Wilson (1977), for a number of accounts of women living in poverty and raising children. It should be noted here that similar conditions do not produce homogeneity among families. Each sole-support mother's life differs in many respects from another's, even in the same school catchment area.

8 Note that this is an example of how the intersecting of a teacher's work process with a mother's work process also produces an intersection with practices of the local state, in this instance those social courses of action which include welfare provisioning. It provides an instance of how teaching work processes intersect with processes of unequal distribution of societal resources. (Does the mother have enough money to buy extra milk for her freezer? Is her freezer compartment big enough? Does the freezer compartment even work?) Not all teachers' work processes intersect with state and economic practices in these ways. The potential is always there, but it is only some teachers whose work processes shift to absorb and interact in these ways. Explicating the intersections with wider state processes is central to a full analysis of the social organization of teachers' work.

Compulsory Heterosexuality: Schools and Lesbian Students[1]

DIDI KHAYATT

This essay sketches schooling processes that shape the problems faced by lesbian adolescents within the Ontario school system. In describing the experiences of these lesbian adolescents, the essay provides an analysis of the social relations of schooling which shape and determine these experiences. What everyday activities in schools shape a young lesbian's experiences of gaining cognizance of her sexual orientation, of coming out, of marginalization and vulnerability, of even contemplating suicide?[2] Given current debates about the quality of education, what can be said of how the quality of life in schools is structured for young lesbians?

In 1990 I interviewed young lesbians in Toronto as part of a study to investigate the barriers to the provision of quality education for lesbian and gay youth.[3] Following the feminist sociology of Dorothy E. Smith, I adopted the methodological procedures of institutional ethnography (Smith 1987a). The process is one of investigating the practices and activities organizing a segment of the social world from the standpoint of those who, in various ways, are involved in its production. In this study, the experiences of the young lesbians along with the work and activities of other students, teachers, guidance counsellors, and administrators provide the data. Through this we can begin to comprehend how schooling practices are integral to the construction of the marginality and vulnerability experienced by young lesbians. We can also begin to see how young lesbians are seldom in a position to break the relative silence which envelopes their lives at school.

SCHOOLS, HETEROSEXUALITY, AND MALE SUPREMACY

In a modern patriarchal Western capitalist society like Canada, hierarchies and multiple forms of oppression and difference are maintained ideologically, socially, economically, and politically. Inequitable social relations, regulated through interlocking ideological practices (laws, policies, procedures, and traditions), are legitimized in the ongoing activities of such institutions as schools, churches, and the media. (For example, see Kinsman in this volume for an account of regulating sexuality through law reform commissions.)

Although many hegemonic principles regulate patriarchal capitalism, one of the most fundamental is heterosexuality. Heterosexuality is an ideology as well as a sexual practice that exists in binary opposition to other forms of sexual expression (such as homosexuality or bisexuality) and that is socially legitimated as a political institution. 'Heterosexism' is defined as 'the belief that everyone is, or should be, heterosexual' (Friend 1993: 211). According to Adrienne Rich (1980: 30–3), 'compulsory heterosexuality' is a systematic and forcible imposition of heterosexuality through institutional and cultural arrangements that privilege people for being or appearing to be heterosexual (see also Buchbinder et al. 1987; Cartledge and Ryan 1983). Compulsory heterosexuality is imposed on women through practices ranging from the enormous social pressures to marry and to be appealing and available to men, to the inscription of heterosexism in legislated entitlements (for example, spousal benefits).

The education system is one of a coordinated web of institutions which actively accomplish hegemonic ideologies. While the production of knowledge in schools is contested terrain (see Apple 1993; Giroux 1992; Weis and Fine 1993), school knowledge and the practices which structure that knowledge generally maintain rather than challenge prevailing social relations. It is true, of course, that people often live their lives in resistance to particular dominant practices. Clearly, young lesbians confront and challenge hegemonic heterosexism when choosing to love other women; their choices produce particular counterhegemonic ideologies. But such struggles against dominant forms are enacted on hostile terrain.

To understand experiences of young lesbians in schools, we need to look at a whole range of coordinated and coordinating schooling practices. These include mandated curriculum content; allocation and control of resources; teachers' knowledge and provisions for teacher professional development; administrative procedures in a school or school system both local and provincial; and the coeducational and/or denominational status of a school. These and other schooling practices embody and enact (both contain within themselves and actively produce) particular forms of femininity, masculinity, and heterosexuality, and therefore what is experienced by students. The overall effect for lesbian students is one of constraint, silencing, marginalization, lack of support, lack of knowledge, and fear.

DOING THE INTERVIEWS

In 1990, after consulting various organizations and support systems in Metro Toronto,[4] I was able to reach twelve young lesbians for interviews. All respondents were self-selected and thus already self-identified lesbians. At the time of the interviews (between 1 May 1990 and 30 April 1991), the young women ranged in age from fifteen to twenty-four years.

In the interviews, we explored broad topics such as when and how the interviewee began to self-identify as a lesbian; what mention of 'homosexuality' did she hear in class, school, or assembly; and what were the attitudes and actions of various peers, teachers, or administrative staff towards the topic. Using these interviews as entry points, in this essay I examine the everyday school world of these students and uncover aspects of the local organization of the schools, making visible some of the determinants of the social relations of which they are a part.

SCHOOLING PRACTICES

Peer Relations: Heterosexism, Isolation, and Homophobia

Relations with peer groups are important to adolescents. Yet relationships must be maintained within the bounds of heterosexist norms. And heterosexist norms underpin everyday taken-for-granted practices in the social lives of adolescents. For example, assumptions about dating, including the organization of school dances as well as everyday talk about boyfriends and girlfriends, assume heterosexual relations. Generally there is pressure to relate to the 'opposite sex,' although single sex schools provide some freedom from this pressure to date: 'unlike a lot of other people that I've met since then who talk of what a really rough time they had in high school because they had to go out on all these fake dates and stuff like that, there was no pressure on us [in our single sex school] to go out on dates if we didn't want to.'

For these young women, decisions to come out in a school context were fraught with concerns about relations with peers. Several of the young women were aware of the discrimination they were undergoing at school, experienced as a general climate of rejection of lesbians and gays, a negativity which forced some of them into a self-imposed isolation: 'I never had any close friendships in high school because I was afraid that something would happen and that I would slip up and say something. I was one of the top students and I was afraid that I was going to lose all these privileges that I had if this kind of thing accidentally came out.' Conversely, a couple of young women felt their isolation was a consequence of having come out:

People loved me, students loved me and I was nominated for student council. Then, in grade eleven, everybody knows that I'm a lesbian [and now] most people seem to back off and don't want to talk to me and say hi – they say hi, but it's not the same ... The funny part is, when I sit down [in the auditorium] no one will sit around me, that's the worst. They'll leave a space, or you know what I mean, and that's hurting me inside, because I think it's my choice to come out or not, but I did come out and I'm glad of it. That's what you get when you come out.

One young woman stated that her experiences at school as an 'out' lesbian were not as difficult as they could have been:

I was very lucky because I've done a lot of work for the school and I've been very active with the school teams, and joining school clubs. So, I'd already earned respect that couldn't be taken away just because I was gay. The fact that I was already very visible in school, when I came out it was just an additional thing – a big addition, but just an addition. But, like I know a lot of lesbian and gay youth who go through high school thinking their life is worth shit, and just go through, and always contemplating: God, I'm so alone, I wanna die. And I hear a lot of this, and I get so angry that there isn't anybody to help them.

The hegemony of heterosexuality is imposed in other ways. Student attitudes isolate and marginalize gays and lesbians. One striking theme in the interviews was the recurrence of experiences where mention of homosexuality within the general school context meant pejorative allusions or verbal abuse by their peers. One example, from among many: 'I remember there was this snowshoeing contest, it was [the school's] winter carnival and I had my favourite plaid jacket and jeans and I was doing quite well in the contest and someone yelled out "fucking dyke," and I remember that comment, you know, because I felt vulnerable enough as it was.' Whether a lesbian is out or not, the isolation (or threat of it) and verbal abuse create a hostile environment. Name-calling is a manifestation of the pressures to conform to certain notions of masculinity and femininity. Such an environment regulates sexuality, enforcing hegemonic masculinity and heterosexuality. But name-calling is sustained, indeed structured, by a range of institutional practices which coordinate sexual regulation in schools. These come into view when examining official schooling practices: curriculum content, teachers' instructional activities, administrative procedures, and teacher rights.

Official Curriculum Content

Almost all the young lesbians I interviewed described the official silence of the school system regarding the topic of homosexuality. This silence was expressed both in the invisibility, intentional or otherwise, of any gay- or lesbian-related topics, and in the suppression or distortion of information regarding lesbian or gay sexuality.

One of most prevalent ways lesbian and gay sexuality is rendered invisible is by simply not mentioning it, by not having any information regarding its existence available in schools, and by not including it in any section of the curriculum. One young woman, asked whether she remembered being taught anything regarding lesbian or gay sexuality, replied: 'Never formally. I can remember one English class, it was a creative writing class, and at the beginning of the class a different student would bring up a discussion topic to give us, topics to write about in our journals, and issues around AIDS came up and homosexuality, but I can't remember it ever being taught formally in a positive or negative context. No I can't really remember it at all.' And another student remembered: 'I never encountered it formally – like, it would come up, but it was never addressed as a topic by the teacher. The teacher didn't take the initiative to say I'm going to discuss this. Not even in sociology, no, it wasn't touched on then. It was an option you could study if you wanted to, and luckily people did, and they informed the class.'

Another young woman described her 'gifted' program as lacking in information regarding lesbians and gays: 'I can remember in our Modern Western Civilization course we learned about how good liberalism was. But the only black person we learned about was Martin Luther King and he was optional. Women: we learned about Mary Wollstonecraft and one other woman. But it was ridiculous that, although the course went up to 1984, we didn't learn anything like Stonewall,[5] we never studied Oscar Wilde, in our drama section, and Jane Rule wasn't touched upon in our Canadian Fiction.'

One place in the mandated curriculum where sexuality can be discussed is in sex education programs. However, control over sex education and specific knowledge about sexuality has always been highly contested in schools. The control of girls' sexual knowledge has been discussed by authors such as Fine (1988) and Walkerdine (1990), who describe how sex education programs emphasize the biology of reproduction, the dangers of sexual activity, and means of pregnancy protection. Critiques of sex education also point to the assumptions of heterosexuality that pervade discussions of birth control. To learn about women loving women, students rely on knowledge gleaned informally: 'There was reference to [women having sex with each other] in another of [Margaret Laurence's] books, *Rachel, Rachel*, which I searched out and read ... That was the first actualization for me that women had sex.'

A further form of control over sexuality education has to do with the rubric under which it is taught. One student came out while attending a Catholic school. In her school, sexuality topics were taught under the rubric of 'religion,' whereas in the public school system the topics fall under health or physical education or family life. The interviewee understood that learning about sexuality in religion class rendered sexual behaviour a moral issue, expressed, for example, in terms of 'sin' and 'purity.' One young woman clearly saw her sexual orientation as evil: 'At the end of grade ten, after I had come to the realization [that I was a lesbian], I would spend a lot of time in the Chapel praying. That's what I thought I should do. I got to the point where I was so depressed with it and feeling so incredibly guilty about it. I was causing this evil.'

Overall, the mandated school curriculum does not include either lesbian and gay social and historical contributions or lesbian and gay sexuality. This silence is reinforced by the resource acquisition practices in school libraries and resource centres. In the words of one of the interviewees:

I was looking for information because when you're coming out you go through a stage where you need to be swarmed by information. And there was nothing, not even in libraries. I looked in the school library and the only place I found anything was in the dictionary. I went to the extent of looking it up in the encyclopedia and actually one of the pages had been vandalized by one of the students. So there was nothing for me. In the Guidance Office, you can stand there and look at all the pamphlets and stuff, but there was nothing.

Further regulation of knowledge is accomplished through administrative control over access to external resources. In the gay and lesbian community, there are people willing to speak, for example, at official school assemblies or in the classroom. But access to such knowledge is regulated by school administrators. For example, one student wanted a gay speaker for the AIDS Awareness assembly: 'I approached the principal for permission, and he said that he wanted a speaker who was not gay. No gay speakers at all. And he said that he was scared of what the parents would say when kids went back home and said, "Oh, there was a gay guy today speaking about AIDS at our school." Like, he was really careful. He didn't want any negative exposure.' The student challenged the principal. She even had several teachers back her, but the administration stood firm. In any case, when the speaker did come to the school, he was indeed gay, but he did not identify himself as such.

Of course, this silence in the official curriculum and in official access to resources does not necessarily mean that homosexuality is never mentioned in instructional contexts. In classrooms, the topic can come up, initiated by either teachers or students. But classroom discussions are managed in ways that maintain the hegemony of heterosexuality and subordinate lesbian or gay issues.

Teaching Practices

Notwithstanding what appears to be an 'official' silence which surrounds the subject, a number of teachers and students do put the topic on individual classroom agendas. However, according to the experiences of the students I interviewed, these cases are mostly exceptions. What is more likely is that when the topic is raised in classrooms, teachers act in ways to trivialize, marginalize, and silence helpful discussion. One young woman described how one teacher presented the poetry of Audre Lorde, never mentioning that she was a lesbian. The same teacher went on to suggest that, perhaps, one of Shakespeare's sonnets might be addressed to a man. The interviewee reports, 'We did talk about a sonnet that Shakespeare wrote, like a gushy one to a man, and our whole class kind of laughed and all that and then she explained that it was to his patron and you're supposed to exaggerate the good characteristics of your patron.' This teacher's response was essentially a denial of the possibility of Shakespeare's homosexuality. Coupled with the students' laughter and joking about the tone of the sonnet, the instructional practices of this teacher meant that an opportunity to have an informative discussion about gay sexuality was not taken up. Instead, by permitting laughter and joking about homosexuality to go unchallenged (or even participating in it herself), this teacher fostered a silencing around homosexuality, one that reinforced rather than challenged the homophobia of the halls and playing fields.

The pretence that lesbian and gay sexuality does not exist in the school system produced feelings of unease for the interviewees. However, worse than such examples of trivializing or sidelining discussion on gay sexuality are examples of outright misinformation. It was the active suppression or distortion of information which generated a climate of fear and rage in those young students. Not only was the homophobia explicit, but often teachers did nothing to counteract it. One young woman described the 'ignorance' which surrounded the topic. Asked to elaborate, she said: 'Well, some say that kids raised by gay parents will grow up to be gay. Or, [being gay] is just a phase, it will pass, it comes after puberty for some people. Some of the stuff is outrageous: there's something wrong with their chromosomes, poor conditioning; all sorts of things ... And, I'd never heard a teacher rebut [this stuff] in any way, in a positive way, and support homosexuals or clarify that, no, that's not true. I never came across that.'

One interviewee who was in the process of coming out at the time, continued to deny her sexuality because, 'I didn't understand how could someone as feminine as I was be attracted to another female. It didn't make sense.' She had nowhere to turn for information to counter myths she held about what lesbians 'were like.' In her case, one of her teachers made the situation worse for her: 'My gym teacher actually confronted me on whether or not I was a lesbian, and of course, I was still denying it; I didn't know, and I thought she was wrong anyway, so I said, "How can you say that?" And she said some comment to me afterward about, "If you were, I would accept it but I wouldn't tolerate it." I mean, if these teachers don't want to tolerate it, they're not going to want to talk about it a whole lot either.'

Neither teacher education programmes nor professional development programs have systematically trained teachers in understanding gay and lesbian sexuality nor in challenging dominant heterosexuality and heterosexism. Just as the mandated curriculum in schools constructs compulsory heterosexuality, so too does the official curriculum in most teacher education settings. So teachers are hampered in their own ability to supplement or challenge curriculum content and student homophobia.[6]

Schools, as transmitters of official ideologies, cannot afford to condone male or female homosexuality. Officially requiring teachers to include homosexuality within the curriculum, or even readily making available information about the topic, is tantamount to acknowledging that there might be an alternative to heterosexuality. To date, virtually all boards of education in Ontario have a tacit (if not official) policy that proselytizing about homosexuality is forbidden in the schools. Certainly, under particular conditions, the topic may be dealt with, but not presented as an alternative sexual option. Yet, some teachers may discuss the topic of homosexuality in their classes, even if it is not in the official guidelines. Very often, however, even those teachers who are politicized or who are lesbian or gay, have to be careful in the way they deal with questions about homosexuality when and if these come up in class. Therefore, it is no coincidence that the students interviewed all remonstrated against the lack of information, and that whatever mention of homosexuality they reported was frequently a student-originated challenge to the status quo.[7]

Administrative Procedures

As described above, the hegemony of heterosexist assumptions and the marginalization and suppression of lesbian and gay issues is exerted though a mandated curriculum, by general resource availability, and through teacher management of classroom discussion. This marginalization is furthered by administrative procedures. Administrative policies (at both the school and system levels) and textually mediated procedures exist on such things as what kinds of counselling and support services should be in place for students and what kinds of incidents warrant official disciplinary action. In both of these areas, there is an ignoring, even an intolerance, of gay sexuality.

Generally, support and referral services available in schools exist because they have been officially mandated. Once mandated, staff are normally educated to recognize students in need of support and are provided with textually mediated processes to make referrals of students who fit the mandate of the services (much as social workers are mandated to recognize children in need of 'apprehension' – see de Montigny in this volume). In the absence of such services, students are left very much on their own. When mandated procedures for events in an institutional context do not exist, the events do not become officially knowable (see Smith 1974c); the student experiences do not enter into the mandated institutional courses of action.

One interviewee explained that she had tried to commit suicide and had been sent for counselling. She also tried other tactics to bring attention to her plight, but nothing seemed to work:

I actually ran away from home three times and used to come back with the police and nobody ever asked me why. My parents didn't ask why. The school didn't ask why. I refused to be confirmed by the Catholic church and nobody asked me why. I didn't go through [confirmation] with my classmates. I decided I didn't want this because it's obviously a conflict. Nobody ever asked why. And I just kept consciously rerouting these anxieties and feelings and intensities into my work and into the social awareness things I'd become involved in and I was very aware why I was doing things.

Another way administrative practices shape the lives of lesbian youth is through the disciplinary procedures enforced (or not enforced) in schools. Although girls and women do not suffer the same incidence of gay bashing that boys and men do, they do live with their share of violence. Many of my young respondents described examples of this violence, both to their gay male friends and to themselves. We have seen some of this in the verbal abuse described above, both in name-calling (faggot, dyke) and in the ridiculing laughter when mention was made of gay sexuality. But it is crucial to look beneath these events to explore institutional practices which substruct them. The vulnerability and marginalizing of lesbian students is produced in part by administrative failure (by both teachers and principals) to intervene and censure these forms of abuse. Administrative practices thus sustain homophobia and embody heterosexual privilege.

For one student whose lover had inadvertently come out at her school, homophobic comments were direct and threatening, yet no teacher came to her defence: 'She would be walking down the hall and they'd say: "Dyke, here comes the dyke, or ..." She lost a couple of friends because of that. So that's a pretty bad experience.' Another student, in the confusion of coming to terms with her sexuality, was reading Margaret Laurence and realizing for the first time 'that women actually did have sex.' However, shortly after this momentous realization, the student encountered what others thought about women loving women. She elaborated:

There was reference to [women having sex with each other] in another of [Margaret Laurence's] books, *Rachel, Rachel*, which I searched out and read. I had these books with me one day and one of the guys got up on the stage and started talking about 'cunt-suckers' and how these poor women, all they do is ... and me, the language he was using, oh my God, you don't mention that and I was taken aback so much. He picked up this book and just happened to open it to this page and he started going on about 'these poor women having to eat pussy all the time' or something along these lines. He was taken to the principal's office and we never found out what happened to him. He was back in school the next day.

While schools may have policies requiring teacher action (often textually mediated through written reports and referrals) relating to violence, racial 'incidents,' and sexual harassment, there are very few school systems that mandate disciplinary action for homophobic comments.

Teachers

Lesbian and gay teachers teach in public schools (Harbeck 1992; Khayatt 1992). Assumptions of heterosexuality underpin the conditions of their work; their sexuality is marginalized, not recognized in any official way (for example, in spousal benefits or family sick day leave). In some jurisdictions, lesbian and gay teachers have begun to receive official protection. For example, in Ontario, Bill 7 protects individuals from discrimination on the basis of sexual orientation in such areas as housing, work, and access to services. Yet particular boards of education, even those which consider themselves relatively progressive, often bury recommendations protecting the rights of lesbians and gay teachers (see Khayatt 1990). Thus, while some minimal rights are being won, lesbian teachers are still vulnerable. Overall, like the young lesbian students, lesbian teachers' lives are constrained and marginalized through administrative and ideological practices. These constraints mean that lesbian teachers experience danger when taking up the topic of homosexuality or heterosexism in their teaching. They are also in danger if their sexuality is known to the students. Lesbian or gay teachers are seldom inclined to bring up the topic of homosexuality in class for fear of exposing their own sexual orientation. This silence among lesbian and gay teachers means that lesbian and gay students do not find official support from them.

In my interviews with the young lesbians, we touched on the topic of lesbian and gay teachers. Since none of their teachers were open about their sexuality, students had to make assumptions. In some cases there was surreptitious recognition of lesbian or gay teachers. For one respondent, the very fact that she suspected that there were lesbian or gay teachers in her school provided her with support. She admits: 'I knew of one teacher who I was about 90 per cent sure he was gay and another teacher I was about 70 per cent sure he was gay. So that was kind of exciting knowing they were there.' However, recognizing that a teacher was gay often did not improve conditions for the interviewees since, for the most part these teachers prefer not to reveal their sexual orientation (Khayatt 1992).

A lesbian or gay student can, in effect, pose a problem for closeted teachers (see Khayatt 1992) in that the student is more apt to recognize such teachers as gay. In general, lesbian and gay teachers almost always work to maintain their own invisibility and are therefore not of any obvious assistance to lesbian and gay students.

However, even if the sexuality of lesbian or gay teachers were to become known, they could not stand as 'official' role models because the subtextual information conveyed in the concept of 'role model' is that it be publicly recognized as such. In other words, teachers would have to be hired officially as gay or lesbian or perceived to have succeeded despite or because of their sexual orientation before they can be appreciated as role models to emulate. On the one hand, suspecting or knowing about the homosexuality of teachers may help gay and lesbian students know that they are not alone, that they may look up to some of these teachers, and that living as a lesbian is possible; on the other hand, it does not provide an example to the rest of school or society that it is 'OK' to be homosexual.

CONCLUSION

The practices by students, teachers, and administration that produced the invisibility of lesbian and gay sexuality within the school contexts of the young women I interviewed were in some cases deliberate and in others unintentional. However, all were effective in maintaining the appearance that lesbian and gay sexuality did not exist. The silence which surrounded the subject, although not complete, generated a feeling of isolation in the lesbian students interviewed. Whereas the social isolation they experienced is evident in their words, their most profound sense of isolation came from being marginalized, from never being able to speak freely about their sexuality, and from almost always feeling that an essential part of their being was either dismissed, despised, or deleted from the everyday life of being a high school student.

Silence is a form of discrimination and marginalization. The schooling practices that produced the silences and mistellings regarding the subject of homosexuality affected the students in myriad ways: some reported feeling terrified about what was happening to them amidst what seemed like universal reticence to mention the topic. Others spoke of a 'chilling effect,' where they themselves hesitated or refused to bring up the subject for fear of being 'branded.' Others mentioned that the silence itself reinforced their suspicions that the topic was taboo, that what they were undergoing was, in some way, bad. One young lesbian, still attending school, said, 'I don't know, sometimes I feel like I'm the only lesbian in the world.'

The stories of the twelve lesbians in this essay are a clear testimony that homophobia and heterosexism are solidly entrenched within the school system and within the larger society. I have sketched some of the institutional practices which mandate curriculum, provide courses of action for resources and support services, name and enforce disciplinary procedures and ensure teachers' and students' rights; these practices reflect a social organization which is hostile to homosexuality and which enacts compulsory heterosexuality. In the essay we have seen glimpses of how the enforcement of heterosexuality is coordinated across sites (religious, educational, legal). This coordination is characteristic of social relations and ideological practices (see Smith 1987a, 1993).

According to the lesbian students interviewed, several options are open to lesbian and gay youth in the school system today: they can conceal their sexuality and remain invisible; come out publicly and put up with harassment; seek a gay or lesbian community outside the school, an option not often possible for rural youth; or leave school. None of these options provides quality education, and most may, indeed, be a cost to society in the long run.

Although the Province of Ontario added sexual orientation to its list of areas as a prohibited ground of discrimination in 1986, this does not necessarily guarantee equal rights of access to quality education for lesbian and gay youth. Despite Bill 7 only one board of education in Ontario (Toronto) recognizes publicly the needs of lesbian and gay youth. No other has made any provisions to allow them adequate support nor a positive and safe environment in which to come out. The bill does, however, leave school districts in Ontario open to human rights complaints. Yet to date, no lesbian or gay youth has challenged a school board for failing to provide a quality education.

Those in the helping professions (see Gay Teachers' Group, 1987; Heron 1983; *Radical Teacher*, issues 24 and 29; Rofes 1989; Lazier 1990) often discuss the barriers to quality education and lack of support systems for lesbian and gay students, arguing that the lack of information in schools is a reflection of a homophobic society which denies the existence of homosexuality. Some of their suggestions are that schools should provide services aimed at lesbian and gay students, that policies should be initiated to help change attitudes towards homosexuality, and that compassion or respect for homosexuals should be taught. All of these steps, they suggest, would stop discrimination against lesbian or gay youth. Certainly, such changes would help, especially in the immediate future. Schools have to be made to deal systemically with the issue of homosexuality. By insisting on the existence and importance of the issue, by challenging stereotypical misconceptions, by rethinking and reshaping institutional practices, only then can we normalize it. This may not eliminate discrimination against homosexuals, but it would make the issue visible, going some way towards ending the current marginalization of lesbian and gay youth and, thus, possibly providing them with opportunities for quality education. However, these measures are not enough. What we have seen in this essay is that compulsory heterosexuality is inscribed in a range of schooling practices, and it is this heterosexism that must be challenged. If we are truly looking to eliminate oppression on the basis of gender, race, and sexuality, we have to challenge the structure of power as it is presently composed, to resist current hegemonic ideologies. In the case of homosexuality specifically, we have to call into question heterosexuality.

NOTES

1 This research was funded by a block transfer grant from the Ontario Ministry of Education to the Ontario Institute for Studies in Education. I am indebted to Bob Tremble, Tony Gambini, Laurie Bell, Kim Mistysyn, and Krysten Wong for assisting with the recruitment of informants; and to Nicole Groten for transcribing the interviews. I am especially grateful to George Smith and Gary Kinsman for their helpful suggestions. To Ann Manicom, my special appreciation for strengthening the essay. The data for this essay have been used for an article published in *The Third ILGA Pink Book*, (Utrecht 1993), and in *Gender and Education* (1994).

2 Gay and lesbian adolescents are over-represented in adolescent suicide statistics. A United States Task Force (1986) suggested that homosexual youth are two to six times more likely to commit suicide than heterosexual youth. The London (England) Gay Teenage Group (Warren 1984: 16) reported that one out of five of the 416 lesbian and gay youth whom they surveyed, 'at some point [had] felt under such intolerable pressure that they attempted suicide.' In Canada, a Winnipeg study revealed that of the forty-five gay and lesbian youth surveyed, two-thirds had contemplated committing suicide and one-quarter of them had attempted suicide (Prairie Research 1989: iii). Of the twelve young lesbians interviewed for this study, four mentioned at least one attempt to kill themselves.

3 In 1990, George Smith and I conducted parallel research to investigate the barriers to the provision of quality education for lesbian and gay youth (see G. Smith, unpublished paper). As the research progressed, it became increasingly evident that the experiences of the young lesbians and gay men differed, including factors such as at what age they recognized their homosexuality, where they found support, and how they expressed their sexuality (Powell 1987).

4 These organizations included: Lesbian and Gay Youth of Toronto (LGYT); Central Toronto Youth Services; the Toronto Board of Education Student Support Services, Counselling and Information on Human Sexuality; Lesbian Youth Peer Support (LYPS); and Street Outreach Support (SOS). Of the twelve women interviewed, seven were white, two had a parent of different race or ethnicity

from the other, three were Asian. They were either middle class or came from low-income families. None lived on the streets. All lived in Toronto at the time of the interviews. Seven were born, raised, and schooled in Toronto, two came from the Maritime provinces, two went to schools in small communities close to Toronto, and one was from Ottawa. Three students attended Catholic schools. These schools are provincially funded but retain a proviso in the Education Act of Ontario that they 'may establish and maintain programs and courses of study in religious education for pupils in all schools under [their school boards'] jurisdiction' (Government of Ontario 1990). To ensure that no informant is recognized as a continuous presence, neither names nor pseudonyms are provided when I quote from the interviews.

5 'Stonewall' was a gay bar in New York City which was stormed by police in the summer of 1969 and where the patrons stood up and fought back. This date, 27 June 1969, commemorates the beginning of the Gay Liberation Movement in North America.

6 It is only in the 1990s that we are beginning to see a selection of materials published for use in schools – for confronting homophobia, teaching about heterosexism, including gay and lesbian content in curriculum, and providing counselling and support services to gay and lesbian youth. (See Harbeck 1992; Chamberlain 1990, as well as issues 24 and 29 of *Radical Teacher*. See also the 1993 collection edited by Sue McConnell-Celi, which includes writing by gay and lesbian teachers and students, as well as an extensive bibliography of curriculum and resource materials both for supporting gay and lesbian youth and for confronting homophobia in schools.) The earliest North American example of such an initiative was Project 10, a counselling service for gay and lesbian youth in Fairfax High School in Los Angeles, and the Harvey Milk High School (school within a school) in New York. In Canada, the most concerted initiative is the development of curriculum materials by the Toronto Board of Education. In 1992 the board developed a resource guide for teachers at the secondary school level, *Sexual Orientation: Focus on Homosexuality, Lesbianism, and Homophobia*. But these initiatives are still scarce, and many gay and lesbian students currently in schools go through much of what the young lesbians in this essay said about their school experiences.

7 Despite the increased availability of material regarding homosexuality, student access to material in the school is still very controversial. Strong lobbying against including information regarding sexualities other than heterosexuality exists across Canada. One such example is an organized group in Toronto called CURE (Citizens United for Responsible Education). Furthermore, in the current difficult economic climate, many of the progressive board-initiated programs are being cut back or eliminated.

'These Things Just Happen': Talk, Text, and Curriculum Reform

NANCY JACKSON[1]

This essay is about the deep malaise affecting teachers in the educational reforms of the past two decades. It focuses in particular on the introduction of competency-based curriculum which has been widely billed as a means to make educational goals more explicit, instructional methods more effective, and educational institutions more accountable. These measures have been embraced by enthusiastic reformers across the United States, Canada, Great Britain, and Australia. But wherever they appear, they have been at the centre of conflict.[2]

The details of my story come from a competency-based reform process in the community colleges of British Columbia in the mid-1980s. I spent portions of two years there doing research as a doctoral student interested in the social organization of vocational knowledge and skill. The college teachers I met during this period were variously excited, angry, and confused about the impact of competency-based curriculum on the definition and organization of vocational learning. But they were universally upset about other, more nebulous aspects of the impact of these measures on their work, as I will explore below. I came to be interested in exactly how it was that competency measures could cause such profound unrest.

I soon discovered that developments in British Columbia fit very closely the framework of reform – and the patterns of conflict – occurring across continents in educational institutions wherever a more 'systematic approach' to education was being introduced.[3] Indeed, in the intervening years, the reforming zeal and the storm of conflict have spread to universities as well, as efficiency and accountability have become the hallmark of good management even in the relatively privileged institutions of higher learning.[4] But by the mid-1980s critics were already describing these developments as the emergence of a new generation of managerial methods which profoundly altered power relations in institutions of learning. According to British observers, these reforms amounted to nothing less than 'a fundamental shift in where and how the education system is controlled and managed' (Walker and Barton 1987: xi). One of the earliest American critics of these developments summed them up aptly as a contest over who will 'rule the schools' (Wise 1979: xvi).

I quickly recognized as well that the problem of 'who rules' was a concern well beyond disaffected teachers and other critics of contemporary education. The crisis of governance in education that I was witnessing is part of a broader picture of transformation in social relations being played out across a range of professions and areas of public administration, as the essays in this volume amply demonstrate (see in particular the piece by Marie Campbell). In this context, the story of curriculum reforms reported here has implications as well for a much broader social analysis of the nature of contemporary institutional life. Since I am interested in both the local and the broad approaches to the telling/reading of this story, let me try to identify briefly where I am headed.

In the most local context, this essay tells the tale of how teachers in one institution had their professional autonomy stripped away as curriculum decision making was shifted to employers and the teachers' authority was subordinated to a process of administrative accountability. The basic outline of this story will be familiar to readers of the critical literature on competency-based education particularly from the school systems in the United States.[5] At a broader institutional or policy level, the story is about how program priorities were rendered more accountable to public policy goals, and how the rationale for course content thus shifted from responding to individual learning needs to serving the needs of industry. This version of the reforms of the 1980s has also been widely written about, particularly by critics in Great Britain and Australia.[6] Both of these lines of analysis are central to understanding the impact and widespread controversy over competency-based education.

But there is yet another version of these events, which I have tried to make central in this essay, and that is an analysis concerned with the social organization of knowledge (Smith 1987b, 1990a, 1990b). Using this approach, the focus of analysis is directed to somewhat more technical questions about the actual mechanisms through which such sweeping changes are effected in an institutional environment. In posing this problem I am reminded of the title of an influential study of state power entitled 'What Does the Ruling Class Do When It Rules?' (Therborn 1978).

My question here is of this general order. What are the practical, every-day activities of 'reform' in the college system through which 'change' occurs in what teachers do, how they do it, and how they feel about their job from day to day? This version of the story directs our attention to a realm of almost invisible but profound transformations associated with the introduction of textually mediated decision-making processes.

A brief version of the analysis to follow goes something like this. The competency-based curriculum reform process introduces to the college environment a textual mode of action which obscures the presence of individual employers, instructors, and students as the living subjects of the instructional process. Their presence is displaced by an objectified system of curriculum planning and implementation in which documents replace individuals as constituents of social action. These arrangements make the instructional process – from planning to evaluation – reportable within a framework of institutional goals and objectives oriented to serving not the learning needs of individuals, but a public policy discourse concerned with economic need, fiscal restraint, and political accountability. Instructors are left feeling alienated and 'confused' by curriculum decisions that seem to 'just happen.'

This latter rendering of events permits us to situate the local experience of loss of autonomy among educators in British Columbia in a broader social and historical framework, as part of the changing organization of the social relations of capital. In this light, the process of curriculum reform examined here can be seen as part of a process of ideological 'retooling' (Smith 1987b) sweeping through contemporary institutions in the context of capitalist crisis. But that may be getting a bit ahead of my story. First, I will provide a little more basic information about competency-based curriculum measures and the college reform process. Then I will say something about how I have approached an analysis of textual modes of action.

COMPETENCY-BASED CURRICULUM REFORM

The competency-based curriculum measures examined here were being introduced at 'West Coast College' as part of a program review initiated by the Dean of Applied Programs. The review was mandated in the five-year planning requirements of the provincial government as a means to determine the extent to which existing college programs were 'responsive' to identifiable 'needs' of industry.

The data presented here focus on a review of the Office Administration section of a Business Department, including two secretarial programs and one for medical office assistants. The programs were either two or four semesters in length and employed about a dozen instructors, half of whom were full-time faculty members with the college. Most of the students were young women seeking their first jobs in the local business or medical community; others were returning to upgrade their skills in the face of rapidly changing information technology. The requirement for a competency-based program review was being presented by the administration as part of a college-wide initiative to get their 'managerial house in order.'

A competency-based review process routinely begins with a 'task analysis' workshop in which local employers are invited to participate in a one- to three-day session to define the 'range and depth' of skills required for entry-level positions in a given occupation. These workshops are highly structured events directed by a curriculum consultant who is a specialist in the use of the competency approach (see Adams 1975; Sinnett 1975). Instructors are not invited to participate but are permitted to send one or two representatives as observers. Following the workshop, the input from employers is elaborated first by the curriculum specialist and eventually by instructors themselves into a set of curricular materials which can be seen to reflect actual requirements on the job. Thus, the task analysis serves as the first step in the process of practical articulation of vocational instruction in colleges to the public policy objectives of 'relevance' and 'responsiveness' of educational institutions to the needs of industry.

The process of articulation described here depends centrally on a documentary process. The outcome of the task analysis workshop is summarized by the curriculum specialist in a document called a skills profile which becomes the centrepiece of the curriculum reform process. This document consists of a detailed description of exactly what an incumbent in a given job is required to do. Examples include 'transcribe dictated letters using a standard wordprocessing software' or 'operate a spreadsheet.' Elements of skill or knowledge considered 'nice to have' or 'nice to know' but not a current performance requirement for the specific job under consideration are not eligible to be included in the profile. This means that the skills profile tends to have a narrow and short-term focus, a feature which is controversial among teachers and even among some employers. The skills profile is nevertheless the authorized standard for instructors to assess and revise their existing course and program outlines to demonstrate that college offerings have been brought into line with identified 'needs' of the employer. The data examined in this essay are primarily from the very last stage of this process, when faculty meet to assess and revise their course documents. I have referred to these meetings throughout as 'revision meetings.'

In the course of my research, I observed both the task analysis workshop for the Office Administration programs, and the subsequent revision meetings among faculty. I interviewed all of the instructors in the program, collected the documents of the five-year planning strategy of the provincial government, and gathered the working documents of the course and programs approvals process within the college. These various texts, and segments of talk which surround their use, form the core of the analysis undertaken here.

TEXT AND SOCIAL ACTION

Although my broad analytic concern is with the transformative power of textual relations, the focus of attention in much of this essay is not on the texts themselves. I will begin by describing the documentary character of the competency-based curriculum management system, and I will report how teachers use segments of these texts in their meetings. But my objective is not to analyse the features of these texts in and for themselves. Rather I want to demonstrate how the texts become an integral part of individual and collective action in the college setting and how they organize the action of which they are a part. To make this visible, I will rely more heavily on analysis of talk than texts.

The everyday working language of individuals serves as the point of entry for this investigation. The analysis proceeds by minutely scrutinizing what instructors and others in the college setting say and do in the course of their working day. Our interest in what they have to say is neither to confirm nor dispute their opinions, likes, dislikes, or explanations. Rather, their reporting serves to uncover evidence of the social organization of the college setting. It tells us what is happening to them, offering a window on the social relations of college life. It is particularly in the taken-for-granted underpinnings of their talk that we will see, among other things, the way in which the action and experience of instructors is being mediated through a textual process. Thus, the analysis of talk reveals the role of texts as constituents of social action.

In a competency-based curriculum process, the task analysis workshop is the first and most critical step in the development of what the department head at West Coast College called 'a totally objective statement' of needs and requirements in the workplace. This statement is inscribed in a series of documents which become the only legitimate basis for action and decision making about the curriculum. In the analysis below, the status of these documents as 'objective' and their capacity to organize and authorize action in this way are the central object of the analysis. I will argue that the capacity of these documents to authorize action does not depend on how accurate or comprehensive they are as a picture of the workplace. Rather it depends on the conditions of their production as an *organizationally warranted account* of the workplace and their officially designated status as the basis for institutional action. To oversimplify for a moment, this means that the documents were becoming the sole means of authorized actions because the college said it should be so. In particular, the much touted 'objectivity' of the review process documents depended on their exclusion of the point of view of instructors, who were seen to have vested interests in the curriculum because their jobs were at stake. By contrast, the documents of the review process were not only deemed to be untainted, but came to be used to constitute the 'actual,' to stand in for workplace reality, for the purposes of curriculum decision making in the college. How this was realized in practice becomes visible in the program revision meetings examined below.

The revision meetings take place as one step in a whole sequence of activity that includes the actions not only of instructors, but also of employers, curriculum consultants, college administrators, and education officials in the provincial government. In this context, the talk and actions undertaken in the revision meetings cannot be interpreted in isolation. Rather, we will see how the activity of instructors in these meetings is organized and coordinated by both prior and subsequent actions of others who stand outside the sphere of instructors' everyday experience. Smith (1987a, 1987b) refers to this phenomenon as a process of extra-local coordination or 'concerting' of action. This process of concerting action takes place through the mediating presence of documents, as I will show in the revision meetings examined below. As a 'stand-in' for workplace reality, the documents become not just transmitters of information, but active constituents of social action, mediating the activity and decision making of people at different moments of the curriculum review process.

CURRICULUM REFORM IN ACTION

To make visible the full impact of the curriculum reform, it is important to be clear about the role of college instructors in setting the content of curriculum prior to the program review. The tradition within the college system was that instructors had the authority to decide about both program and course content, with a system of approvals at the department and divisional levels by committees consisting again of faculty members. Decisions about content were based on the instructors' professional knowledge in their respective fields, which they maintained through a variety of means. They were required by the college to maintain a program advisory committee of local employers with whom they consulted on an intermittent basis. They also maintained individual memberships in professional associations and, in some cases, part-time consulting work in the business community. Most instructors also reported frequent contact within their fields through informal social contacts as well as through phone calls or meetings with employers either sponsoring work-week assignments for their students or seeking to hire new graduates. These various contacts provided what an accounting instructor called 'a little path of intelligence' about changing requirements in the job market.

There are friends of mine who are accountants, office managers, and in related fields. Our kids are the same age so we will meet at a band concert at school or something and I'll ask 'What do you think about this' and they'll say 'Oh, it's definitely this way' or 'definitely that way.' Then there's another fellow, an accountant, who has taught quite a bit and has quite a large sphere of people he talks to. We chat a lot, and we both have friends in public accounting practice, doing consulting, and so on ... These guys know what's going on ... So, you see, there's a little path of intelligence ... So when it comes to what I've done with my course, it is coming right out of their mouths.

In fact, instructors' knowledge of their fields was the principle resource used by the college administration in putting together the competency-based review process. Instructors provided the names of employers to be invited to the task analysis workshop. Because of all this, most instructors at West Coast College were expecting no great surprises to emerge from the workshop. They anticipated that most of the changes called for would be ones that they had been considering or even recommending for some time. Instead, they indicated that the biggest change would be in the power of the new approach to get things done. For example, office administration instructors pointed out that for more than two years they had been dissatisfied with the marketing course provided for office administration students by the marketing discipline. However, faculty agitation for change had been seen as a matter of them trying to take the course back in order to protect employment within their discipline. Their complaints were seen to be based in self-interest, resulting in a deadlock between opposing parties.

Under the new system, once the course was shown to be inappropriate in relation to the skills profile chart, instructors expected that the changes would be addressed as matter of course. In cases like this, instructors anticipated that the new methods would bring action where their own voices had been unsuccessful. Some of them spoke about this optimistically as a matter of increased 'leverage' for change.

Instructor: Basically I think some of the things that they came up with reinforced a lot of what we as teachers have been pushing for a long time, for three or four years. And I think getting that feedback ... was good. I think it sort of gave us some impetus to get busy and say okay, you know, there are changes that are necessary. And because of the status of task analysis with the higher levels here, you can almost say that this is what task analysis wanted ... It is a little bit of leverage.

Instructors' talk of 'leverage' is a useful focus for our investigation. As we pursue their sense that the task analysis will 'get things done,' we see that this feature of the approach is the same dynamic that makes the process contradictory in relation to their interests as instructors. The power to get things done associated with the new curriculum methods arises out of a new organization of decision-making relations. In the new mode, the knowledge that instructors have of the workplace comes to be externalized, vested in a documentary process which is then used to subordinate their work to the decisions of employers and administrators. The activity of instructors becomes one step in an organizational course of action which originates and derives its sense elsewhere, as I will illustrate below.

REVISION MEETINGS: EXTRA-LOCAL ORGANIZATION

The revision meetings at West Coast College consisted of two days when instructors got together to revise their course outlines in light of the outcome of the task analysis. These meetings were a critical moment in the process of effecting change, since it was the first opportunity for most instructors to examine the new skills profile or hear about the outcome of the task analysis workshop. By the end of these two days of meetings, instructors were expected to produce revised Course Information Sheets outlining course content in line with the new skills profile, and have these documents ready to forward for approval at the departmental and divisional levels.

There are many moments in the interaction of instructors during these meetings that begin to make visible the extra-local organization of the revision process and the contradictions embedded in it for teachers. The first and probably most pervasive feature of the revision meetings that illustrates both of these elements is the way the voice of employers organizes the scene from offstage. The voice of employers enters the revision meetings as a ubiquitous 'they' (for example, 'they wanted us to discuss') which can be seen in the excerpts below to serve as a central organizing device in the discussions among instructors. This dynamic secures the orientation of talk and action in these meetings to a duly constituted abstraction representing 'employers in general' as the source of legitimate authority on the requirements at work and to the dominant discourse on 'the needs of industry' which is the driving force behind the program review.

The articulating presence of the abstract 'they' is starkly illustrated in the following verbal summary of a portion of the new skills profile developed for the Medical Office Assistant program. This summary was done by the chairperson of the revision meetings as part of an introduction of the results of the task analysis workshop. The chairperson had been one of two departmental observers at the task analysis workshop itself.

Maybe I will just review the type of content included there to give you some kind of feeling. In this one, they wanted to talk about medical institutions in the Lower Mainland, they wanted to know about their location, their principal focus for work. They wanted to have students aware of their hierarchical structure and the communication structure within these institutions ... They also wanted them to be aware of the different types of orientation packages they face when they enter those institutions ... who they report to, etc. They wanted team dynamics addressed ... They want you to address in this course the 'typical office assistant' that is, the kinds of jobs, the kinds of skills, the kinds of personality, the kinds of knowledge that the individual will need to get a job at the end. They wanted them to be aware of the professional associations that they can use as a support group ... Then they talked about the students setting down career goals for themselves ... They wanted time and stress management skills looked at a little bit. And they wanted us to discuss things like responsibilities to the employer.

This excerpt of talk illustrates the structure of 'us and them' that dominated the meeting. The word 'they' appears fifteen times in a roughly two-minute segment of talk. This is, of course, partly a feature of the character of this talk as a condensation, a summary, but in this form, the essential relations are also made very stark. The word 'they' appears in the paragraph above as the subject of almost every sentence. This is more than a grammatical observation; 'they' are indeed the acting subjects and authors of the decision-making process which is being put in place through the program review. The new process situates the instructors collectively ('us' and 'you' in the summary above) as audience to the decision-making subjects ('they') who are employers. The results of employers' actions come to instructors as news, information conveyed to them from outside their sphere of immediate experience and action. For some instructors, this moment brings the first jarring realization that they are being systematically displaced from their position of authority on matters of curriculum. As we will see in their words quoted below, they are not entirely clear how this has happened to them, which is of course exactly the question I want to pursue. Finding the answer depends on examining closely the interaction of talk and documents.

The results of the task analysis process are officially vested in and conveyed through the skills profile chart. This is demonstrated by the way the skills profile serves to mediate and organize the remaining stages of the program review process. As I will try to demonstrate below, its power to do so depends on its capacity to embody – to stand in for – the complex process of debate and decision making that went on among employers in the task analysis workshop. This constitutive character of the documents does not happen by itself; it is produced – made real – through the talk of instructors in the revision meetings. It is this achievement that allows these documents to organize activities in the new setting.

During the review and revision process, the information contained in the skills profile is summarized, interpreted and reinforced in various ways through personal communication by those faculty members who attended the task analysis workshop as observers. Their verbal summaries and interpretations of the document carry the special force of speakers who were present at the events of which they speak. They also carry the weight of their delegated administrative responsibility for overseeing the 'implementation' of the review process, of setting the meeting on track by reminding others of 'what we should be doing.' In these senses, their voices 'realize' in the new setting the decisions of others on which they are reporting. At the same time, their talk and actions in these meetings are part of something more. They put into practice a transformation in the relations of curriculum which is more than a matter of reporting what went on elsewhere; it is an active part of constituting the new relations in the setting where they speak. The chairperson's account of these changes is thus part of their reflexive accomplishment, their self-realization in this setting, as a new form of relations, even among instructors themselves. This is illustrated in the following segments of talk from the first day of revision meetings.

The first discussion of the day was about requirements in the area of communication skills. After several minutes of discussion, the chairperson produced the following interpretation of what had gone on in the task analysis workshop:

What the task analysis really stressed was communications, being able to communicate with other office workers adequately, in oral and written form ... What they say here [reading from the profile chart] is 'demonstrate the ability to communicate effectively ...' And they really did stress this, to the point where, I would say, the first hour of the Office Administration task analysis was basically spent discussing just communications from all angles – telephone, interpersonal relationships, working with a team – all of those things.

This kind of intervention and interpretation is part of making real in the setting occupied by instructors the new organization of decision making. It establishes that what will count as important has already been determined elsewhere, as has the sense of relative weight or urgency among items. This information is conveyed to instructors as a form of instructions to act, not an invitation to debate and decide, as in the past. Faced with this growing realization as the discussion progressed, one teacher soon voiced the following protest: 'I am a little confused here; it is as though we have already changed communications into two courses, and yet *we have never decided* whether we need that course more than we need Typing I. *I am a little miffed about that. It seems that these things just happen.* The way you are talking, we are just going to get the two communications courses, and Typing I has just been swept under the rug' (emphasis mine). Of course, this instructor is exactly right. Under the new system, instructors are put into a situation where curriculum decisions 'just happen.' By the time they are involved, the moment of decision is past, a *fait accompli.* This is underscored by the response of the meeting chair to the protest quoted above: 'I think *it is given* that we need two levels of communications courses ... *If you read through both documents, it's there*, without a doubt' (emphasis mine).

Curriculum decisions that 'just happen' represent a whole new way of doing business for college teachers. In the past teachers faced all kinds of constraints and compromises in determining their course and program content but they were nevertheless the active, decision-making agents. The knowledge which came from employers about job requirements was appropriated by instructors for their own use. The new system precludes this form of appropriation, imposing a new organization in which knowledge of work is vested in an organizational process to which instructors are subordinate. This process of subordination is mediated by the task analysis documents. As put by the meeting chair above, still in response to the voice of protest above, 'If you don't want to take my word for it, you can look at the documents.'

PRODUCING DOCUMENTARY ACTION

The kinds of decision making assigned to instructors is profoundly altered by the new curriculum procedures. This is clearly visible throughout the revision meetings, as instructors prepare course changes to go forward to committees at the department and divisional level where institutional approval formally takes place. According to the chairperson of the revision meetings, the first step of this process is for instructors to rearrange existing instructional blocks to see where they fit into the skills profile and then to make whatever additions or deletions the profile requires. Finally, they prepare the Course Information Sheets which provide an overview of each course in the required standardized format.

For the revision meetings examined here, two senior instructors have done some preliminary work of matching existing course content to the skills profile charts in order to 'expedite the process' among the larger grouping of faculty attending the revision meetings. They described this work as 'identifying' blocks of curriculum in the existing programs and in the new profile, seeing what's 'missing,' what's 'covered,' and what 'coincides.' The process is like completing a puzzle: 'checking' one document against the other, seeing that items are 'listed,' 'covered,' or 'don't fit.' The chairperson asks the assembled instructors to check this preliminary work, to verify that what they have produced 'actually conforms to what is in the profiles' or whether something has been added or deleted in error.

After introductory discussions, the chairperson gives instructions for the faculty to break into groups and work on Course Information Sheets for different segments of the program. Her instructions to the group are as follows:

Your job this afternoon and tomorrow will be first of all to name the course, to identify a calendar description, to verify the content ... *I think the content is almost basically done for you, you just have to type it in.* The objective statements are basically given in the [task analysis documents] package. *All you have to do is make sure that they match.* Then you are going to have to determine the mode of instruction, for example, lecture, or lecture/lab, and last thing, the evaluation process. Oh, then texts. I have an office full of texts for you to look at. (emphasis mine)

The approvals committees for which the Course Information Sheets were being prepared had already adopted the use of some standard competency techniques, such as the requirement to use behavioural language, and some instructors had previous experience of the need to conform in order to get their courses approved. As the revision meeting broke up into smaller working groups, the chairperson offered the reminder, 'Make sure you don't miss anything; they are getting really sticky about everything matching – boy oh boy!'

Anticipation of a 'sticky' committee process can be seen as a major factor in determining how time was spent in the small group meetings. For instance, a lot of time and effort was spent struggling to produce the required form of verbs for the Course Information Sheets, as the following passage demonstrates:

Instructor A: OK, well, this is a main objective. ... The student will demonstrate the ability to communicate using written business messages. Now, do we have to say 'by choosing' or do we start out 'choose and produce' ... or can you use 'choosing, using' ...?

Instructor B: Oh, yeah, that's no problem. It's got to be a verb that continues with this ...

A: Yeah, that's a gerund, though ... can you use a gerund instead of an active verb?

B: It seems to me that ... you're supposed to have 'choose, use, handle, discuss ...'

A: Yeah, but can you use 'choosing, handling, correcting'?

B: Oh, I see what you're saying ... that's no problem.

A: Or do you put 'The student will be able to ...' several times down the page ... ?

B: No, you would have 'The student will be able to ...' and ... then a colon ... and under that have A, B, C, D ...

A: Oh, I see, well that would be a lot easier ... so after the colon would be 'A. Demonstrate the ability to ta-da-ta-da ...' Yes, I'm following you now. It's easier to work with this way ...

Attention to a particular use of verbs is a small detail from which we can learn a lot. Requiring certain verb forms is a standard feature of competency approach, and on the surface it appears to be largely a concern for precision and economy of words. Getting the specified arrangement of gerunds and infinitives and such gives a degree of clarity, simplicity, and uniformity to course outlines. Achieving this format is reported by some instructors who have been trained to use the system as relatively unproblematic, even helpful for their own thinking. For those who have not had such training, the required use of language often poses a considerable stumbling block – an example of 'impenetrable jargon' (Cantor and Roberts 1979: 63) or educational 'mumbo-jumbo' as some of my respondents complained.

The emphasis placed on verb forms is, however, much more deeply rooted than the concern for economy of words. It is traceable to the basic principles of behaviourism required to achieve a thoroughly systematic form of curriculum management. Only those elements of achievement that can be externalized or objectified for the purposes of observation and measurement are technically eligible to be used as learning objectives. Thus, active and transitive verbs are the essential currency of the approach. This requirement is particularly critical if the systems approach is to be extended beyond the planning and design phase of instruction into the evaluation phase as well, where measurable outcomes are essential. In the Office Administration programs, such strict applications of the rational or scientific approach to evaluation were not being introduced at this time. But instructors were aware that administrators in the Applied Programs Division favoured such an approach and that they were already moving the division in this direction.

The series of competency steps which culminate in measurable outcomes constitute critical ground on which any further aspects of a curriculum management system might be laid. They achieve the essential step of making instruction answerable to individuals other than instructors, thus laying the cornerstone for programs that can be seen to be 'responsive' to external policy makers. For these reasons, the competency approach is seen to provide a framework of institutional relations in which the problem of accountability can be addressed rationally and systematically. This accounts for its enduring popularity with administrators.

The importance of seeing the wave of competency-based reforms as a critical shift in the social relations of curriculum, rather than simply an exercise in updating curriculum content, cannot be overstated. It is the organization of the means to define curriculum – not once but again and again – which is at issue in the reform. This difference is reflected in comments of the department head, who said to me that he was not very concerned with the specific recommendations on course content that would come out of the review process in the office administration area because he believed that 95 per cent of the content already was what it should be. On the other hand, he stressed that while the changes being implemented looked 'simple, almost trivial' they nevertheless represented a 'major, major shift in direction for the institution.' He continued, 'Because in the past the faculty have been responsible for the definition of program content and outcome. You cannot have that – you cannot put the wolves in charge of the chicken coop, let's face it.'

Indeed, it is a 'major shift' to define teachers in general as in a conflict of interest position vis-à-vis curriculum. This amounts to a radical reconceptualization of the teaching function that might well have something to do with a generalized malaise in the teaching profession of late. But once again, my primary interest lies not in weighing the merits of this position but in understanding the practical mechanism for implementing such a change within in a local college setting.

The program review process turns out to be a very powerful tool for implementing a change of this magnitude by quietly but swiftly putting into practice an immediate reorganization in the local relations of decision making. Instructors come to a meeting one day to revise their courses and discover that curriculum decisions have already been made by employers at a workshop to which they were not invited. What's left for them is to complete the paperwork. Of course, instructors helped organize the workshop, just like they had organized lots of previous meetings with employers. But this was to be a meeting with a difference. The 'meeting' was the first step in the creation of a textually mediated social organization. In these new arrangements a textual mode of action displaces the living subjects of the curriculum process – individuals who make decisions and teach classes. The documents come to speak with an authoritative voice, not as an aid to the transmission of information, but as actual constituents of the decision making process. Curriculum choices cease to be attributable to any person or moment in particular; they appear to 'just happen.'

CONCLUSION

Curriculum decisions that 'just happen' are an everyday experience of textually mediated social organization (Smith 1987a, 1990a, 1990b). In the college setting, competency-based curriculum measures constitute a textual method of 'knowing' and 'deciding' which is formalized, abstracted from the intentions of particular individuals. Authority over curriculum is lodged within the documents of the institutional process, and the documents themselves become constituents of institutional action. It is precisely this arrangement of decision making that constitutes the much-touted 'objectivity' of such forms of 'rational action.' Decisions come forward in the passive voice.

To return, then, to the story line I introduced at the beginning of this essay, I have argued that the local conflict over curriculum in community colleges turns out to be about many things in addition to teaching and learning. It is part of a broader transformation in methods of institutional governance appearing not only in education but in business, law, health, and social services among other areas. These are changes which make organizational action more accountable to a framework of externally set goals and objectives. Thus, competency-based curriculum continues to have the effect on several continents of harnessing educational practices more tightly to short-term skill requirements in the workplace. Like similar reforms in other sectors, these changes serve to articulate everyday lives to the social relations of accumulation and the related discourses of power in contemporary capitalist society (Smith 1987a, 1990b).

And so it happens that workers in many fields, perhaps the professions in particular, find our experiences reflected in the lives of these college teachers in British Columbia. Our own participation in sophisticated documentary forms of action in the places where we live and work is highly contradictory. Our skills and knowledge are being displaced and obscured by textual processes – budgeting, planning and design, workload measurement, caseload management – which come to dominate and circumscribe our work.[7] Thus, we become the agents of a course of action which does not reflect our own understandings and which remains highly resistant to our criticism. Like the instructors in British Columbia, we are left 'a little confused' and 'a little miffed.'

NOTES

1 Thanks to Marie Campbell, Ann Manicom, and Marilee Reimer for helpful comments, and to the Social Sciences and Humanities Research Council for funding to support this research.
2 For overviews see Grant et al. (1979), Short (1984), Cantor and Roberts (1979), Muller (1990), Collins (1993), and Jackson (1988a). On the antecedents of contemporary competency measures see Glaser (1962), Grace (1948), and Travers (1973).
3 For discussion of these processes in the United States, United Kingdom, and Australia, see Wise (1979), McDermott (1976), Walker and Barton (1987), and Connell (1985).
4 For analysis of these changes in university management, see Newson and

Buchbinder (1988), Bates (1992), Walker and Barton (1989), Preston and Walker (1993), and Carnegie Council (1980).
5 See Apple (1986, 1982, 1980), Apple and Weiss (1983), and Kliebard (1986, 1975).
6 For broader critiques of policy see Collins (1993), Bates (1992), and Field (1991).
7 Furthermore, as I have argued elsewhere, those educators who raise questions about the process or about the character of learning opportunities for students that result from these methods of decision making are charged with ignorance and self-interest and sent out for in-service training (Jackson 1990a, 1988b; Macdonald-Ross 1975). Thus, not only are the process and content of curriculum transformed, but also the basis of professionalism in education.

Activating the Photographic Text[1]

LIZA McCOY

It would be difficult to get through an ordinary day without encountering a photographic image. Still or moving, the products of photographic technology – television, photographs, cinema – have come to figure prominently in discourses of information, entertainment, and persuasion, and they are an indispensable feature of what Dorothy Smith calls the text-mediated relations of ruling (Smith 1990a).

This social organization of photographic representation can be empirically investigated. I have been exploring an approach to the study of still photographs which is founded in Smith's innovative sociology and draws on ethnomethodology and the semiology of the Bakhtin Circle. Unlike traditional semiotic analysis, which proceeds by detaching photographic texts from local situations and searching for meaning as if it occurred independently of perceiving subjects, the approach I am using begins with photographs embedded in the social situations of their use. This is consistent with the ethnomethodological concern to explore people's sense-making practices in concrete settings. The aim is to discover how photographs come to mean through interpretive practices that activate them as records, evidence, art, fantasy, or 'memories.'

In the language theory and semiology of the Bakhtin Circle, a sign or text comes to mean when a person involved in everyday ways of making sense 'draws the work into some particular social situation' (Volosinov 1983). This drawing-in establishes relations between local circumstances and relevances and the material resources of the photograph. Although each drawing-in is historically unique, it occurs within courses of action that organize the interpretive practices available to viewers.

My empirical investigation of photographic use begins with the individual act of drawing-in, but it does not stop there.[2] The aim is to explicate the social organization in which individual acts of interpretation are possible, and occur – along with their consequences. An important link is provided by Smith's notion of discourse as a 'field of action mediated by symbolic forms' (Smith 1990b). Here discourse is more than an intertextual relation; it is what is getting done. Text-mediated courses of action or social relations rely on individual moments of interpretation, where texts are activated within discourse by competent users through the employment of known-in-common interpretive schemes. Photographs intend these schemes through their production and structuration, although photographs can be and often are viewed in discourses other than those they intend (that is, their resources can be activated according to a variety of interpretive schemes).

'Looking at photographs' is not a single, neutral practice. As a form of drawing in the photograph, the looking people do is socially organized. By 'looking' here I mean not simply the fact of visual perception, but a social practice of viewing. Vacation snapshots and other private photographs, for example, are frequently viewed during occasions of interaction characterized by a certain kind of talk. Someone shows and someone else looks. The person showing directs the attention of the viewer, providing explanations that identify what is to be seen as going on in the pictures. The person looking asks questions and makes comments – appreciative or otherwise – about the pictures and the events they are understood to depict. Of course, not everyone engaged in looking at vacation snapshots will collaborate in this kind of drawing-in; if they do not, however, other participants in the setting may infer that they are uninterested, or just plain rude.[3]

Other photographic genres come to be seen in settings where quite different practices of looking draw them into specific courses of action. The viewing of mug shots, for example, often occurs within a regulated institutional process designed to link the local experience of eyewitnesses with objectified, institutional records for the purpose of discovering possible suspects.

THE PHOTOGRAPH AS RECORD

Since the development of photographic technology in the nineteenth century, theorists have been fascinated by the peculiar ontology of the photograph, and they have tried to get an analytic grip on the relation of the photograph to the event or thing photographed. Photographic representation does indeed differ from other forms of visual representation in its production. Light reflecting off or emanating from objects enters the camera through the lens where it is refracted to throw an image onto the light-sensitive emulsion of the film. Chemical processing fixes the negative image which can then be used to make positive prints. (The technique of capturing or producing an image in this way, the camera obscura, was known hundreds of years before a method of fixing the image was invented.) The philosopher Peirce (1965), in his typology of signs, called the photograph an index, along with footprints and weathervanes, an index being a sign that refers to its object by virtue of having been affected by that object. Such signs are also sometimes called traces, since the material properties of the sign contain in some way a physical trace of the object.

In his early work on the photograph Barthes (1977) called the photograph a 'message without a code' – the idea being that the photographic image conveys literal reality or information. Barthes was aware of what he calls the connotative or coded, social level of the photograph, but he was after some kind of pre-social, underlying, universal relation of photograph to thing photographed. He identified it as a relation of recording rather than of transformation, such as would be involved in a map, drawing or painting.[4] At about the same time, other theorists (for example, Damisch 1978) began pointing out just how transformative photographic technology actually is. The principle behind the construction of the camera obscura, the camera and the lens, conforms to traditional Western conventions of objectivity and one-point perspective and cannot be supposed to record the 'real' in any direct way.

This recognition of photographic technology as a cultural construct has had the side effect of producing a notion of the naive viewer who thinks that photographs work one way when they in fact work another. The purpose of theory is seen as offering the correct understanding of this relation: that the 'real' work of the photograph is to be 'unreal' even though we mistakenly think that the photograph is 'realistic.' Thus, according to Baudrillard (1988: 14): 'The immense majority of present day photographic, cinematic and television images are thought to bear witness to the world with a naive resemblance and a touching fidelity. We have spontaneous confidence in their realism. We are wrong.'

I am proposing something of a shift. I am interested in the socially organized and organizing ways that people make and use photographs. Rather than talking about how we *think* photographs bear witness to the world, I look instead at the ways we are able to *treat* photographs as witnesses to the world and what happens when we do. With this kind of shift, which owes much to ethnomethodology, our everyday practices of drawing-in the sign come to appear as 'accomplishments' rather than the 'spontaneous confidence' of the ignorant. The reality that I want to discover is the social reality of what we do with photographs, wherein the 'real' is an object of knowledge and where the sense we make of photographs justifies and organizes courses of action. The indexical features of the photograph, in the Peircean sense – the image's relation to what came before the camera – are more usefully investigated as they are of concern to people in actual settings.[5]

In this essay, my focus is on practices of using photographs and in particular on the socially organized ways viewers constitute what the photograph shows or is 'of' – that is, on the moment of activating the photograph within a particular discourse. The first practice I will discuss is embedded within a discourse of ruling and concerns what we usually refer to as mug shots and identity pictures (the ones attached to drivers' licences, passports, student cards). The second practice concerns the making and viewing of wedding pictures, in particular the formal, professionally produced pictures arranged in sequence in the wedding album. These two practices occur within different discourses but occupy the same experiential field. By that I mean that a competent viewer knows how to participate in both kinds of looking, and on any given day can successfully pass quite rapidly from one discourse to another: imagine a police officer whose daughter's wedding picture is proudly posed on her desk beside an open file displaying somebody's mug shot. Our policewoman views the two pictures almost simultaneously, yet her viewing of each is embedded within different courses of action and has entirely different consequences.

PHOTOGRAPHS AND RULING

Contemporary Western society is characterized by an organization of ruling (or managing, governing, administering) that relies on the circulation of textual realities through which the world can be known in common in objectified ways that transcend the particular local knowledge of individuals (Smith 1990a). The expansion of text-mediated discourses of ruling has largely occurred over the past century, in response to increasingly complex circumstances, and it is enabled by the development of technologies that permit the rapid reproduction and circulation of texts in multiple sites. Photography has been one such enabling technology.

In the nineteenth century the development of photographic techniques ran roughly concurrent with the establishment of organized police forces, which began first in urban areas and then eventually spread out into national and international networks. The increasing availability of photographic expertise and equipment contributed to the development of record-keeping methods that maintained a centralized knowledge about criminals and criminal activities outside the local knowledge of individual jailers or members of the force.[6] English prison records from the 1870s, for example, include photographs of the convicted person affixed to a page detailing the particulars of the crime and the punishment meted out, along with a verbal description of the person's appearance and the registration of all known names and aliases (Tagg 1988). Photographs of other institutionalized persons, such as people in asylums and children in orphanages, also began to figure in the development of another textual reality, the case record. These early uses of photography in text-mediated discourses of ruling intended a surveillance of the poor, the marginal, and those in trouble with the law; but over time the continuous expansion of a textual order of identity and entitlement has brought just about everyone before official cameras.

For the purposes of ruling, identity is a textual phenomenon. From the time we are born an interlocking chain of documents establishes and maintains our identity – for a person generally needs to possess one document, such as a birth certificate, in order to obtain another, such as a passport. The regulation of people according to the documented features of their textual identity is thus concerned not only with controlling those seen as troublesome, but is integral to the allocation of entitlement. Entitlements based on nationality, place of residence, proven competence, age, and so forth are vested in textual realities rather than in the local knowledge of members of the community.[7]

It is an in-built weakness of such a documentary system of identity and entitlement that the elaborate textual order is not grounded in any secure way on the actual bodies that drive cars, enter restricted premises, travel beyond national borders, or take books out of university libraries. Authorization documents are eminently 'transferable,' despite all those notices on the back that tell us they are not. Hence the use of photographs to enable a link between the textual person established through official documents and a bodily person moving and acting in the world. This text–body link is the interpretive accomplishment of individuals who view these authorization photographs within courses of action through which entitlement is verified, challenged, or otherwise regulated.

The photograph is a form of text itself and a constituent of the textual order of identity and entitlement. It is physically part of the authorization document yet it is treated as mediating between the verbally inscribed text–person and the bodily person presenting the document. Here, what Peirce

186 Liza McCoy

would call both the indexical and iconic properties of the photograph become relevant. The iconic properties of the photograph, its visible features, are activated by the viewer as resembling – or not resembling, as the case may be – the bodily person presenting the identity documents. If the bodily person looks like the person in the picture, well then he must be the person entitled to use the card.

Of course, not just any photograph will do. To guarantee authority, the photograph itself must be authorized. This is generally done by producing the photograph as part of an authorization procedure. When a person, supported by documentary evidence of her textual identity, if necessary, presents herself for the purpose of obtaining a certain textual entitlement (such as a driver's licence or bus pass), another person, acting for the entitling agency, takes a photograph of her. This process of picture-taking produces standardized photographs. Each subject is positioned at the same distance from the camera, instructed to face front, and the camera can be raised or lowered so that, no matter what height the subject may be, the resulting photograph shows a head and shoulders centred within the rectangle. By holding constant the background, pose, and relative size of the person, the differences that count in this discourse – facial features – are rendered more clearly visible. Later, affixed to the appropriate document, the photograph can be read not only as the record of an actual face, but as the record of a face at an actual moment in time. The photograph as read makes the link thus: official photograph-past moment of authorization (trace relation); photograph-bodily person (resemblance); hence, this person was there, at the moment of authorization. That is, first you recognize the photograph's official character as part of an entitlement document. Sometimes that is all that is necessary; the next step of visual verification of resemblance is usually carried out only when there are grounds for suspicion or for purposes of harassment. But when it is done, the recognition that the person resembles the picture (for that is the direction of resemblance that matters), serves as proof that the bodily person was there at the moment of textual authorization and is therefore entitled to use these documents.

Outside of the discourse of ruling, identification photographs can be read quite differently. My example of the police officer concerned one person in a particular situation who can almost simultaneously read two different photographs according to entirely different discourses. Here's another example where one person in a particular situation reads the *same* picture according to entirely different discourses: Once when I climbed on the streetcar and flashed my Metropass, the driver complimented me on my present appearance in relation to my recorded, previous, appearance. 'Your hair looks a lot better like that,' he said. As part of doing his job, he read my Metropass-with-photo as an official text entitling me to ride the streetcar without depositing a fare. He did another, unofficial reading on top of this which he made available to me through talk.

This second reading was organized by the relevances of the private or 'family' picture discourse that I mentioned earlier with respect to vacation snapshots. In this discourse, appearance becomes an interactional object. People compliment each other on 'good' photos (and a 'good' photo in this discourse is not the same as a 'good' photo for strict entitlement-verification purposes). In this discourse, what the photograph is 'of' and what its salient features are, are negotiated through talk.[8] Private pictures are generally not anchored by any verbal text that comes packaged with the photograph. Whereas identity and entitlement documents establish a single official, objectified relation of viewer to photograph or textual person, private pictures generally come to be viewed in contexts where the relation between viewer and photograph is negotiated and established, through talk, for each separate occasion of viewing. Often this involves the identity of the person in the photograph, although on terms very different from the discourse of ruling. For example, a woman in a photograph may be identified as 'my sister' or 'your Aunt Joyce' or 'John's daughter' depending on who is showing and who is looking. Identity in this discourse is not the fixed, objectified same-for-everyone identity produced in the discourse of ruling. Rather it is a contextually determined identity involving shifting levels of intimacy and varied expectations and obligations. 'Aunt Joyce' and 'John's daughter' are quite different social identities.

WEDDING PICTURES

Formal, professional wedding pictures are activated through the kind of show-and-tell talk I have been outlining above but they differ from snapshots in their appearance and are constituted through talk as a particular kind of record. To see how this is done, let us begin at the wedding itself, where the photographs are produced concurrently with the events they are to represent.

At a wedding people organize a series of actions that aim at discursive ideals of love, romance, family, and so forth. By creating images on and with their bodies they produce the local realization of these discursive forms. I am referring here to what I call the wedding discourse, and by doing so I mean to call attention to all the ways we know what happens at weddings and what they are about. This includes religious prescriptions,

representations of weddings on soap operas and in films, in specialty magazines such as *Brides*, and in wedding albums; it also includes our various
experiences of weddings and conversations about weddings. The textual
portion of this discourse is heavily oriented to idealized versions of what
the participants feel and how they look and behave. What the photographs
taken at the wedding do is realize the discursiveness of the local event by
producing it as a local instance of the ideal.

At a traditional wedding where people have hired a professional photographer, occasions are scheduled into the day for the making of photographs.
The form of these pictures precedes their realization at any one wedding
and enables the representation of a particular wedding in the recognizable
terms of the discourse. Certain moments are recorded through a range of
standard options, other moments are not recorded, and the wedding itself is
structured to provide those moments that intend the photographic record.
The photographs thus refine and enhance the features of the wedding, lift-
ing them to levels unattainable in the actual event. An ideal narrative is pho-
tographically separated from the scaffolding activities that put the wedding
in place, to reveal a collection of appropriate wedding moments: The Bride
and Her Mother, Leaving for the Church, Exchanging Rings, Cutting the
Cake.[9]

As part of my investigation of wedding pictures, I tape-recorded an occasion where a woman is showing her wedding album to two women friends
(see McCoy 1987). I wanted to do a close analysis of the way an album
could be activated as a meaningful record in an actual setting. Here is a very
small excerpt from the friends' conversation, but one that proved significant for my understanding of how these pictures are activated. At the particular moment of this exchange, the album is open to its last page, which
shows a picture of the bride, Rachel, and her new husband, Hugh, Cutting
the Cake.

Friend: Did you smush cake in each other's faces?
Rachel: Nope, we didn't do that. We just pretended to cut the cake. The top two
tiers were real and the bottom one wasn't and we handed out cake to
everybody, and then the top tier went back to Norway for my godmother
who couldn't make it over and the – this tier I saved for the christening of
our first child.

Here we have a photograph that bears some kind of trace relation to an
actual occasion of posing, and this is common-sense knowledge to the people in the setting. But the event portrayed in the photo, enacted through

the pose, did not actually occur. It is not uncommon for wedding pictures to have a time-shift relation to the events of the wedding: some pictures are reconstructions, some are taken before the occasion officially happens. In this case, not only was the picture posed before the reception began, but the preconstructed event never happened. In conversation while showing the album, the owner is quite matter-of-fact in her explanation that the cutting was pretend. She goes on to detail what was done with the cake and what the guests actually did get to eat for dessert. Her explanation is not treated, by her or by the other participants in the conversation, as a declaration that the picture is a false record. Within the setting and the discourse, it is not. What is recorded, or produced, is the essential ideality of the wedding. Through the perceived indexicality of the photograph, the evidence that something really did come before the camera, the ideal wedding moment appears, not as imitation or deception, but as a revealed aspect of the real.

In relation to this 'real'-ized or naturalizing ideality, how the event actually happened is simply the scaffolding work of putting a wedding in place. This scaffolding work, which has been cleared away from the formal account of the wedding as ideal, is nonetheless of critical interest to viewers. Traditional weddings are for women major projects of planning; a woman's wedding is in part a public display of her taste and powers of organization. One advantage of formal wedding pictures is that, through their visual plenitude and careful composition, they provide a record of the wedding in its character as a carefully planned event. Women especially when viewing albums will treat the photographic resources as supplying evidence of the bride's choices, to be noticed, appreciated, and discussed. Here is another excerpt from the same conversation. The picture being looked at shows the Bride and Groom Leaving the Church. A few bridesmaids are visible in the background.

Friend: What were the bridesmaids wearing?
Rachel: Uh, emerald green velvet, forest green velvet. Unfortunately, in the photographs it looks black.
Friend: It's really nice. Were you wearing a stole?
Rachel: Yeah, my mum's stole. Because the dress was satin I didn't want the snow to leave marks.

What the bridesmaids were wearing is not a chance event; the bride has chosen the colour and style of her bridesmaids' dresses (a fact acknowledged in the friend's appreciation, 'It's really nice'). And notice that here

Rachel does call attention to what she produces as a regrettable difference between the record and actuality at the level of colour faithfulness, since her choice of forest green velvet is not properly available to viewers.

A common feature of the talk people do while showing pictures is the recounting of 'disaster' stories or humorous anecdotes. The contrast between these stories and the highly formal photographic record can be striking, but as in the case of the wedding cake picture above, the disaster stories are not necessarily told to contradict the pictures, nor are they received as such. It would even appear as if the existence of the formal record 'allows' such stories to be told by balancing them with a stronger 'truth.'

Friend: Did you enjoy the day?

Rachel: I had a great time. I didn't at the beginning because I was late. Ellen [maid of honour] and I got stuck downtown and the photographer had been there for half an hour and I walked in and it was five thirty and I was getting married at six and my mother just looked at me and said, 'Get dressed.' I go, great, great, this is the mother and daughter talk before I get married – 'Fine,' and stormed into the room.

This story was told at a point in the conversation when the friends had finished going through the album and had begun to talk more generally. It did not occur during the discussion of any specific picture. There is, however, a photograph of Rachel and her parents that was taken at home before the wedding. They have their arms around each other and are smiling broadly. There is no apparent evidence of haste or ill temper.

To get more deeply at the way these highly formal photographs are appreciated, it can be useful to compare them with a genre of photograph circulating in another discourse: documentary photographs. In this latter discourse, evidence that a photograph was staged or that the photographer cleaned up or manipulated the scene in some way might very well be seen to invalidate the photograph's 'objective truth' or to disallow its status as a documentary rather than art photograph. Documentary photographs are generally produced in order to tell one group of people, who were not there, something about the lives and setting of another group of people. There is often an uneven relation of power: those who are 'known' through documentary photographs are often the poor, the marginal, the foreign – the picturesque Other. In contrast, wedding pictures are produced to serve as records for the very people who figure in the pictures as subjects, who are ongoing participants in the relationships being presented in ideal terms.

In this context, pictures are recognized as offering 'essential' truths, not only about past events but about the continuing present. Hence, the concern that people and rooms be photographed at their best, with hair freshly combed and clutter removed beyond the sight of the camera. One is attempting to 'capture' an essential state that transcends ordinary untidiness or momentary flashes of temper. Photographic 'honesty' in this discourse is associated with results, rather than with techniques of production as in the documentary discourse. Those who view wedding pictures are not in a position to be fooled or misled about people and events they know directly. The elaborate staging of these pictures, on the contrary, allows for the 'discovery' of essential states of family harmony, beauty, order, love, or the capture of a characteristic expression. Thus, the people who commission and prize such pictures can say, as I have been told during my research, that the wedding album represents the wedding 'the way it was.' The ability to read the album as such a record is the accomplishment of viewers employing the interpretive scheme of the discourse.

CONCLUSION

The approach to photographic representation that I have put forward here is not limited to investigations beginning from an interest in a specific genre of photograph. Because the products of photographic technology play such a prominent role in discourse, researchers embarked on diverse investigations may discover that photographic texts figure somewhere in the courses of action or discourses they are investigating (for example, in school textbooks, as scientific 'evidence,' or in news reports). The notion of photographic representation as socially organized offers a way to investigate visual texts as they are activated or drawn in to particular social situations through distinct practices of looking.

NOTES

1 This essay is a revised version of a paper originally presented at the Meetings of the Canadian Sociology and Anthropology Association, Learned Societies Conference, Queen's University, Kingston, Ontario, June 1991. Natalie Beausoleil, Alison Griffith, Joseph Schneider, Susan Turner, and Yoko Ueda all provided comments that have assisted me in the revision for this collection.

2 As a matter of investigation, I often begin from my own experience, 'collecting' moments of drawing-in that I have witnessed or participated in. In this way I activate my 'member's knowledge' as a resource. In analytic traditions that

extract photographs for study, what often happens is that the researcher's competence as a viewer of photographs is smuggled in and imputed to the photograph as 'its' meaning. By starting with actual occasions of use, and consciously examining my own competence – or lack of it, as the case may be (I would have to learn how to read the kind of aerial photographs used to plan bombing raids by the military) – I can work towards an understanding of photographic meaning as a social event.

3   An anecdote may serve here: Once I was showing some photographs I had taken to a friend. He flipped through the pictures while continuing to talk about something I identified as having nothing to do with the pictures. 'You aren't looking at them,' I complained, and I took the pictures out of his hands and proceeded to go through them myself, verbally drawing his attention to what I considered their salient features and eliciting from him some verbal indication of approval or interest. On that occasion, 'looking at pictures' clearly meant, for at least one of the participants, something more than causing pictures to pass before one's eyes. My friend's 'looking at pictures' was satisfactorily accomplished when he made his looking available to me through talk.

4   In his later work, Barthes (1981) repudiated the notion of a message without a code and took a more phenomenological approach, declaring that the essence of the Photograph is its simultaneous reference to reality and the past, which he calls 'that-has-been.'

5   This point is also made by John Tagg (1988).

6   A related interest lay in producing objective knowledge about criminal 'types' on the basis of comparisons involving photographs of people who got in trouble with the law. See, for example, Shapiro (1988).

7   For example, I am legally entitled to drive a car because I have passed certain official tests of my competence and carry a valid licence complete with photograph, and not because my father, who taught me, has deemed me capable.

8   The streetcar driver verbally proposed a reading of the picture as showing me with an unflattering hairdo. Sometimes I am riding the streetcar with a friend who asks to see my Metropass photo, and as I show it I usually say something like, 'This is me nine years ago.' In that case, I am proposing that the photo be identified as 'of' something different from what the streetcar driver proposed. To say that we all see the photograph as being 'of' me is to miss subtle but significant differences.

9   Instructions for how to do this are detailed in the trade literature. See, for example, Schaub (1985).

Downgrading Clerical Work in a Textually Mediated Labour Process[1]

MARILEE REIMER

A growing literature exists linking gender and skill categories as these are socially and interactionally constructed; for example, see Cynthia Cockburn's (1985) *Machinery of Dominance: Women, Men, and Technical Know-how.* This research tends to focus directly on the attribution of skill and on the presence or absence of socially recognized sets of skills in the workplace. Authors who focus on women's work in the clerical field have taken up the social construction of skill in relation to comparable work or pay equity, for example, Acker (1989) and Glenn and Feldberg (1983). However, they do not have a sustained focus on the enterprise of constructing work activities into jobs and its centrality to the gender organization of corporate hierarchy.

This essay takes up a more general feature of our modern knowledge of work, in terms of the institutional construction of work as jobs or positions in corporate work organization. The very 'skill' categories which might be questioned within government and corporate organizations are lodged within the discourse and practices in which work and gender are constructed as jobs. That becomes the problematic of my social organization of knowledge analysis. In this essay, I identify how the use of these skill categories in job descriptions restricts the naming and claiming of advanced clerical employees' valuable contributions to the work and how, thereby, their jobs are formally downgraded.

The goal of the Canadian pay-equity movement is to achieve greater equity in the pay and recognition of women's work. On the job, women's skills typically have been 'invisible' and until recently, this invisibility of skill has also characterized sociology's treatment of 'women's jobs.' An ever-growing literature refers to the multifaceted ways in which 'women's skills' are devalued (Abella 1984; Acker 1987; Armstrong and Armstrong 1984; Cassin 1990a, 1990b; Edwards 1979; Glenn and Feldberg 1983; Hammell 1991; Remick and Steinberg 1984; Steinberg and Haigner 1987). Historical analysis of the images of skill in women's and men's work shows how the attribution of skill to work is a social and political achievement (Gaskell 1986; Jackson 1990b). The pay-equity research is beginning to make clear that inequality continues to be produced in an organized fashion.[2] Job evaluation, a key process in which work is made accountable, is far from being a 'gender neutral' process in which women's jobs receive equal recognition and remuneration to that of men (Acker 1989).

Despite the development of pay-equity policies and 'gender neutral' job evaluation schemes, the skills associated with typically women's work continue to be difficult to perceive. Clerical work is a case in point. It is difficult to overcome the common perception of clerical work as relatively mindless routines. This is a perception that I wish to challenge, showing instead how the undervaluing or invisibility of clerical work within government administration creates a gender division that underpins the recognition and validation of career accomplishments. To do that, I need to reframe the analysis of clerical work to include the larger work process in which its outcomes are produced. It is only then that we can see how such asymmetry in the recognition of men's and women's achievements arises in this kind of work.

Through an institutional ethnography, I focus on clerical employees' administrative work processes using their experience as the entry point of analysis (Smith 1987a). The research was done in the Ontario public service where, over a six-month period in 1982, I interviewed twenty-five clerical employees and twenty-five personnel managers, officers, and classification specialists with the Civil Service Commission and observed the ongoing work activities of a policy department (a department I refer to here as 'policy') in an anonymous ministry (Reimer 1987). In total the policy department had thirty-one full-time civil servants, including six clerical staff, the Director and three assistant directors, sixteen Policy Advisers, a Policy Assistant, and four Research Assistants. The all-female clerical staff included the Unit Leader (Clerk 5), the secretary to the Director (Secretary 4), two secretaries to the Assistant Directors (Secretary 4s), two junior secretaries (Secretary 3s), and a 'GO Temp' (Secretary 4). The management positions were all male, with the exception of a female Policy Adviser and a female Policy Assistant.

I argue that two structures of accountability determine the administrative work organization as they also determine how clerical contributions to it are officially recognized. Both originate in personnel management and, specifically, in job descriptions. Job descriptions situate positions hierarchically for purposes of valuation and pay. They also determine how any piece of the work in a government office is attributed officially, that is, to what level of employee. My analysis of concrete clerical activities seeks to display the work's embeddedness in policy development. I contend that the actual contributions of advanced clerical employees, as opposed to what can be known about the work from job descriptions, make it clear that theirs is an interdependent policy development process between management and clerical employees.

ADVANCED CLERICAL WORK: 'DISAPPEARED' AND UNDERVALUED

While it is useful to look at clerical work in its context in the ongoing government administration of which it is a part, it is not easy or straightforward to see what clerical employees actually do. The products of clerical work seems to disappear into a managerial product as it takes shape within the routine documentation of work activities in government. To discover the actual character of these jobs it is necessary to understand how they are organized vis-à-vis managerial action, 'properly' the domain of higher level employees in administration. This targets the employment relationship because that relationship provides the basis for how the work is organized, managed, and recognized. More precisely, it is the system of documenting the work that produces a differentiation of clerical from managerial action as a routine feature of the employment relationship.

Herein lies the distinctiveness of clerical work as typically 'women's work': the differentiations produced in the job descriptions normally seal off clerical employees from advancement into higher level administrative jobs. The invisibility of their active role in managerial action is an outcome of the way work is documented as part of a hierarchy of authority, where only designated positions are accountable for initiating, directing, and managing policies and programs. Although the examples I use here provide an especially vivid display of clerical employee involvement in higher level administrative work, many of the secretaries and clerks I studied had requested and been denied reclassification. Such decisions were taken, not by reviewing what the workers actually did in those jobs, but by comparing their duties and responsibilities with a hypothetical performance of the previous incumbents in these positions understood through abstract job descriptions. The contrast is clear between my data about clerical work and its definition as separate from other administrative work and as relatively unspecialized and routine. My inquiry reveals that clerical work is not that different from other administrative work once it can be liberated from its descriptive categories and seen as integral to the achievement of management and professional objectives and responsibilities.

My analysis explicating the social organization of the undervaluation of clerical work has two parts: first I describe the system of documenting the work which makes it disappear into the domain of managerial action; then I give two examples of what clerical employees actually do in this government policy department, and show how this work is officially attributed to others.

ACCOUNTING FOR CLERICAL-ADMINISTRATIVE WORK

Clerical work is an outgrowth of the continual division between mental and manual labour, which is central to the drive to cheapen labour costs under capitalism (Lowe 1979). The division between mental and manual labour is produced within the processes of accountability of mandated government action, and the documentation of 'jobs' is basic to how this is done.

Early work on job descriptions in the Ontario Public Service began in the post–Second World War period when the conventional divisions between positions were established. Clerical positions were organized within the standardized categories and descriptions of deskilled forms of labour. A classification system was designed based on functional divisions between work and worker traits. Clerical positions were analysed in terms of worker functions or involvement with 'Things, Data and People' (G. Smith 1979: 10). The key distinction which produces hierarchy within administration is that clerical jobs are differentiated according to 'types of activity' while professional, technical, and managerial positions are grouped according to 'subject matter' areas. The job descriptions create the analytical divide between positions characterized in terms of knowledge of specialized 'subject matter' versus those schematized in relation to proceduralized activities, functions, and routines.

Job descriptions construct, textually, an ordering of positions, the work attached to them, and the recognition given for that work. Some government job descriptions require knowledge of concrete programs and organizational objectives and some do not. Incumbents of the jobs that require such specific knowledge are made accountable for the action that requires the use of that knowledge in managerial programs; those whose job descriptions do not call for such knowledge, including clerical employees, are not made accountable for knowledgable action (Reimer 1991–2).

Government job descriptions reveal a textual ordering of government policy work that can be schematized in terms of the temporal sequences or phases, as follows (Reimer 1987: 177):

Temporal Sequence of Government Action

Phase One	Phase Two	Phase Three
Policy formulation	Program management	Administrative support
	Public accountability for ministry	Program delivery

Phase One, involving policy formation, is the domain of politicians, legislative committees, and policy makers. The mandate of a ministry is established in this phase, and this is referenced in the job descriptions of high level managers and other management module positions.

Phase Two is mandated at the level of each government ministry. In this phase of action, positions which are mandated to act on behalf of government are assigned responsibilities for achieving departmental objectives through the formulation of management programs. The job description of the Director of the policy department has the most explicit statement of the ministry mandate and the particular responsibilities this entails for the department. A major aspect of this work is providing input into legislative committees on behalf of government. Thus, a mandated relationship is established between the Director's position and the particular program activities. For example, under 'decision-making' this involves 'recommending policy positions the Deputy and/or Minister and/or government should pursue on a particular [Ministry] matter' (Reimer 1987: 277). The job description specifies that these activities must be carried out 'recognizing consumer interests' and those of industry, specifying the constituencies to which the policy process will be made accountable. For program management positions the relation of the position to the departmental mandate is established in the 'Purpose of Position' section of the job description. There, the character of the work as 'policy development' is stated, for example, for the Policy Assistant to the Director 'to provide administrative assistance to the Director; to coordinate the program and policy development activities of the department' (ibid.: 138).

Subordinate to Phase Two are all of those activities which are designated 'administrative support' and as enabling the 'decision makers' to do their work. Designated as Phase Three in this diagram, administrative support is identified by personnel managers as 'reactive' work, as opposed to 'proactive,' and therefore dependent on the guidance and supervision of management-level positions. This is where clerical jobs fall. Within this group are secretaries and clerks 1, 2, 3, 4, and 5.

Accountability for program management and hence for decision making is constructed textually as the domain of management module positions (Phase Two). All clerical positions are constructed as operating strictly in a relation of subordination or delegation to management activities and essentially as a separate order of standardized routines and technical functions. For example, the most advanced clerical module position, the Clerk 5 or 'Unit Leader,' is organized in relation to the mandated course of action, but in the 'Purposes' section of the job description, that position is characterized as providing 'administrative, clerical and secretarial support services for the Director' and principals and coordinating 'the provision of such services in the group to which assigned' (Reimer 1987: 281). This characterization establishes the position as supportive to, but outside, the group of positions which are mandated to act on behalf of government within the programs of a given department.

The job descriptions for the Unit Leader and other clerical positions fall into the category of 'generic specifications' and are not individualized for each job as the management positions are. The clerical activities listed as 'duties' produce the delegated relation of the position to the mandated courses of action as sequences of routinized functions which are carried out under the supervision of a manager. Thus, a division of labour is constructed conceptually within the job descriptions which defines how the work done in any position relates to mandated governmental action. My analysis of two cases of departmental action (the 'Government Press Release' and the 'Elderly Homeowner') challenges this ideological construction.

THE POLICY DEPARTMENT: PRODUCING PUBLIC ACCOUNTABILITY
IN THE MEDIA

The work of making government action accountable to the public is central to the work of the policy department. In fact, public accountability for the policy of the government is the key outcome or product of the policy department. The outcome of most of the work carried out in this depart-

ment eventually comes under public scrutiny either in the provincial legislature, the news media, and/or by the relevant industry officials. Since
policy development activities are always open to scrutiny, producing the
work properly comes to mean achieving in documents the proper forms of
mandated action (Reimer 1991–2; 36).

All government programs are conceived, managed, and accounted for in
official texts. The mandate for policy development and its entry into the
media discourse is established within the documentary processes of government legislation, orders-in-council, management-by-results systems, and
so forth, all taking place within specifically defined and routine forms of
administrative and managerial action.

The mandate of 'policy' includes providing policy recommendations for
the government and ongoing support for their success. Taking place within
the parameters of a legislative process in a highly politicized area, policy
support for government activities are both functional and technical in
nature and the topic of continual political attention in the media. The director's job specification established his responsibility for this mandate under
the section 'consequences of error,' where he is held responsible for
anything which might have 'serious impact on the Ministry's programs/
objectives ... [or be of] immediate embarrassment to the government'
(Reimer 1987: 280). Potential problems of this nature are managed through
the advice provided by the policy department and the articulation of the
department's policy recommendations with government positions.

This department is a particularly key player among the varied middle
level bodies contributing to policy at the ministry level. The expertise of
senior policy advisers in this department is relied upon heavily because the
political appointees to ministries change fairly often and are not specialists
in the areas to which they are designated. On a daily basis, for example,
policy letters researched and written in the department are signed by the
political appointees. Similarly, with speeches, policy statements, and the
like presented in the legislature, the policy department has significant, if not
total, input into the body of the message to be delivered. The Director also
sits on the Cabinet committee concerned with ministry matters and is
directly involved in high level policy formulation, for example, (at the time
the fieldwork was being conducted) government imposed wage and price
constraints.

The ebb and flow of program demands are geared to the political impact
of policy development and the ability of the government to display the successful aspects of its program publicly. Concretely, this translates into the
ongoing development of statements, defence of government actions, and

announcements by the minister in the legislature, the media, public forums, and official meetings where representatives of the department appear. It also involves the timely communication with Cabinet, management board, the premier's office, and other levels of government when advice and information are sought for budgetary announcements, orders-in-council, or such issues as wage controls and taxes on industry (Reimer 1991–2: 37).

For the department, the work of preparing back-up information, briefings, and so forth for the minister in the legislature receives top priority. This work is organized in terms of a highly interdependent approach between secretaries and policy advisers, which the Unit Leader (Clerk 5) described in terms of an 'overlap' between clerks' work and that of the policy advisers. The Policy Assistant, the Director's secretary, and the Unit Leader work as a team: the secretary goes through all the mail in the Director's office and informs the Unit Leader of anything coming up that she needs to know about. The Policy Assistant will look through the Director's tray and get started researching or preparing briefing materials for anything with a deadline.

This coordination of activities requires advanced clerical employees to keep abreast of the activities of the Director's office and the department in order to get the policy advisers and staff organized to meet deadlines. When the legislature is in session, for example, the final deadline for a speech going to the minister must include time for him to 'digest' it. The Unit Leader begins by checking the morning paper to find out how many issues are up, because if there are many, she may have to have everyone including staff and advisers preparing for the legislature first thing in the morning. Such a day would usually require her arriving early.

All such action is authorized in relation to ministry mandates. As indicated previously, the manner in which responsibilities are formally designated accords with the authority assigned in job classifications and job descriptions. Nonetheless all employees who do the work must use specialized knowledge of policy and of its impact on the public. For example, part of the secretary 4s' work involves managing an internal dialogue among government bodies and officials, as well as sectors of the public such as members of the business community. The dialogue is much more attenuated, but nonetheless exists, in relation to community and consumer groups who attempt to have an impact on governmental decision making. What becomes public in these dialogues, and the form in which it is packaged, is largely a managed production carefully tailored to the political discourse of the media. What reaches the voters is a form of public accountability designed to keep the government in office. Clerical employees participate in this work of public accountability with a trained and acute knowledge of the political discourse which is played out in the media. To do so successfully, everybody must, for instance, be cognizant of how their ministry's work is organized in terms of the oppositional character of the legislature. As a secretary explained, 'Even though the MP's conduct themselves like children in the legislature booing, horsing around, trying to catch each other up, at all costs the Minister must be prepared ... and able to answer any embarrassing questions. Anything that appears in the papers, or the MPs are contacted about by their constituencies, can come up in the House. The MPs bring it up to the appropriate Minister, and they should be able to answer. This is how the government works. It's like a circle' (Reimer 1987: 254).

This comment captures the sense in which the ministry's work is oriented to the media discourse produced in the form of newspaper articles, the proceedings of the legislature (in the provincial *Hansard*), public hearings, commissions, and conferences. The government's representation of its own actions and ability to account credibly for government policies will have an impact on its own political future. The ability to shape public discourse is a powerful resource which the bureaucracy has a major role in accomplishing.

The production of public accountability also involves an ongoing dialogue conducted in 'policy' with various levels of the business community and segments of the public which initiate communications with the government. Some of these groups appear to have an ongoing and consultative relation to the ministry, and part of the secretaries' and clerks' work is to facilitate this dialogue. In order to do so they must be knowledgeable of the actual day-to-day program activities of the department and able to provide information regarding these activities between the department and high level officials. In relation to company executives in certain segments of the industry, for example, this means understanding that the squeezed profit levels they are experiencing would be a high priority concern in a period of economic constraint.

How such a priority could translate into action requires knowledge of the manner in which policy activities are related to the legislative process and inner workings of Cabinet (Reimer 1991–2: 37). Secretaries' and clerks' knowledge of how to organize and coordinate dialogue with industry representatives depends on knowledge of the extended activity sequences of policy development and legislative process. Staff who must organize or participate in such action sequences, which together produce public accountability, must know the historical background and ongoing action of the whole department to actually do this work. This is illustrated below in the vignette called 'The Government Press Release,' where the clerical responsibility for handling phone calls can be seen as specialized and not routine work.

The Government Press Release

The Director's secretary received a phone call from a government agency executive prior to a policy announcement on the level of price restraints for government-regulated resources. Making government policy is often an interdependent work process between ministers, heads of government agencies, and Cabinet members in which administrative employees play an important coordinating role. Given the fact that policy development is subject to scrutiny by the press, this coordinative work goes beyond merely answering the telephone – the task which appears in the clerk's job description. It involves piecing together sequences of action according to an informed understanding of the contingencies of the policy development process. Prior to this policy announcement, one such agency head phoned to say he was finished with the first draft of his portion of the follow-up announcement. Knowing that a decision had been made regarding the technical aspects of the announced price levels, the Director's secretary informed him that this had occurred. She knew that this was 'useful' information to this agency head, because, if the press called him regarding the announcement, he could coordinate his comments with the final decision of the government. As well, knowing that the policy advisers were waiting to find out whether his phase of the follow-up announcement had gone as planned, the secretary relayed this information immediately to the advisers who were writing the next phase of the follow-up announcement. This 'phone work' requires an insider's knowledge of the policy development process and, in particular, an appreciation for 'timing.' The secretary explained the background of this issue to me in the following way: 'The whole picture took six months ... the Board held hearings and then we worked on the report, and made recommendations. The industry asked for a price constraint level of "x," the Board recommended "y," and the average they came up with was "z." Monday night the estimates meeting lasted until 9 p.m. because we had to submit the estimates to Management Board. Yesterday the announcement was made' (Reimer 1987: 264).

All of the policy activities discussed were confidential Cabinet committee decisions to which only a select number of individuals had access. Given the need for ministers and government representatives to coordinate information requested by the press or in the legislature, the timely exchange of information of this sort avoids 'gaffs' on the government's part and provides the maximum amount of time to prepare briefing materials. Since the schedule is often gruelling for advisers involved in attending meetings, preparing announcements, and so forth, the informational and bodily logistics of policy development become a separate phase in the coordination of program events.

This Government Press Release example captures the typical administrative activity of organizing and coordinating the dialogue internal to government officials. Secretaries and clerks doing this work must have concrete knowledge of program activities and, therefore, of policy issues. This means knowing how these must be coordinated as the concerted actions of official spokespersons of ministries, agencies, and offices, as well as knowing who is properly part of the internal dialogue of government and business. It means making judgments about who should be excluded because they are linked to the attacks of the official opposition upon government policy in the legislature.

Clerical employees must approach the forms of accountability to non-business sectors of the public quite differently from the forms of accountability to the relevant industry. Their consultative relationship with industry executives, involving an ongoing and collegial form of dialogue to support and protect business interests, does not apply to various other segments of the public, for example, senior citizens, rural ratepayers, and provincial government civil servants. The general public stands in a relation of 'non-expert' to the policy advisers in the department.[3] Business groups, on the other hand, receive more specialized attention which accords with the objectives of government in the recessionary period prevailing at the time of this study. This set of policy concerns is articulated in the director's job description in a section specifying the kinds of judgments required, for example, protecting profit margins when setting prices on government-regulated resources.

If clerical employees are going to contribute to the production of accountability to different publics, they must be knowledgable about what information is not to be made public, particularly in relation to groups receiving a low priority in the policy development process. Media coverage remains a tightly controlled operation in this ministry, with the government often downplaying issues which might prove an embarrassment, for example, an industrial accident and the responses of lobby groups to it. The clerical employee's ability to centralize information in the policy department plays an important role in informing the director and advisers of all urgent matters of this sort. The various documentary forms of information included press releases, telex messages, excerpts from *Hansard*, media summaries, and policy strategy statements. The Unit Leader and Director's secretary examine all of these, as well as all letters going to the minister. Knowledge of ongoing events allows advanced clerical employees to bring information to the advisers' attention in order to act in a timely manner and to prepare for confrontations in the legislature. It is this kind of knowledge and judgment which makes telephone work far from the routine clerical task of the job description.

The Elderly Homeowner

A second vignette, the Elderly Homeowner, displays a secretary's sensitivity to the political logistics of handling a potentially explosive complaint made on the day wage and price constraints were announced. A senior citizen came in to speak to the minister with a complaint regarding his expenses on government-regulated commodities. He was complaining because he would be forced to sell his home because of the inflated prices which made his total expenses prohibitive. Rather than telling him that the minister was not in or that he should contact the ministry more closely concerned with his problem, the secretary immediately acknowledged the sensitivity of the situation and ushered him in to see the ministry lawyer. She also contacted an adviser and discussed the need to inquire with the appropriate ministry in order to calculate the man's expenses related to the constraints and to notify the Cabinet committee on constraints policy to inform them of this situation.

In explaining the political sensitivity (and confidentiality) of this event, the secretary told me that 'this man will not be stopped' and would likely contact his Member of Parliament on the matter. Handing me the letter to Cabinet to read, she explained that this would give me an idea of some of the work they do on behalf of citizens such as this man. Once his expenses were checked out he still had to pay his bills, which were properly calculated. She said that he was a perfect example of the low-income, senior citizen who was left unprotected by the constraints policy.

As the secretary was aware, the Opposition would have liked to have heard about this man's complaint on the day constraints were announced. However, by providing him with immediate attention and attempting to deal with the issue within government, this possibility was avoided. Also, the possible political liability of such cases could be weighed by entering his situation immediately into the policy-making process as a factor for consideration by the Cabinet's constraints committee.

In this case, we can see how administrative employees actively organize the policy development process to deal with situations which are possibly damaging to the government's defence of its record. Knowledge of the content and ramifications of the as-yet unannounced pricing policy was required to identify the situation as one with immediate consequences in the oppositional forum of the legislature. Although the secretary brought attention initially to the need for a timely response to the situation of this elderly homeowner, it is only the directors or advisers who can 'input' this information into the policy development process. In this case, an adviser sent a letter to a Cabinet committee. Recognition of acts of 'inputting' or 'initiating' depend on documentary formulation of jobs. The director's and adviser's positions mandate them to act even though the action sequence may originate with the secretary 4 or clerk 5, and depend on their timely recognition of the pertinent policy 'input.'

ACCOUNTING FOR ADMINISTRATIVE WORK IN GOVERNMENT

In the Elderly Homeowner case, as in the Government Press Release, producing accountability included the timely provision of policy information to the executives of a government agency and mobilizing advisers to inform a Cabinet committee of possible policy consequences of price constraint levels to elderly homeowners. Again, job descriptions and action mandates tied to job classifications render invisible the program and policy work in administration which clerical employees perform, contributing to their image as low level and relatively unskilled. By comparing the organization of the 'Major Responsibilities' section of a managerial position, for example, that of Policy Assistant, with that of the Unit Leader, it is possible to see just how the mandate of the former provides for and subsumes the activities listed in the job description of the latter.

The work in question is authorized under the following responsibilities in the Policy Assistant job description: 'Establishes and maintains a network of information sources within own Ministry, other ministries, outside agencies ... involved in [policy] issues to ensure requested information will be provided' and 'providing effective administrative services for confidential matters ... which provide the Director with significant input to achieve program goals and objectives' (Reimer 1987: 278, 280).

When this same work is performed by Clerk 5s, the Clerk 5 job description organizes her activities as clerical operations under the guidance of a manager, such as the Policy Assistant: 'requesting or giving information on projects, liaising with own principals ... and those in other ministries to ensure requested information will be provided' (ibid.: 281). The mandate for participating officially in the managerial process as an agent on behalf of government is stated in the job description (for example, of a Policy Assistant or Adviser) in relation to specific programs and departmental objectives. These include knowledge of the department's specific management systems and procedures and expected program results. The subject matter or knowledge of management systems is central to the description of management positions.

In the clerical position description, all 'functions' listed reference a different order of activity altogether: for example, 'to provide administrative, clerical and secretarial services.' All aspects of the 'skills and knowledge' section reference support services and generic procedures instrumental in providing them, for example, 'familiarity with a centralized administrative system ... ability to liaise effectively with all levels of management' (ibid.: 280).

The fundamental difference between the positions classified in higher level administration and those identified as advanced clerical is the absence of recognition of the kind of program knowledge required to perform the job. Because the job description does not reference program objectives nor the kind of knowledge, judgments and decision making involved in achieving them, the grounding of clerical activities in organizational processes and programs is not established for evaluation. Failure to recognize clerical employees' knowledge and involvement in managerial programs is a central organizing feature of the clerical job descriptions. This textual organization creates positions outside of the mandated courses of action, the incumbents of which, therefore, officially perform only delegated responsibilities.

What the personnel management documents prescribe, the accounts of the labour process within managerial programs accomplish as 'fact.' This subordination is achieved textually within the documentation of authored reports, records of ongoing activities, and presentations of work in official contexts. Two results occur. When clerical employees are not named as authors of the work, it appears as delegated, low-level routines and functions. In addition, advanced clerical work contributes to a documentary 'track record' for the incumbents of positions which are located within the managerial career trajectory.

CONCLUSION

In the case I have analysed, clerical work is documented in such a way that the specialized knowledge and contributions of women in advanced clerical positions are drawn upon while not being made accountable as performance in a position. Any evaluation of their jobs would build on that understanding and misread the nature of the work. Rather than stating a particular set of routine skills practised in such a position, an accurate evaluation would have to document the specialized work of advancing an overall mandate of programs and policies. Specifically this would involve acknowledging the ongoing organizational context (programs, policies, objectives) of which it is a part and the concrete knowledge required to produce it.

Gender-neutral job evaluations will never be truly gender neutral until the underlying conceptions of jobs and job hierarchies are abandoned. This depends on an analysis of the manner in which inequalities between men and women are organized within jobs evaluation systems and in the jobs themselves, as in this case, embedded in the textual basis of official government action.

NOTES

1 Parts of this essay appeared previously in M. Reimer, 'Women's Invisible Skills and Gender Segregation in the Clerical-Administrative Sector,' *Optimum: The Journal of Public Sector Management* 22–4: (1991–2) 29–41, reprinted here with the permission of the Minister of Supply and Services Canada, 1995.

2 According to a recent ruling by the Ontario Pay-Equity Tribunal, jobs in the clerical, retail, and service sectors have been undervalued because of their being 'women's work' ('Ontario pay-equity ruling sets precedent for women,' *Globe and Mail*, 16 August 1991). Skills that are often overlooked when performed by women in these sectors include 'those required to adjust to rapid change, juggle priorities, coordinate schedules, deal with upset or irrational people, provide emotional support to distressed or ill people, clean up after others, and work with constant noise and interruption.' Also unrecognized are the alternative forms of organization of women's work, for example, working in cooperative team structures in order to coordinate activities with other workers or with people receiving services. The unprecedented ruling directs an employer to ferret out and acknowledge the invisible and overlooked skills of forty nurses in the Ontario Nurses Association. It may be applied, as well, to hundreds of thousands of Ontario women who have not yet negotiated pay-equity settlements. This case also set a precedent as the first litigated case over gender neutrality in job evaluations. The legal recognition of hidden skills in female identified work sectors is a watershed in the sociological literature on the work process where the skilled character of typical women's work has long been disputed.

3 A section from an adviser's job description illustrates the status of non-business, public groups as 'non-experts': 'The public has unrealistic expectations
about the extent to which the program will make a contribution to Ontario's
future. Current 'mythology' stems from the ill–informed or biased lobbies, public fear of the program, media hype, poor or non-existent data' (Reimer 1987:
267).

The Power of Being Professional

GERALD A.J. DE MONTIGNY

To do social work is to engage in socially organized practices of power: the power to investigate, to assess, to produce authorized accounts, to present case 'facts,' and to intervene in people's lives. The exercise of such power, although having its dramatic moments – such as the apprehension of a child – is also realized through more subtle and less visible moments of practice. This essay seeks to explore the subtle uses of power which are realized through the textual or documentary practices of professional accounts.[1] The proficient use of documents and texts in the form of legislation, policy manuals, memoranda, case files, and various reports occurs almost automatically as skilled professionals perform their daily work. Indeed, the very possibility of professional authority depends to a large degree on the ability of practitioners to employ textual realities to mediate the details of their daily practice.

This essay explicates the practical exercise of textually mediated power by examining a specific textual fragment. I begin with a single line which was buried inside a case file, in the Running Records: 'The apartment smelled of urine.' This factual observation was made by a colleague in her capacity as a child protection worker responsible for managing a particular Family and Child Services case. By analysing this entry and the background work which provided for its cogency I will explicate the implicit structuring of power which is integral to a professional standpoint.

Foucault's notion of a 'mechanics of power' (1980), the exercise of power as realized through specific tools, is used to focus on one particular tool for the exercise of power, that is, textual production in the form of organizational records. Specific acts of textual production are moves through which forms of professional power are constructed.

It is through texts that mundane activities ultimately appear or stand as proper social work, hence, as matters of record. A home visit becomes an entry in a Running Record, an apprehension becomes a Report to the Court, a decision to request custody of a child becomes a Notice of Hearing, and so on. Furthermore, as textual entries are aggregated into files they become the record of the work carried out for an organization. Through various organizational procedures, including file storage, file audits, mandatory reports from local offices to central offices and budgeting, the routine record-keeping activities of social workers become the statistics for the office, and ultimately for the department.

THE CASE EXAMPLE

Consider the simple notation in the Running Records, 'The apartment smelled of urine.' Behind this seemingly factual statement there existed a complex work process, and in the sections which follow I will unfold the social organization of that process. This essay employs the methods developed by Dorothy Smith to explore 'the status of knowledge as socially and materially organized, as produced by individuals in actual settings and as organized by and organizing definite social relations' (Smith 1990a: 62). The simple facticity of the entry relies upon a complex organizational division of labour, elaborate professional knowledge, everyday organizational relationships, and a multitude of cultural and class assumptions about proper and improper smells.

Curiously, although the entry was recorded by a colleague in a file on her caseload she did not personally determine that 'the apartment smelled of urine.' I was the social worker who did the investigation. How was it that this social worker could treat my experience as factual?[2] What gave my voice authority? What gave her the authority to record the 'facts'? To answer these questions I turn to examine the background work which provided for the possibility of such 'factual' recording.

At the office, I received a phone call from a person who claimed that the next door apartment was emitting a horrible stench. The neighbour worried, 'There's a three-year-old kid living in the apartment. I don't know how he can survive in that stench.' As the Intake Social Worker I was required to investigate the situation; I was mandated to determine if there was a child in need of protection. Later that day I drove to the address provided by the caller. As I entered the apartment building, descended the stairs, and neared the apartment door I could definitely smell a 'disgusting' odour. When the door was opened by a thin middle-aged man, a wall of stale air and urine hit my nostrils. I coughed involuntarily. The lining in my nose burned. Trying not to inhale – impossible – I blinked my watering eyes and introduced myself. The man at the door invited me in. To my surprise the man seemed quite comfortable and oblivious to the noxious odours where he lived. I asked, somewhat obliquely, 'Isn't it a bit thick in here?' He returned a blank and uncomprehending stare. After I explained that I was there because of a complaint about the smell, the man explained that what people were smelling was 'probably pee from my grandson's bed.'

I asked the man to tell me about his grandson, the problem with bedwetting, and what he had done to correct the problem. Apparently, the man's two-year-old grandchild lived in the apartment along with the child's mentally incapacitated mother. The grandfather explained that he was struggling to care for his daughter and his grandchild despite having recently suffered a severe and incapacitating heart attack himself. He observed that the child was not yet toilet trained, and that the child continued to wet his bed every night. I asked the man what he did when the child wet his bed, and so the interview proceeded, with a review of measures to deal with bedwetting.

In the press to get on with the work of social work I glossed over the obvious disjuncture between my experience of stench and the man's experience. For the man, the smell of his apartment was unremarkable. Yet, for me the smell of the apartment was focal. There was an unexplicated disjuncture between my experiences and the man's. And what counted in the Running Record was my experience not the man's.

The 'fact' that the man at the door did not share my sense of stench became a sign that he lacked common sense. I could invoke a common-sense embedded in social work understandings to argue that for any normal person the stench in the apartment would be intolerable. I knew that the apartment really stank, and that it was a sign of inadequate child care. I knew that the man violated or ignored the common-sense boundaries of personal hygiene and child care. He had not properly managed smells and bodies. The man had failed to properly diaper the child before putting the child to bed. He had failed to change wet bedclothes. He had not wiped urine off the carpet. He had not taught the child to use the potty.

As a social worker I was equally certain that the smell was a problem requiring some form of professional management. I knew that the case needed to be managed by providing the man with parenting skills, for example, toilet training the child, changing soiled bedding, doing the laundry, using disinfectant to clean soiled areas, and so forth. The smell was inscribed into a professional code as a matter indicating parental failure and therefore as properly deserving social work attention.

PRODUCING THE TEXTS

As an artefact of organizational work, files and their contents are visibly ordered as organizationally relevant and as addressing organizational work. In my office our position as social workers invested us with the power to inscribe our accounts and assessments as 'realities' in the documentary records. The Running Records on client files were a location for noting the more ad hoc details of our practice; they operated as a textual dialogue, recording our thoughts concerning a case. The details contained in the Running Records could be referenced to establish the chronology of events, early identification of problems, tentative theorization of issues, intervention activities, and case planning. When a formal report was required the Running Records could be referenced as an invaluable source of background information.

Running Records and most other documents placed on client files were usually written by the social workers. Clients did not author the reports on file about their lives. Smith observes that in such records, 'The patient herself and her friends, family, or co-workers appear only in "reported" speech' (Smith 1990a: 99). As 'reported' speech, what clients actually say is located inside professionally determined schemata and documentary forms. For example, the grandfather's statement that the smell was caused by the child's bedwetting might be framed on file as indicating an inappropriate tolerance of offensive smells, a failure to maintain proper hygiene for the child, parental inattention, and so forth. The application of such background organizing frames to the grandparent's utterances would be outside his control as a client.

Files purport to represent the lives of clients. In my office the information on file had the appearance of a series of documentary facts. However, inside the spaces of the file, the actual voices of the clients were silenced. Both the creation of the file's contents and access to those contents depended on a formal relationship of employment with the child protection agency. In this sense what counted as a proper file was thoroughly implicated in the work of the organization (Smith 1990a; Zimmerman 1974). The putative objectivity of file information rested on the implicit warranting of professional knowledge and on the acceptance of organizational mandates.

The cogency of the case record as a moment of social work was implied by the simple matter of its location. Turning back to the example, 'The apartment smelled of urine,' we recognize that it was located inside a case file in a child welfare agency.

Wheeler suggests that 'a file or dossier is likely to attain a legitimacy and authority that is lacking in more informal types of communication' (Wheeler 1976: 5). Yet what is it about the file which gives it such authority? Wheeler observes that records are formalized forms of communication, that they have a permanence which does not exist for speech, that they are transferable, that they have a 'facelessness' unlike personal communication, and finally that they can be combined in a variety of ways. Certainly, while these are all essential aspects which contribute to the authority of records, what Wheeler does not address is the underlying reliance of record-keeping practices on methods of representation. Simply, inscriptions in the record stand as representing the lives, events, circumstances, and actions of clients. The methods of representation (Foucault 1970; Lowe 1982) are themselves embedded inside a standpoint of power and authority.

It is this social organization of certainty that I now wish to examine. It was within this standpoint of certainty that I breathed the air, determined that it was foul and that there was a problem that I had to investigate. As noted above, when doing the work I did not entertain the possibility of a reality disjuncture (Pollner 1974). I knew there was one reality: the apartment stank from urine, and the urine was the result of a failure to properly toilet train or to clean up after the two-year-old child. Furthermore, when I reported my findings back to my colleague who carried this family on her caseload she obviously treated my report as factual, as was indicated by her notation on file.

A critical analysis of this work process raises several pressing problems. First, how was it that I was the proper interpreter of reality? What gave me a sense of certainty and authority? Second, what devices did I employ to report my experience as a series of facts to my colleague? Third, how was it that my colleague was able to rely on my narrative to produce her record on the client's file? What was the nature of the relationship between us which allowed her to treat my story as factual? Fourth, what were the organizational factors which effectively silenced the client's account? What were the organizational sources of power which authorized social work accounts over those of clients?

AUTHORITY AND CERTAINTY

If I had been asked to explain how I knew that the apartment stank, I might have shrugged my shoulders. As the investigating worker I did not bother to ask why I noticed the stench. Both the question and the answers I provided presupposed my power to define the everyday world of this man and

214 Gerald A.J. de Montigny

his family from inside an authoritative professional location. Furthermore, as a skilled social worker I knew how to take up the man's failure to notice the stench. I could invoke a series of professional understandings to explain that the man had become accustomed to the rank odour, that he had an inappropriate tolerance for filth, that he had poor parenting skills, and so forth.

The certainty of sense which I brought to this doorstep was woven into a position of authority, knowledge of complex professional explanations, and membership within a world characterized by the demand for a singular and univocal account of that world (Pollner 1974). A proper professional account had to frame the problem of smell inside an acceptable professional schema. An improper account of the problem would reveal my reliance on, for example, negative cultural assessments, racist schemata, or an excessive standard for hygiene. Simply put, a proper account had to make the problem the client's, not mine. For example, if a social worker made disparaging remarks about 'curry smells' in the homes of people from India or 'fish smells' in the homes of coastal aboriginal people, these comments would probably be regarded as inappropriate. A proper problematization of smell needs to be free of racial stereotyping or negative cultural assessments.

To raise the issue of smell and odour is an enterprise fraught with peril. Social workers must be clear that they are not unreflectingly imposing narrow cultural or class standards and values onto groups of people who do not share these standards and values. In circumstances where a social worker finds a smell to be offensive, yet the smell is clearly part of a family's cultural way of life, confusion might arise about what to do. The social worker could reorganize this confusion, recognize the difficulty of making an 'objective' assessment, acknowledge cultural biases, and reframe the encounter as a value dilemma. Or the social worker might recognize the risks of being called racist and simply not report her observations. The social worker could justify a decision to not intervene as not wanting to impose her or his values on the clients. However, in the case at hand, such concerns were adumbrated largely because both the client and I, the social worker, were white, and because a neighbour had phoned to complain about the odour from the apartment.

Despite the dangers and difficulties of appropriately framing accounts of smells, social workers must be able to identify smells which can be treated as indicative of pathology and disturbance: for example, the sweet smell of alcohol exuded through bodily pores, the smell of urine and faeces, the smell of garbage, the smell of uncared for pets, and so forth. Such smells may indicate serious individual or family problems such as alcoholism, child neglect, possibilities of infection and disease. Further, social workers must be able to recognize those smells which enter people's homes from outside, and over which clients have little responsibility – pollution from pulp mills, smelters, abattoirs, sewage outfalls, and treatment plants.

As a trained social worker with experience in child protection I had come to know how to detect neglect. I could examine a child's body for sores, scratches, rashes, and malformations. I could assess the child's developmental progress against a knowledge of 'normal' developmental milestones, for example, turning over, crawling, walking, talking; see Griffith, this volume. I could assess a parent's affect, intellect, capacity to parent, bond with the child, and attitude towards intervention. I could examine the home environment to look for signs of neglect – food scraps on the floor, filthy toilets, diapers in corners, empty refrigerators. Finally, I could sniff about for odours which might reveal 'unacceptable' filth, chronic alcohol or drug abuse, and child neglect. Thus, the apparently simple issue of smell was entered into a series of professional schemata for determining neglect and for deciding what measures were required to protect the child in the apartment.[3]

The notation that 'the apartment smelled of urine' taps into deeply rooted cultural premises surrounding urine and faeces as inherently defiling (Clark and Davis 1989: 651): The 'rules and conditions surrounding the specifications and processes of defilement constitute a cornerstone in the construction of culturally defined forms of identity and solidarity for individuals and social collectivities in any and every culture.' Among white, middle-class members of our society the smell of urine is never acceptable and is almost automatically attributable as a failure. The ascription of defiling characteristics to a client separates respectable social workers from disreputable clients. Such construction of clients as defiled undermines their authority and claims to competency. The ascription of defilement is an integral tool in the interchanges of power between social workers and clients.

AFFIRMING RELATIONS OF POWER

My talk with my colleague the next day was embedded inside the organizational work of child protection. As the worker on intake who had responded to the complaint, my job was to apprise my colleague of my analysis of the case. Once she was brought up to date, she would be able to resume her control and management of the case. Our talk was shaped by our location inside the office and by our self-referencing of professional discourse and the standpoint of agency authority. Our conversation was centred on issues of possible child neglect, determination of risk factors, and future courses of action for case management.

An integral aspect of our conversation was that my colleague and I had known each other as co-workers for sometime. Through shared participation in work and social activities, we had built up a professional relationship of mutual respect and trust. Furthermore, just as I was able to regard my colleague as a social worker, through knowledge of her formal credentials, her speech acts, and her participation in the routines of the job, so too did she regard me. Our work-life together supported our capacity to treat each other's utterances as properly professional and, hence, as truthful and authoritative.

Indeed such background relationships are essential for cementing into place the capacity of co-workers to treat each other's work as properly organizational. For my colleague to treat my utterances as trustworthy she had to assume that my report was not organized by personal concerns such as revenge, partiality, self-interest – wanting to see a friend gain custody of the child or maliciousness or subconscious impulses, for example. My motivations had to be properly organizational (Weber 1978). Personal motivations would certainly raise issues of appropriate professional distance, personal over-involvement in the work, inappropriate projection of one's own issues onto clients, and so on. To develop trust in each other, professionals perform discursive work and produce a continuous series of presentations of self which demonstrate the proper professional and organizational motivation.

In summing up, the simple 'facts' which my colleague entered in the record glossed the complex professional sense-making practices which I had brought to the doorstep that day. They glossed the mundane management of self which provides for accounting for a sensory barrage of day-to-day work. The record glossed the complex relations between colleagues in an office, just as it glossed the background relations of power which define who contributes to the creation of a record, who has access to the record, and the organizational uses to which the record is put.

INSCRIPTIVE ACCOUNTING PRACTICES

Through textual accounts I and others in my office constructed our work, and accordingly ourselves, as proper social work professionals. By inscribing our work into record we displayed our proper professional location. Our record keeping was itself a sign of professional practice, as it demonstrated our ability to use professional language, to organize our daily activities into proper professional routines, and our willingness to incorporate professional understandings into our practice.

What the social work profession is, at the moments of its practical accomplishment, is bound to members' textual accounts. Social workers' textual practices for generating accounts, such as reports to court, file notes, and requests for service emerge out of organizational work processes. Work at hand is connected to organizational courses of action which are themselves outlined step by step in documentary form as policies, directives, and legislation. The textual mediation of everyday practice insures that it proceeds according to predetermined plan, inside determinate courses of action. Texts impose an ordered, manageable, and controllable character onto the equivocal, messy, chaotic worlds presented to social workers by clients.

To be a proper professional, members produce the self-negation of their particular situated place in an experienced world.[4] Of course if their place in an experienced world is negated, then they must exist somewhere. The solution is found through practices which construct their existence as social workers. Being a social worker allows members to locate themselves inside a conceptual topography which they inhabit with other social workers. In concert, members can move about together and replicatively find their way through the turmoil, chaos, and confusion of daily life. Once inside a professionally generated professional topography social workers encounter, and teach others how to see, a world of social problems, whether child abuse, neglect, alcoholism, or family violence.

Making proper professional accounts requires inscriptive work 'in which events in the ordinary world are reconceptualized and entered into documentary reality' (G. Smith 1988: 171). This inscriptive work is ideological,[5] and it is located inside relations of management and control. It is work which manages and administers a lived world such that it becomes visible, reportable, and actionable professionally (Latour and Woolgar 1979; Smith 1984). Social workers in their day-to-day practice transform (material) activities into usable documentary forms. These activities become textually bound to a course of action outlined in policy and disclosed in a report.

Social workers use the ideological practices of documentary inscription to gloss the particular and equivocal character of situations and to generate professionally ordered and sensible accounts. Incidents yield a harvest of particulars which can be arranged and ordered according to the 'mystical connections' derived from the imperatives of the organizational and professional work at hand (Smith 1990a: 49–50; Marx and Engels 1976: 62). 'Mystical connections' arise when social workers reorganize the particular 'facts' generated from the situation at hand according to the theories, frames, and models of discourse to produce factual accounts. The authority of professional accounts silences alternative accounts (Pfohl 1985).

Experience in daily life is fluid, subject to ongoing reinterpretation. Yet, the fluid movement must be professionally arrested such that a moment in daily life becomes a meaningful incident for social workers, defined as child neglect, child abuse, or wife battering. For example, a front-line social worker investigates a suspected case of child neglect to produce a series of organizationally relevant particulars which either sustain or refute the application of the formal category 'neglect.' The social worker invokes a repertoire of discursively organized questions: What kind of case is this (neglect, physical abuse, sexual abuse, wife battering, alcoholism)? What family dynamics are at work? Is there a history of dysfunctional family transactions? What motivations do these people have for their actions? What are the 'facts'?

The ideological practices for constructing textual accounts allow social workers to claim that they record the 'facts' of the matter. Participation in professional discourse enables front-line social workers to effect conceptual repair to the tensions and conflicts which arise in day-to-day practice. When conflicts arise, as they invariably do, social workers defend their work by locating their practice and their arguments inside a professional authorized discourse. Professional discourse found in social work textbooks, for example, allows social workers to affirm their practice as valid and helpful: 'Social Workers are professional helpers designated by society to aid people who are distressed, disadvantaged, disabled, defeated, or dependent. They also are needed to help people lessen their chances of being poor, inept, neglected, abused, divorced, delinquent, criminal, alienated or mad' (Siporin 1975: 4). The depoliticized language of 'helping' enables social workers to speak with apparent innocuousness about 'client systems becoming linked to resource systems' (Pincus and Minahan 1973: 18) even when their work requires revoking clients' parole, apprehending children, assessing involuntary psychiatric patients, counselling prison inmates, or denying social assistance.

By accounting for their authority and power as 'designated by society,' as helping or as treating, social workers affirm the propriety and value of their work. Social workers thus 'know' that they do not work to regulate the working class for capital, rather, they work for the good of individuals in society. The discourse of helping works to exempt social workers from the thorny problems of ruling others' lives.

CONCLUSION

By focusing on the apparently simple line in a Running Record, 'The apartment smelled of urine' this essay has sought to explicate the underlying social organization of 'facticity.' Through 'factual' representations accomplished in texts, social workers affirm their power to account for clients' lives. Power when explicated in terms of actual socially organized practices ceases to be reified or mystifying, but rather can be recognized as embedded in the complex organization of professional practices and organizational life. Power is realized through the processes of formal education which teach students how to see and how to think about the world as social workers. Power is realized day by day as individuals work together and build relations of trust and mutual reliance inside the logic and sensibilities of organizational life. Power is realized as social workers construct their accounts about client lives and thereby appropriate for themselves the right to tell the story and to decide what gets counted as relevant.

Social workers are expected not only to perform but to enter themselves into the good sense, cogency, and legitimacy of their work. To do social work demands appearing to colleagues and supervisors to be a controlled, self-administered, objective, and impartial professional who preserves the values of the profession and competently conducts the work of the organization. The successful production of a professional 'being' is accomplished primarily through textually mediated practices. In texts social workers construct a reality which can be ordered, regulated, and administered. In texts they find spaces and places of sanctuary and distance from clients. Through our texts, I and other social workers affirm our power to manage the worlds of daily life.

NOTES

1 This essay originated in the work of my doctoral dissertation entitled 'Accomplishing Professional Reality: An Ethnography of Social Worker's Practice.' As the title suggests, the research examined the construction of professional reality in day-to-day front-line practice. Accordingly, the data for the research was rooted in my own practice as a child protection social worker. The case material discussed here has been altered to protect the confidentiality of my clients.

2 Smith (1990a), in her analysis of the incident on Telegraph Avenue involving a

confrontation between street people and police, observed that 'the account (of the confrontation) is specifically detached from particular subjectivities, in part by being presented as the product of an official inquiry, but in part by grounding itself in the observations of police officers ... It treats police officers as interchangeable; it does not establish which individual saw or was active in what ...' (ibid.: 64). As will become clearer later in this essay the same organizational relations are at work in the construction of this factual account.

3 See Griffith's account (in this volume) of developmental discourse, not as used by social workers, but in relation to schooling. This illustrates Smith's point about discourse knitting together work processes in different professional sites; see also Manicom, this volume.

4 Indeed, many social workers remember the admonitions in their initial social work training and in agencies to write reports in the 'third person': 'The worker apprehended the child' rather than 'I apprehended the child.'

5 Social workers' practice arises in a class society and is rooted in the problem of managing a class society. By defining social workers' practices as ideological I point to the character of their practice which denies actual social relations, their particular location, the social organization of their power and authority, and which as a result claims to represent the 'facts' of the case in an objective fashion. Hence, ideology designates practices of individuals which have as their effect the erasure of their socially organized ground. Ideology specifically addresses those knowledge practices which split the knower from the known.

Teaching Accountability:
What Counts as Nursing Education?[1]

MARIE L. CAMPBELL

Nursing education is currently coming under intense scrutiny from within the profession. Long-standing doubts about the salience of behaviourist curriculum approaches are surfacing. This essay makes a contribution to such critiques and may help nursing educators make sense of some of their own misgivings about nursing education. It directs readers' attention to the increased attention being given to nurses' *accountability* and to training for such accountability. Nurses *practise* accountability by following procedures for making their work known and knowable to others in documents, that is, meeting their 'formal obligation to disclose' (Lewis and Batey 1982: 12). Special skills are required for doing this kind of accountable nursing. This essay looks at what students learn, both explicitly and implicitly, from instructional programs organized around accountability.

The instructional program studied is a three-year college diploma program in an Ontario College of Arts and Technology which prepares its graduates for registration (RN) examinations. While more and more nurses are acquiring university degrees, either as their first professional credential or in post-RN baccalaureate programs, still, in 1992, the largest number of registered nurses in the Canadian labour force were diploma-prepared and most of these are graduates of college programs.[2] The research reported here was conducted over a period of two years, including a nine-month period of intensive ethnography of college instruction and students' practical nursing experience in local hospitals.[3] The research explores how students in this program are taught 'to nurse' and to 'be nurses' within the specific context of a curriculum organized around the Roy Adaptation Model of Nursing[4] (Roy and Andrews 1986).

In nursing, theory-based practice is part of an increasing professionalization of the work which depends on building an intellectual bridge between nursing work and scientific knowledge. Presenting nursing as an academic discipline which requires students to learn to think and do nursing in relation to abstract theories of nursing is a professional achievement of the past several decades. These nursing models and theories and a growing body of nursing research are intended to support rational and scientifically sound nursing decision making and action. 'Nursing process' (Little and Carnavali 1976) refers to systematic documentation of what nurses do which aims at making those links visible. According to Smith (1990a) such documentary developments are also a feature of contemporary organization of Western capitalist society where action of all kinds is increasingly 'vested in texts and accomplished in distinctive practices of reading and writing' (ibid.: 62). It is quite clear that beyond clinical decision making, nurses are now expected to make accounts of their work to satisfy a number of different 'needs to know,' not just communication with the health care team. Patient treatment records offer health care managers the means to speak authoritatively about all aspects of care, including nursing.

Accounting, as it is conceived in this essay, has a special meaning beyond the one that nurses give it. Ethnomethodologists and phenomenologists draw attention to how language is embedded in social context (Heritage 1984; Wittgenstein 1958). 'Accounting' and 'accountable' are used in these methodologies as technical terms relating to how people themselves understand and communicate the contexted sense of their actions in the everyday world. Smith (1984) extends this understanding and shows how the everyday world and people's actions in it *are administered* through complex textually mediated social organization. She argues that the documentary accounts which are unremarkable but ubiquitous features of our world stand in for experience and (re)present that experience on behalf of people who are no longer present. Smith's analytic interest shifts 'to the status of knowledge as socially and materially organized, as produced by individuals in actual settings, and as organized by and organizing definite social relations' (Smith 1990a: 62). The inquiry Smith proposes begins with the text, '[with] words or other symbols on paper, on film, computer monitor' and investigates the actual social organization which 'structure[s] the relation between knower and known' (ibid.: 62–3).

The present study focuses on nursing students' sense making at the level of their experience as learners and attempts to discover how their sense making is 'ordered,' especially through text. The essay looks at what it means for students and instructors, and later, nurses and other health personnel and patients, to have relations among them structured by documentary practices. On the one hand, nothing could be more commonplace for nurses and nursing students than making reports of what they do. Nursing instructors, too, regularly work with the written word, treating texts of conceptual models, guidelines, and specific curriculum objectives as routine components of their instructional systems. On the other hand, and forming the central problematic in this essay, is the view that something very different, and not at all commonplace, happens when a textual account is substituted for an experienced actuality in the learning environment.

Learning to create the smooth appearance of 'good nursing' in documentation is a practical skill built into the curriculum. The study reported here looks closely at how this curricular approach supports a transpersonal and extra-local organization of nursing and how that is accomplished through nurses' own orderly and trained sense making. The next section begins an explication of this abstracted mode of action which permeates the nursing instructional program.

TEXTS, PLANS, AND ACCOUNTS OF ACTION

Nurses' education, for more than a decade in Canada, has been the basis for a particular development of professionalism. Curricula organized around a conceptual model or models of nursing have developed a cadre of nurses whose practice follows specific professional tenets. A conceptual model offers educators a methodical approach for teaching a body of knowledge and a professionally approved method of determining *how* and *when* to take *what* specific nursing actions. Implicit in the use of a model of nursing as the basis of instruction is a belief in the 'planning model of action' which Suchman defines as 'something located in the actor's head, which directs his or her behaviour' (1987: 3). It would appear that the nursing instruction I observed relied on this view of action.

The planning model of action postulates a causal relation between a course of action to be taken and its representation, first in a plan and then in an account of what was done. Suchman elaborates, 'Given a desired outcome, the actor is assumed to make a choice among alternative courses of action, based upon the anticipated consequences ... *Accounts of action taken ... are [assumed within the planning model of action to be] just a report on the choices made*' (ibid.: 51, emphasis added).

There are more questions than answers within social science theory about the actual relationship between projected and reconstructed courses of action and the real thing, that is, between plans and accounts and actions *in situ*.[5] In a telling example, Suchman argues that in paddling a canoe through rapids, rationality may help to anticipate action before the fact and reconstruct it afterwards, but 'when it really comes down to the details of [getting your canoe through the rapids] ... , you effectively abandon the plan and fall back on whatever embodied skills are available to you' (ibid.: 52). She argues that 'it is frequently only acting in a present situation that makes its possibilities become clear, and we often do not know ahead of time, or at least with any specificity what future state we desire to bring about' (ibid.: 52). Suchman agrees with Garfinkel (1967: 96) whom she quotes, saying 'It is only when we encounter it, and identify it as desirable, that we are able to say that this is the goal toward which our previous actions, in retrospect, were directed "all along"' (Suchman 1987: 52).

This essay argues that the accounting mode of instruction requires students in the program studied to learn to act in ways which prospectively and retrospectively 'reify' nursing actions based on the curriculum's plan of what nursing is. Students' sense of an interaction with a client is *mediated* by what must be said/written/done about it to produce it as adequate in an instructor's reading. Becoming skilled in mediated action gives nurses the means of 'repairing,' in records and other documents, nursing conditions that are always inadequate as to time available, material resources, knowledge, and so forth and of producing a seamless accountable version of what was done. Because an underlying reality will always remain unaddressed and unreported, accountably 'good nursing' can nevertheless fail as patient care. This kind of preparation of nurses to contend with everything and anything that confronts them, and to resolve it into elements of a comprehensive conceptual frame which stands for 'good nursing,' actually constructs 'good nursing' *in documents*. Indeed, the training for doing good nursing demands that students learn to produce both learning and nursing as what Smith (1990a) calls textual reality.

INSTRUCTION AS ACCOUNTABLE PROCESS

The curriculum of the nursing program I studied is laid out in Workbooks, one for each of the five college-based semesters. Clinical practice is interspersed with classroom instruction throughout the course of studies but takes on increasing importance in the third year of the program. Besides teaching the knowledge necessary for making nursing judgments and offering students sufficient opportunities to practice nursing skills in the workplace, a major goal of the whole instructional program is to inculcate in students the use of the Roy model as a planning device.

In this curriculum, the concepts of the model are translated into a set of instructions for students to follow as they 'assess' their patient. To assess is to conceptualize the relationship between the patient's nursing-relevant characteristics and a proposed course of nursing actions. This curriculum approach has the practical goal of making the nursing knowledge that students are taught generalizable and portable across all nursing workplaces and situations. Students are expected to use the model in all their clinical placements, even where nursing staff use different approaches to thinking and recording nursing.

For students, using the Roy model and the nursing process means having an empty frame that they fill with specific content about a patient as they decide what to do and how to sequence action. 'Using the model' means speaking in the model's language in response to instructors' questions about the patient and the proposed action. It means acting in a way that provides for its proper recording which, in turn, facilitates ongoing medical and nursing care and administration. As discussed in more detail below, 'using the model' means producing a documentary trail for various organizational and instructional purposes, including evaluation of students' learning.

THE ACCOUNTING APPROACH TO TEACHING AND LEARNING

Documents link instructors into a coordinated course of social action in which statements in the Regulated Health Professions Act of Ontario[6] and the Ontario College of Nurses' Standards of Practice are realized in college curricula and teaching. Professional standards determine the general shape of instructional programs, for example, how many hours of what kinds of experiences are offered to students. Nurses' professional education is governed through documents, producing sufficient uniformity across multiple sites to prepare students to sit for a single Canada-wide registration exam. Documents actually coordinate the activities of instructors, students, hospital staff, registering body, and so forth, building a documentary trail through which students can, in due process, assume the duties, obligations, and rewards attendant to being Registered Nurses.

In addition to being accountable to the College of Nurses and the ministry through documentary processes at the college level, instructors produce records to be accountable for student progress in instructional programs. Putting things on paper (or into computer files) accomplishes accountability when those records become part of special management or monitoring systems. For example, students' progress through the program is systematically tracked on paper and an authoritative documentary account is accumulated. As we shall see in the remainder of the essay, Performance

Evaluation becomes not just evaluation of student progress but the accomplishment of it. Accounting for progress becomes 'work' which directs both students' and instructors' attention to certain issues and actions throughout the program.

THE MODEL IN USE: ACCOMPLISHING 'PROGRESS'

The Evaluation Form may be used to guide an instructor's choice of patients to assign to students for their weekly clinical practice sessions, as indicated by the following comment: 'Every time that I would select a patient I would be looking at the choice in terms of Semester Five Evaluation ... It tells me what the students are supposed to be able to do' (Instructor Two). Knowing what students are 'supposed to be able to do' helps the instructor identify patients whose care includes those particular interventions, a particular level of knowledge, and so on that will fulfil their own teaching and students' learning objectives. Instructors can set students an assignment in which they can check that item off on the Evaluation Form. This does not mean that students are not having other experiences than the targeted ones, but both instructor and student learn to orient their attention to the learning experiences that 'meet objectives.'

Both instructor and student are required to 'make something' documentary of a patient assignment, as a teaching and learning experience which can then be evaluated. We will look at one instance of a student attempting to meet the instructional objective of writing a Nursing Care Plan. A care plan constructs 'the nursing process' in documentary form, as it is required of students to do nursing accountably. In a care plan, nurses enter the 'nursing problems' which they observe through assessments and for which they take responsibility to act, independent of doctors' orders.[7]

We look in on the student (S) as she puzzles over how best to write up the attention she has given, and will give, her patient who has leg pain of unknown origin. She considers different nursing care options she could offer – advice to 'dangle' legs, relaxation techniques, distraction, maybe some kind of warm treatment which doesn't need a doctor's order. At present, the puzzle is how to write it as a plan. As she works on the plan, she refers to a Roy Adaptation Model 'Indices Card,' about which she is telling the researcher (R):

S: [The Indices Card] tells me all the Adaptation Problems – pain is a major problem with her. And so – seeing that there is nothing they can do about her pain – they don't know what's causing it – so, I see a major adaptation problem with her 'powerlessness' because nothing can be done to relieve it. Like there is no surgery she can have to get rid of it.

R: This is one adaptation problem you came up with on your own?

S: See, this is one of Roy's ... under self-concept.
(Reads out loud, as she writes on the care plan.) 'Expected Goal': Patient will verbalize and demonstrate ways to relieve her pain ... 'Deadline' ... (sighs and explains) ... Deadlines are hard to set for this because you really don't know ... Like, you know, with different patients, she may not be accepting to what I help her with. Or she may take it in but not even bother trying.

R: So how do you end up deciding?

S: (laughs) Well, you don't. I'm putting 'ongoing' now. I'll go in there and find out how she does and then go from there. It's hard to say, because usually you have a 'deadline' like 2 days, and if she doesn't reach it, then you have to go back and extend your deadline. And I only have her for today.

Here, the student's 'work' is to demonstrate the adequacy of her action. She is using the Roy model's programmatic schema to 'see' her patient and identify what is appropriate to do. She considers her patient's situation and finds a concept, 'powerlessness,' from the model that fits it. For constructing the plan, she uses Kardex headings which follow the 'nursing process' taught in her nursing program and used in that ward. It would appear that the student has been able to represent herself as competent. But she discovers a variety of troubling realities intervening. The patient has to cooperate, and the student has reason to think she may not. She recognizes that the plan is not complete without a deadline, and without meeting a deadline, her plan and she as a nurse/student cannot be seen to be fully successful; her own student schedule prevents her from achieving a successful result. The point here is not whether her instructor understands this and adapts her own expectations of the student, but rather that the focus of the student's 'work' is accomplishment of the proper textual product.

Instructors must attend to students' development of good skills in documenting their work. Monitoring students' recording is one way that they can keep in touch with students' learning within the exigencies of fast-paced hospital action in which students participate both as learners and as quasi-hospital staff: 'Different teachers have said ... that clinical practice is really very hard for them to evaluate because for one thing they are not always with us; they don't always know what we're doing ... A lot of times, it's finding out what we are doing by what we chart, afterwards' (Student One).

Charting is not just any written version of 'what we are doing,' as this student expresses it. The skill required and being taught is the ability to sort through the range of experiences one has as a student and decide what happened that can be represented as an instance of the curricular plan being put into action. Students must learn the concepts and language that will meet expectations for this kind of textual construction. They must grasp the interpretative frame so that they can build satisfactory versions of their experiences into the account. What satisfies, of course, relates to the documentary courses of action, either administrative or instructional, into which the accounts must be inserted. Learning to account, getting the idea of what's being asked and how to do it, does however make a difference to student careers. As students gain skill in seeing their actions in terms of abstract course objectives they are better able to participate in a formal process of self-evaluation, about which one student says: '[Self-evaluation] allows you to think and pull out stuff that you have done that the teacher hasn't seen you do. She hasn't seen you in conversation with a patient, she hasn't seen you with members of the health team like physiotherapy ... it gives you a chance to make yourself look good because she reads them' (Student Three).

This is an important lesson. The student quoted above is learning that constructed accounts have important future uses. This insight, learned regarding Performance Evaluations, is an orientation to the highly textually mediated realities of hospital nursing which these students will be entering as experienced practitioners of accounting. For example, they learn, in doing self-evaluations, how to make questionable experiences 'count' as compliance with the categories: 'Sometimes, I know, I've looked at a category and thought, you know, "uhmm, I haven't really done it" but you sort of stretch what you've done to fit the category ... Generally, Personal and Professional Growth are the ones that you find you tend to be really shovelling it' (Student One).

Learning to account for one's work in the specific terms of the curriculum 'plan' is a different kind of learning than learning to carry out the nursing activities themselves. Nursing students may be able to do the work but still not be able to do an adequate accounting of it. The latter requires additional attention from the instructor: 'Some of the students will say ... "I really don't understand this; what do you mean?" So, in conference I'll say, "This is what this objective is focusing on. Can you think of an example of *how you might have done that* in the last three days?" and I ask them to hand them in to me and I look at them' (Instructor Two, emphasis added).

This is a lesson in abstract thinking. Students learn abstract thinking when they begin to see pieces of their everyday activities as instances of the concepts on their evaluation forms, when they learn to abstract out of practical work experience those events which 'fit' the conceptual framework that has been provided first in the curriculum and then in the self-evaluation form. This is the preparation which will make students competent 'accounters' of themselves and their work when they are graduate nurses in the nursing workforce.

This essay can only begin to suggest how important it is to present-day management of health care that nurses entering the workforce be prepared to create objective knowledge of nursing in texts. Official texts speak in the absence of nurse speakers, a feature of hospital documentation that is essential to contemporary organization and all kinds of medical and administrative activities (Campbell 1988, 1992). When students are prepared to be competent accounters of *learning*, they are already orientated to a documentary practice of nursing that hospitals rely on increasingly, for organizing and coordinating administrative and therapeutic action.

LEARNING ACCOUNTABLE NURSING

Instructors place a great deal of trust in what I am calling 'the curriculum plan' and 'the accounting approach to instruction.' Ensuring that students meet objectives establishes the credibility of the instruction as adequate preparation of students to nurse. Instructors trust that having students work with a model of nursing provides something of a guarantee about the actual nursing 'product.'

Representation of anticipated and reconstructed action when it is seen as synonymous with doing it, 'realizes' the causal connection between theorized curricular plan and nursing action. To instructors this approach is a big improvement over trying to teach students 'everything that they need to know,' which as Instructor Four says, is impossible: 'More and more we have to have a person who can think on their own; ... the volume of scientific knowledge goes up so rapidly, we have trouble keeping up.' Used as a guide to action, the model-based accounting approach helps students make sense out of any array of problems and possibilities that confronts them. That is what these instructors value about their curriculum's model of nursing: '[The model] gives [students] a structure and a way of completing an assessment. So they are not just focusing on a number of things, they are sort of trying to group behaviours together ... so you are not just going in to a patient's room and saying "where do I start?"' (Instructor Two).

One instructor uses the model explicitly in coaching sessions: 'I'll sit down with them and say "I'd like to talk to you about Mr ————." I want them to give me an assessment, ... to go through all the "needs" and "modes" and to tell me what they have observed in these "needs" and "modes" ... I'll put [the Indices Card] in front of them ... It keeps them on track and helps to direct them' (Instructor Six).

Mediation of students' action by the plan inherent in the curriculum's model of nursing helps students identify and tie together the otherwise loose ends of observations, demands and responses into a course of relevant action: '[The model] is good because it's comprehensive; it's theoretical, so it will fit whatever the practice setting' (Instructor One). And, '[Ours] is a nice model because it's holistic' (Instructor Four). Having looked at a patient or situation in this mediated way, and identified and performed the called-for actions, the model's 'holistic' structure reassures both instructors and students that they have responded adequately. It helps students create the appearance of completion in the nursing action taken, by showing how discrete interventions add up to the model's formulation of nursing. Instructors need this reassurance because they recognize the increasing difficulty of actually teaching students to nurse within the constraints of program time and material resources: 'Our particular model is really strong in terms of assessment because it not only tells me – it classifies – it describes the patient in a way that tells me (the student) what sort of information I have to collect' (Instructor Five). This describes a particular kind of sense making in which students learn a process of objectification, a mental step which establishes the causal connection between plans and action. Its value, over an alternative use of plans, where they are treated as simply one resource among many available to nurses, is in narrowing the discretionary field of action. The planning mode of action helps students avoid being distracted by all kinds of issues extraneous to the economy of action demanded in the nursing workplace of the 1990s. An instructor puts her finger on the key point: 'Interactions nurses have with patients must be goal-directed. There's no time for social chit-chat ... your interactions with the patient must be meaningful. You are either giving information to the patient or you're collecting information from the patient or you're doing a technique' (Instructor Five).

Besides the smooth appearance of adequate learning which the model as a plan helps to construct, instructors see this mediated practice of nursing articulating students smoothly into the contemporary practices of managing nursing and hospitals: 'They're able to operationalize that [model] in relationship to patient care in a very succinct, concise manner ... [They can make a] very concise Nursing Care Plan and pass information on to the next people looking after the patient' (Instructor Seven).

Conciseness is a necessary feature of contemporary nursing. Assessments and reports must be made quickly and only the 'relevant' details included. Learning a form of nursing practice mediated by textual accounts helps new generations of nurses adapt to demands for precise accounting that will stand as adequate nursing against legal, professional, and other administrative tests.

Instructors in this study are not without concerns about their program's graduates. They mention students' lack of 'critical thinking' (Instructor Eight) or 'failure to understand the implications of their actions' (Instructor Two) or 'not realizing what data is significant' or not 'being able to prioritize' (Instructor Two). Instructor Three worries about rigidity being produced by too prescriptive use of the curriculum model. In trying to describe the attitude she finds too prevalent among her students, another instructor notes their main preoccupation: 'They just sort of bustle around and do the IV's and the tests and all the things they need to do to sort of "cover their ass"' (Instructor Eight). This comment may capture exactly what is productive and, conversely, what is counterproductive about the conceptual and practical skills which the accounting approach to nursing instruction is teaching. When students learn to equate good nursing with meeting documentary objectives, as graduates they will be skilled in constructing care as a textual reality. They will know how to make nursing interventions that are adequate for all practical purposes and which this instructor calls 'covering their ass.' The significance of this as an organizational skill should not pass unnoticed. The management of contemporary health care agencies uses text-based techniques (for example, Quality Assurance) for recognizing as organizationally adequate just such documentary action (Campbell 1984).

The textually mediated practice of nursing has new importance in the information-structured hospital. The health care literature confirms that hospitals are relying ever more heavily on systematically produced information (for example, Krawczyk 1989; Meeting et al. 1988). Becoming information workers not only absorbs nursing time but it *directs nurses' attention to particular elements of patient care and features of the patients themselves that provide the correct data for the required accounting*. As argued here, making sense of nursing situations when nurses are responsible for its accounting (that is, nursing as mediated action) is a different kind of undertaking than making sense of nursing situations in the everyday world of illness, pain, fear, medical emergencies, and so on. Learning to nurse in today's health care agencies requires that students gain the ability to do both kinds of sense making. An accounting approach to instruction, however, subordinates one to the other. It trains adequate account-makers and teaches them how to cover all the documentary bases, *creating the appearance* of adequate nursing action. Concerns about experienced reality, both the students' and the patients,' are left officially unaddressed.

There are a number of reasons why nursing educators should not be satisfied with the accounting approach to teaching nursing. For one thing, regardless of the intent of individual educators, nursing as textually mediated activity undermines and replaces care-centred nursing. Second, the accounting approach to nursing obscures and organizationally obliterates nursing knowledge and nursing action beyond that which is mediated and documented. Nursing sense making for situated, as opposed to textually mediated, action remains a necessary, if undervalued, part of nurses' work and nurses' education. However, it is not an explicit or high profile part of this nursing curriculum. Yet it is a component of nursing knowledge and skill on which hospitals, doctors, and patients continue to rely. Nursing 'on the ground' requires nurses to perform both kinds of reasoning. Any claim to higher value for their work depends on identifying, and getting recognition for the nursing action whose sense arises out of the intensely social situation in which nurses work so skillfully.

NOTES

An earlier version of this paper was published as 'Accounting for Learning/ Accounting for Care,' in E. Ksenych and D. Liu, eds., *Conflict, Order and Action: Readings in Sociology,* Toronto: Canadian Scholars' Press, 1992, pp. 213–31, and this version appears with their permission.

1 The research on which this essay is based was supported by a grant from the Social Science and Humanities Research Council of Canada to Nancy Jackson, McGill University, Principal Investigator, and Marie Campbell, University of Victoria, Co-investigator, under the 'Education and Work' Strategic Grants program.
2 My research does not compare college against university nursing programs, nor does it evaluate the college program that I studied. Instructional practices similar to those I describe are being followed in colleges or universities across Canada and the United States, and my findings are generalizable to such settings.
3 Participant observation of one section (thirty students) of a third-year nursing class was conducted over nine months during 1989–90. This included observations of classroom and lab teaching in the college and of clinical instruction in local hospitals during the fifth semester of the college program. Participant

observation of eight preceptor–pregraduate pairs (staff RNs and students) was also conducted throughout the final (sixth) semester. Katrina Costello's research assistance is gratefully acknowledged. In-depth interviews were conducted with fifteen of these students and eight of their instructors during the fifth and sixth semesters; nine graduates who had been interviewed and observed as students were re-interviewed after a year of working as Registered Nurses.

4 The Roy model is one of a number of so-called models of nursing available to curriculum developers.

5 See Suchman's (1987) discussion in her Chapters 3 and 4, pp. 27–67.

6 At the time of the study, the previous act regulating health professionals in Ontario, the Health Disciplines Act, was in effect.

7 The Care Plan format provides a sequenced documentation of a set of actions – identifying and remedying a patient's nursing problem. A signed Care Plan holds the designated nurse accountable for following up and seeing that the planned remedy had an outcome related to the documented 'expectation.'

Rendering the Site Developable: Texts and Local Government Decision Making in Land Use Planning

SUSAN M. TURNER

When people are concerned about changes taking place in the physical environment around them and want to have some say in development decisions, they encounter and are drawn into standard official planning processes. Land use planning is a complicated set of activities and relations within which developers propose plans, agencies and municipalities approve them, and interested and affected citizens are invited and required to participate in the process. This set of relations is not well understood. It is especially difficult for citizens wanting to intervene in ongoing planning processes to grasp how they work. Planning processes rely on the accomplishment of decisions made 'in public' and with the input of citizens to authorize development activities. But citizens learn in their experience in 'the process' that how they know the world in their everyday relations is not how it is put together in the relations of planning. These are different worlds.

Although there are documents and texts to explain decision-making processes, they explain planning as a series of steps that have to be gone through. These steps, however, involve peculiar procedures for producing and reading texts and diagrams that organize the kinds of things that can be said and done in planning. It is important to see this level of work involving texts in the organization of the developable site.

This essay[1] examines the verbal descriptions, maps, and diagrams representing the site in a particular zoning by-law approval process in a mid-sized Ontario city, at the specific moment of a city council meeting.[2] The analysis is part of a larger study of the organization of land use planning in Ontario, which explores how the institutional processes that produce development and change in the physical environment are put together.[3] Here I focus on the interpretive practices employed in public decision making. The activities I examine result in legal changes to the restrictions concerning what can be done on a piece of land to develop it. This essay provides an empirical account of how standard forms of decision making are produced in people's readings of the texts which are embedded in standard courses of action. In planning processes, visual texts stand in for the actual site. City councillors look at a text and talk about what is in it. The lines on the diagram or map play a part in shaping readings which have consequences for what happens in the council setting and what will happen to the site. What the documents people use 'mean' and how they produce or authorize planning actions and decisions are a feature of people's local experience. Understanding what the texts 'do' is a practical problem for anyone participating in the planning process.

APPROACHES TO TEXTS AND INSTITUTIONAL ACTIVITIES

Recent political and urban studies have theorized land use planning as a tool for special interest groups to wield power and make profits, and for state control (Stone and Sanders 1987; Magnusson 1990; Clarke 1990; Fainstein 1989; Kiernan 1990; Sancton and Montgomery 1990). In these approaches, however, the texts people encounter and use in actually doing planning are not treated as part of the institutional activities referred to (but see Richardson 1981; Hartland 1989; Sancton and Montgomery 1990). Studies which recommend research in concrete settings to examine organizational decision making (Kolb and Van Maanen 1985; Duster 1987; Clark 1989; Salter 1988) fail to examine the texts people work with in those settings. Researchers into organizational activity rely on records and verbal accounts as evidence of decision making and organizational activities, but how records and documents operate in actual work processes remains largely uninvestigated.

The approach I am taking to texts relies on an ontological shift made by Garfinkel (1967a) and extended by Dorothy Smith (1987a, 1990a, 1990b). Organization is conceived as the actual practices of people putting together the observable world, and the objects and the relevances that they orient to in their cooperative activities. Central to the forms of routine organization are communication and co-understanding via language. Smith directs inquiry to the organizing capacities of language and texts in relations of ruling, which she formulates as that complex arena of activities in which an objectified world in common is created in texts for the purposes of coordinating and governing some aspect of the society we live in. The development of professions and professional discourses is based on 'knowledge devices,' like site plans or case histories, that provide material about the object of the profession's knowledge. Particular knowledge devices are embedded in and integral to forms of organization where immediate contact with that aspect of the world to be processed, land or people, is not the responsibility of those who make decisions.

In relations of ruling, special conceptual and graphic procedures operate to order and select particulars for textual accounts so they can be manipulated and treated as relevant to the work of people in numerous sites. The surface characteristics of these texts are wholly determined by their location in sequences of account producing and reading that are integral to actual organizational forms of management and intend a legally defined course of action. Discursively organized individual practices of reading and writing and speaking about texts in numerous settings carry out those management activities, and organize social relations.

Investigation into discursive organization is supported by Bakhtin's (1981, 1986) conception of written and spoken verbal utterances as 'links in a chain of speech communication.' Bakhtin's notion directs us to the relatively stable topics, ways of talking, forms of argument, and so on, within a particular professional discourse, which provide for ways of knowing and the bases on which decisions are made. This is the way language organizes particular courses of action. The analysis is not to search utterances for individual intent or type of political ideology. Language organizes relations and courses of action which can elude people's individual intentions. The way to take up texts and utterances, then, is to look at how they actively draw people into relations and organize what can be thought, said, and done in getting on with the practical tasks in a setting, and lay the ground for what can be said and done next.

The analysis presented here proceeds by introducing the key texts – site plans – that figure in the process of approving a zone change for land development and examining how those texts are spoken about and rendered meaningful in the public setting.

THE SITE IN THE ZONING PROCESS

A site plan is the product of extensive constitutive procedures.[4] The productive work of planners, lawyers, engineers, clerks and secretaries is coordinated around a plan and brought through the public political process. These activities are administered through the Ontario's Planning Act. The act is often seen simply as rules to guide behaviour. On closer look, the act holds sets of instructions for producing many texts and for their reading, discussion and review by people in multiple locations and at certain times. It includes specific instructions for producing the *plans, drawings* and *conditions for approval* that must accompany a zoning by-law.[5] Specific planning procedures vary from city to city, but they have in common a reliance on standardized methods of description and sequences of coordinated action through which people take up and address texts in concrete settings.

Zoning is a method of describing, municipally knowing, and doing something with land. It is central to how urban development gets done. All land is zoned by categories that determine what can be built on it. An owner who wants to do something with private property different from what its present zoning allows must apply to the local government to change the zoning. The application activates the zoning by-law approval process. Usually the property owner or developer brings a proposal to the city planning department and pays a fee. What the owner wants to do gets shaped up with city planners into a formal application. The application documents are circulated for comment to city departments, external agencies, and owners of properties surrounding the site. Comments are sometimes written into the planner's report. By the time it gets to city council, the plan is a set of well-worked-up texts.

At least one public meeting is held, where the developer or his hired lawyer or planner (in this case, both developer and lawyer were men) describes the plan and is questioned by councillors. Citizens may attend and can present information and comments. Council can amend the conditions before approving them. The council makes a decision to approve, refuse, or defer making a decision on the application.

THE SPOKEN LANGUAGE–TEXT RELATION IN CITY COUNCIL

My analysis concerns the activities in a city council meeting through which the approval of diagrams and conditions for a zone change takes place. The actions I focus on happen after all the preliminary planning work is done. The site is already created, already textually constituted. At this point in the process, people who have not been involved in its technical preparation talk about the plan and are making a decision about it. They make their decision on the basis of textual representations that stand in for the actual site, and they rely on the verbal statements of the lawyer or developer, professionals, and citizens. The facts of the case are textually represented. The texts are already authorized accounts, but council must approve the accounts and pass a by-law in public. In order to make a decision, the people in this setting have to take up the documents and attend to what is in them. In doing so they bring about a relation between the actual physical land worked up as the *site* in the texts, their own and other individual action, other texts and prescriptive legal texts, and the production of the routine, formalized features of planning. To do 'what counts as' planning in this public setting, participants must engage with the technical details in the texts and what is said, and do something with them.

In the approval process I am examining, a developer wants a zone change to build twelve luxury homes in a wooded ravine abutting city parkland. A group of citizens is trying to protect the ravine, which has value to them as a natural area and buffer of trees for the neighbourhood, and is asking that the plan be amended to prevent development down into the ravine. They suggest that houses be built on the high, flat area surrounding the ravine, and the ravine itself be left untouched. To enter this request textually into the proceedings, to make it something that can appear as a measurable and enforceable restriction, the citizens refer to the site plan, which contains graphic features meant to represent topological features of the site. These take the form of wavy lines that are known as contour lines and which are to be read as showing changes in height or depth relative to other areas on the two-dimensional image. This is a way of representing three-dimensional features. The citizens have indicated a contour line which they understand represents the 'top' of the ravine. It is labelled '326' on the diagram. They have submitted a copy of the site plan with this 326 contour line highlighted in yellow marker (see Figure 1).

What happens at the city council meeting is an experience that will be familiar to people who have been involved in public decision-making processes. It is the experience of seeing and hearing reading practices organized within different social relations holding different intentionalities come together and seem to collide in the setting. In the moments of council talk examined here, citizens, having lobbied council for a year to preserve the site and the small wooded ravine, have made their presentation and, sitting in the gallery of the council chambers, watch and hear the developer's lawyer first, and then councillors, 'get it wrong.' Citizens hear their own statements reported and inserted into the discussion so it goes off in the wrong direction. Councillors appear to read the diagram 'wrong.' Citizens hear council become unable to read the contour lines on the diagram as meaningful to their decision. This disjuncture in readings reflects and expresses the intersection of social relations of two fundamentally different kinds and in which 'the ravine' figures differently.

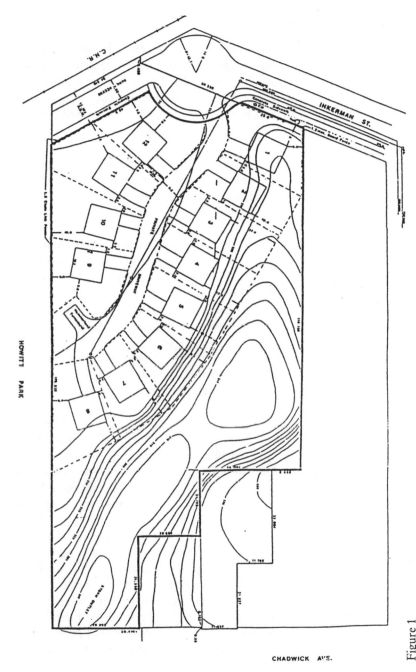

Figure 1
Proposed Site Plan. 326 marks contour line being discussed.

ANALYSIS

Councillors have in front of them the description made by planning staff, the diagram, a list of thirteen conditions and the citizens' recommendations and map with the 326 contour line highlighted with yellow marker. The excerpts of talk that follow are presented in chronological sequence, but are not necessarily continuous. Other exchanges may have occurred between the excerpts analysed here.

1 Councillor (C) Y's is the first reading of the diagram by a councillor. It sets up a reconceptualization of the site in terms of properties in a plan of subdivision and reformulates 'what the citizens want.' Mr H is the lawyer for the developer.

C Y: Mr H ... the 326 foot contour line that runs through two of the homes as I see this, possibly three, touches on a third one ... this yellow line on the single sheet ... what I don't understand Mr H is if the neighbours are in general agreement, uh I don't see how they can be, and I'm confused with this because they're saying they're in general agreement but they want the development to leave the land below the 326 foot line free, and yet it's not just the 326 foot line that I see here, you've got a dotted line on this diagram that seems to come alongside the ends of the properties as I look at it. I may be incorrect in looking at it but that's what I see. In other words the park area that is shown here is quite a bit less than what is below the 326 foot line.

Councillor Y does a reading of the diagram in terms of properties and flat zones. What lines *do* on the flat plane is restricted to that surface. 326 *runs through homes* and a dotted line *comes alongside the properties*, leading the councillor to clarify the *size* of the 'park area' with the developer's lawyer. Homes and properties are given, substantial. This reading relies on an archimedean standpoint viewing the world from somewhere in the air above the site and on the graphic restrictions of the flat surface. That perspective is a feature of the technologies of planning and design professions and their textual organization of work processes that manipulate messy ground surfaces to fit to human projects (Roweis 1988). From the standpoint located in those work processes, the citizens' attempt to restore the messy ravine character to the site is confusing. The relevance of the lines on the diagram is established in terms of the visibly constituted properties of 'the development.' While the city's planner told citizens in conversation the dotted lines 'don't mean anything on this plan,' they intend the reading Councillor Y and Mr H give them here.

2 The developer's lawyer can next be seen to be doing the lawyerly work of making deals. Mr H gives a legal description of what the plan would be if it were to proceed another way than it is right now. 'If we can work out a method' and 'my client is quite ... willing to settle' reveal the actual negotiating process that is going on with city planners. Plans must be dealt with within thirty days. If not, or if the council refuses his application, the developer can appeal to the Ontario Municipal Board for a hearing *de nova* in which the documents are brought in and reviewed by the board and where the board's decision is final. This time frame, combined with the practice of working plans out in the 'informal process' before they become 'public,' produces the quite routine feature of planning that plans are still being negotiated 'informally' while they are being pushed through the public process. What has been called the 'Let's Make a Deal' character of planning in Ontario (*Globe and Mail Report On Business Magazine*, April 1991) is merely a routine feature of its textual organization. Here the lawyer for the developer can be seen to be involved in this routine course of action.

Mr H: Oh quite so. Quite so. The dotted lines, if ... if this is to proceed under ... [plan of subdivision the lots would be] 50 by 100 feet. If we can work out a method without putting it under the Condominium Act, then the, those would all be parts 1 through 3–4 through 12 on a reference plan and each of those parts would then be conveyed to separate people. Instead of the condominium corporation owning that, individual people would own that. Now, my client is quite happy, or quite willing to settle on a line below which no construction will go, but it may be not necessarily always the 326 line. At some points it could be the 326, but when you get up to number 1 it may have to switch to the 324, 323, that house may be farther down the hill. That's all. But to arbitrarily pick out of the air 326 and put a yellow line on it and say we don't want anything below that, is a bit difficult to deal with, because you can't necessarily site all all all your houses.

C Y: Right, I understand that. In effect are you saying that the dividing line between the parkland and the development is the dotted line? [Mr H: Yes.]

Councillor Y's earlier reading of the dotted lines lays the ground for Mr H's legal description of the properties as a registered reference plan 'with individual people owning that.' Mr H employs the perspective of the developer or architect whose business is siting a number of houses on a site. He contrasts that reasoned business with the neighbours' action of 'arbitrarily picking a line out of the air' and making unreasoned demands based on that. The developer is, in contrast, willing and flexible to indicate some line as a dividing line, but there is the problem Mr H draws council into of 'siting all your houses.' Siting the twelve houses is the business of the developer who must make a calculated profit. Those twelve home sites have been drawn up with the city's planner. In this reading Mr H intends the siting process to hook up with another approval process with fewer restrictions than those under the Condominium Act – the approval of subdivisions under the Planning Act – that does not require public participation and also involves fewer 'up front' finances.

3 This next reading is by the director of planning for the city, Mr V. He is looking at the diagram with the yellow line on it. He employs the legitimate zoning categories and descriptive terms for producing and reading a site plan. 'Ravine' is not a standard category. The phrase 'ravine or passive parkland' used by Councillor Y in his question to the director of planning marks the shift from the organization of a reading that relies on the actual physical features of the ravine – which the director can do – to the course of action in which a reading of flat zones is an integral constituent activity.

C Y: I'd like to pursue the question with Mr V about this dotted line and if what is below that does provide about 1.1 acres of ravine or passive parkland, or is it a lot less than that and in which case how much less?

Mr V: (inaudible) ... drops down, so that's the beginning of the ravine. The 326 contour line uh, represents that. If you look at the plan and you look at the units that have been designed on the plan as exclusive use areas, those areas extend further south or further down from the yellow line, and those exclusive use areas would be exclusively used for the units, for the occupants, so therefore the backs of those dotted line areas would not form part and parcel of the open space. So and I if ... just by taking a look at what's left over, and just eyeballing it it looks like it'd probably be an acre even if that, that would be open space.

The planning director begins his reading by noting that the 326 contour line represents 'the beginning of the ravine.' Councillor Y's 'ravine or passive parkland' opens up the identity of the site to the next reading. The planning director relies on the opening to shift to an order of language and discourse in which units and occupants are brought into relation with a properly constituted 'open space' zone. He relies on that shift to then take people through a reading of the plan which instructs them to look not at the physical features but to 'look at the units that ... extend further south or further down from the yellow line.' His phrase 'designed on the plan' relies on and refers back to the extensive work processes that have put this plan together before it arrived in this setting. Council must rely on the technical and professional competence of the staff it has hired. That competence is also embodied in the texts. In this way the issue of individuals' competence in doing planning arises, but not the organization of the process itself. And the technical ability and work of staff is coordinated with the developer's business of siting the houses.

As the planning director invites viewers to look to the areas 'that would be exclusively used for the units, for the occupants,' he brings into the setting as relevant to council's decision making an important construct. The construct of 'future occupants' is one that the development industry relies on, draws into their discourse and planning process, and describes as having needs the industry is meeting. Descriptions of future home buyers, owners, and occupants and their lifestyles are a textual feature of the development discourse and organization of research, marketing, and real estate promotion and sales, central to these other industries as well as planning. Here, their needs are formulated as part of the interpretive frame for council's decision making.

4 Councillor L then produces a reading which relocates the problem of picking a line back into the context of council's mandate. Council is responsible for implementing 'development *control*,' ensuring the site is 'suitable' for development (Government of Ontario 1989).

C L: There's only one problem with that. If we say no development below the
         326 foot contour line our site plan is no good because we have develop-
         ment below the 326 foot line. So we have to change that number. We have
         to pick another number. 320 or something a little bit further down. Maybe
         (inaudible) can comment on that.

The words 'our site plan' situates council as having a vested interest in the task of siting the houses.

5 This situating work links council to the developer's problem and gives the planning director the opportunity to restate it:

Mr V: Councillor L has raised a very good point. If we take the plan as presented,
         and uh, we're assuming fairly large units here in this development, and

we're also assuming a fairly large exclusive use area. These are not your standard townhouses or your standard townhouse lots. These are single-family condominium developments, and they will equal a fairly large single-family house on a fairly large single-family lot. I don't see how we can accommodate a plan of twelve units picking the 326 contour line because that line goes into three units and also the recommendation was that no patios or anything else be constructed within that and if you look at unit number 3 and 4 and 5 and 6 and that would preclude them having any patio or anything else in that area and that would make it very difficult for this plan to proceed.

The planning director frames his statement with two interesting interpretive features: what 'we're assuming' is large lots, single-family homes and what appears a crucial corollary, patios. Mr V again points to council's reliance on the technical competence of its staff and to council's task in this process, when he begins, 'If we take the plan as presented ...' and states the condition citizens want 'would make it very difficult for this plan to proceed.' It is a feature of the text-making aspect of planning that city planners are in a position to be able to defend, and advocate, plans they have worked up with developers. Citizens make the process difficult.

6 Councillor Y tries to get approval of the plan so it can both *proceed and* guarantee that 'the ravine which remains' – is literally left over – is protected.

C Y: Mr V what could we write into the conditions ... to safeguard the ravine, below whatever line there has to be ... in order to allow the condominium development? and the line that has to be is this dotted line that I asked Mr H about. What can we write into the conditions to safeguard the ravine which remains? [3.1-second pause]

Mr V: The only thing we could do would be uh to pick a contour line an/and – put it in as a condition – an agreed to contour line ... um and I'm having difficulty try'na pick one, because the contours 'hhh are not uh that straight, they do curve over as you get further over to Inkerman Street and they really drop off there. So w-hh it's ...

Mayor: The trouble is we're trying to redraw the thing tonight in the council meeting.

Mr V: That's correct –

The planning director's hesitation marks the disjuncture between two orders of relations in which the physical site is linked to the text. Both are

available in the surface features of the 'proposed site plan.' Mr V's competence spans both orders of diagrammatic representation. Untrained readers
can do readings which link the text to the site and produce differing, conflicting, outcomes. The readings I have examined however, emerge in the
course of action which 'implements' the city's land use policies and manages the relations between private landowners and a general 'public interest.' Readings rely on the ability to recognize the flat zoned features as a
future state of affairs *and* on an understanding of how the diagram operates
in processes of regulation and distribution of rights regarding uses of land.[6]
The mayor's "The trouble is we're trying to redraw the thing ... ' refers to
the proper separation and coordination of activities regarding the production and readings of the diagram.

THE OUTCOME

The councillors' practices of reconceptualizing the dotted line as legiti-
mately *separating* the 'parkland' from the 'development' *and* as *protecting*
the 'ravine which remains' enable them to approve the plans and pass the
by-law for twelve houses, with a slight amendment to bring 'any other
arrangement' the developer negotiates back to council.

    In terms of consequent actions this condition unhooks the plan from the
Condominium Act and allows it to proceed as a regular plan of subdivision
under the Planning Act. This has an effect on further planning decisions. As
a plan of subdivision the legislative framework shifts, and the internal road
linking the houses becomes the property and responsibility of the city. As a
city road, it must meet certain engineering standards, such as having a
width of sixty-six feet to facilitate entry by snowplows. Meeting that
requirement results in the house lots being pushed further back down into
the ravine. In conjunction with drainage and backyard standards, this
necessitates a three- to five-metre high retaining wall, and the destruction
of the ravine. On the diagrams on file at city hall, the dotted line now marks
the location of this three- to five-metre high concrete retaining wall. These
events have entered city mythology as a successful 'case' of citizen participation – citizens got low-density single-family homes and a big piece of
land zoned 'parkland' – and the twelve 'estate lots' being sold are advertised
as 'in a ravine setting.'

DISCUSSION

Citizens' readings of the proposed site plan rely on locally observable facts and not on organization sequences which are accountable to and warranted by the organization of local economic development and city administration. The readings examined are organized by their location in different orders of relations, and the struggle for interpretation and the meaning of what is in the texts, marks that shift.

While citizens assume that the physicalness of the ravine represented by the contour lines could be seen as a basis for altering site plans, what is formulated as an interpretive frame for council's actions and decisions is something quite apart from that. Councillors work back and forth between the textual realities in the site plan and the legal course of action they are putting together. Speakers take up the diagram's surface features and engage in the conceptual construction of and orientation to an in-common world, which then operates to warrant their decision.

The reality to which action and decision are oriented in the samples of council talk analysed above is a symbolically constructed *virtual reality* of subdivision life, accomplished in the distinctive practices of people's readings. Engaging with the technical features of the diagram and site plan, speakers draw into relation future subdivision occupants, and produce them as legitimate buyers who need patios, in contrast with neighbours who capriciously draw lines on a map to get more parkland for themselves.

The constitutive work of lawyers, planners, engineers, and clerks has brought the site into the text and inserted it into an extended process. The councillors' task is different. It requires not just reading the plan as a technical document of the site and the plan, but as a particular piece of the organization of the approvals process. That process is a matter of public concern. It draws people acting in a variety of social relations into the decision-making setting. Council is accountable for managing the business of the municipality and incorporating 'citizens' concerns' into their decision making. How 'citizens' concerns' and the social world are represented in the textual organization of the planning process is a feature of how councillors read what is in the site plan diagrams and orient to their administrative and management tasks.

Here we have seen decision making being produced out of the way the diagrams are drawn and read within extended courses of action in which council's task is situated. This moment, usually invested with so much 'political' power with regard to the distribution of rights over land use, can be seen to be highly constrained by the routine surface features of the texts and resources participants rely on to activate them in the council setting. Councillors' 'preference' for development can be seen as reflecting a certain kind of political ideology, and what people do in the setting can indeed be called politics. However, all of this is mediated by and worked through a textually ordered set of procedures which is not neutral. It allows some things to be seen and done more easily than others. Councillors can treat the site plan as given, and issues of politics and intentions will arise, but in the relations of planning the text can be seen to be an active constituent in the business of rendering the site developable.

NOTES

1 This essay is based on a paper presented at the Canadian Sociology and Anthropology Association Meetings in Kingston Ontario, June 1991. The present version has benefitted from the comments and editorial suggestions of Liza McCoy, George Smith, and Gillian Walker.

2 I was one of the residents involved in the case. My investigation began with receiving a Notice of Public Meeting regarding the proposal to develop in the ravine. I had to read texts, attend meetings, and seek information about the process the way any activist who is drawn into planning processes does. From 1986–91, I documented meetings (including council meetings which are video-taped and run on the local cable television network), news media accounts, background documents, and informal conversations.

3 I have formulated how all this goes on as the main business of planning (Turner 1989).

4 Much of the physical production and transference of plans is carried on by clerks and secretaries in the offices of lawyers, planners, developers, city hall departments, land registry offices, intermediate level governing agencies, and provincial ministry offices. This work is generally not visible or accessible to the public. Often the documents comprising a plan are the work of the developer's consultants and are considered privately owned and therefore not 'public' documents. Under Ontario's Municipal Freedom of Information and Privacy Act (1990) however, all documents pertaining to a matter brought in any way to public attention are legally accessible.

5 Section 40, in Part V of the Planning Act, 1983, Land Use Controls and Related Administration, requires particular local municipal practices in passing a zoning by-law. Section 40(4) says 'no development can take place without the approval of one or both, as the council may determine, of the following: 1. *Plans* showing location of all buildings and structures to be erected and showing the location of all facilities and works to be provided in conjunction therewith and of all facilities and works required under clause (7)(a). 2. *Drawings*, showing plan, elevation and cross-section views for each building to be erected ... which drawings are sufficient to display, (a) the massing and conceptual design of the

proposed building; (b) the relationship of the proposed building to adjacent buildings, streets, and exterior areas to which members of the public have access; and (c) the provision of interior walkways ...' etc., and clause '(7) as *conditions* to the approval of the plans and drawings referred to in (4) the municipality may require the owner to [provide, pay for, and maintain facilities and to enter into agreements with the municipality to ensure the provision of facilities, payments, and plans].'

6 Liza McCoy's explication of the organization of identity through photographs embedded in different discourses is especially insightful (see her chapter, this volume). In the organization of planning relations, the diagram is the interactional object of a series of procedures which produce a legal and standardized document. The 'final' registered subdivision plan's surface features include the Land Registrar's 'certificate,' the Owner's 'certificate,' the Surveyor's 'certificate' and the Plans Administration Branch of the Ministry of Municipal Affairs' 'approved' stamp, and the signatures of the registrar, president of the development corporation, the surveyor, and the manager of the Plans Administration Branch of the Ministry, which produce the body-text link authorizing and representing their activities connected to the plan. A chart of detailed 'curve data' represents the measure of lot and road locations. These engineering data need no formal authorization. No contour lines appear on the registered plan. Contour lines of a site are required on plans accompanying subdivision applications. Inserted into the series of procedures producing the legal document of subdivided and properly serviced properties, contours offer up the natural topography in terms of the relevances of development: drainage, road and service locations, and gradients (Government of Ontario 1986: 16). Then they disappear.

Literacy, Experience, Power

RICHARD DARVILLE

This essay develops an analysis of the organization of literacies in our society, from the perspective of adult literacy work. It develops the analysis using the method of the social organization of knowledge, and, like other studies written from feminist, gay, and working-class perspectives, proceeds from outside the ruling institutions, and recognizes language and documents as entrées to inquiry into them. The essay is, in part, an effort to come to terms with some years' experience teaching literacy and writing for literacy students. It also reflects many hours of conversation and debate with literacy workers and others interested in the fractures of language in our society.[1]

The essay works with two major themes in the ongoing discussion of literacy: first that literacy is not simply one kind of skill or activity, and second that literacy can be a form of empowerment, through which people gain control over the conditions of their lives.

It has become a commonplace assertion that literacy is plural and literacies are always particular. Literacy is not an entity in itself. Procedures of reading and writing are constituents of forms of social organization – of social practices, and the relations among people brought into being by those practices. Careful historical and ethnographic work has begun to display how people use different literate practices, and are engaged in different relations, when literacy is a matter of religious ritual and study, or when it serves a community's own informal communication and record keeping, or when it is used in governmental and business administrative processes (Scribner and Cole 1981; Graff 1981; Heath 1982, 1983; Street 1984; Weinstein 1984; Reder and Green 1983; Lunsford et al. 1990).

To come to terms with the forms of literacy requires clear conceptualization, so that in seeing literacy as more than one thing, we do not abandon ourselves to seeing it as an unthinkable proliferation of things. This essay elaborates a distinction, particularly relevant to literacy work, between two forms of literacy. In one form, prototypically narrative, people write down words that are anchored in lived experience. In a second form, writing is anchored in organizational or professional processes. We can label these forms narrative and organizational literacy.

There is a long-standing discussion in literacy work (most clearly crystallized in the work of Freire 1972, 1985) about how developing literacy can be a process of empowerment, in which people can 'name their world,' gain distance from and reflect upon the realities of their lives, and secure a critical understanding of the patterns of domination that underlie daily experience. In the discourse of literacy work itself, empowerment is often associated with narrative, as the most direct means of the expression of experience.

But empowerment is a relation, not a state or condition. The task of understanding the patterns of domination that underlie daily experience forces an engagement with forms of literacy that are part of the power of those who have power – for example, regulations, applications, contracts, invoices, identification cards, licences, business letters, memoranda, laws, and judicial decisions. In asking what people learn when they become literate as an empowerment, we need to examine how the lack of these forms of literacy constitutes disempoweredness in our society. We need also to examine how narrative literacy may either resist the dominant literacy or be its unwitting support.

This set of themes defines the audience for this essay. The essay is written for literacy workers and others (in community organizations, trade unions, and social movements) who write for people who do not routinely use print. It is also for social theorists of domination in advanced societies.

LITERACY LEARNING AND THE LANGUAGE OF EXPERIENCE

In the face of diverse forms of literacy, it is striking that literacy workers often choose, and are advised to choose, to work with a concrete and especially a narrative form of literacy. This strategy is most prominently articulated in the 'language experience' approach, which recommends the use of reading and writing which tell learners' experience. The anchoring of reading and writing in learners' action and experience could be produced with other literate forms, such as lists, recipes, instructions, or aphorisms. But stories are prototypically recommended.

Learners beginning to write often say, 'I can't think of anything to say.'

Literacy workers ask for their 'stories,' listen to them and say, 'Just write that down.' As learners write, they write in a language they already possess. Teachers selecting materials for learners' reading and writing, even beyond the most basic levels, often stick with narrative forms of literacy. They select topics and materials that anchor language in familiar action and experience. The experience involved may not be learners' individual experience, but that of 'ordinary people' (even if fictional) who live through the events of their lives, face a dilemma and make a choice, encounter a danger and come through it. In such stories meaning is embedded in the action and experience of credible and familiar individuals.

Literacy workers commonly find that this point of departure is a powerful stimulus to learning. In working with language experience stories, learners can focus their attention on what is, common-sensically, the first difficulty in literacy, the skill of getting the words off or onto the page. As people work on reading by reading familiar stories, they know what happened next in the story, and so anticipate what words will come next on the page. Their momentum in reading leads them to forget their hesitations about it. They follow the story, to see what happened, and find themselves reading words and ideas which they might not otherwise have been able to read.

Having heard or read one story, students, like the rest of us, will often set off telling stories of their own that pick up on some element of the first story. It seems to 'just happen' that stories lead to stories. People see in stories the grounds for an association of experiences they can tell. Thus, certain stories are 'generative,' as certain words are generative in the Freirian conception of literacy teaching.[2] They 'codify' or objectify key elements of experience and allow reflection on them. Stories enchained to highly charged stories of their readers' lives open up the expression of life experience.

A teacher can learn what story frames and character types are charged for learners by listening carefully and by using various stories and observing learners' responses; and the teacher can self-consciously use the spontaneous topical association of stories to generate elaboration of the life and language experiences with which learners are grappling. The use of generative stories can work powerfully, even explosively. These stories open up experience to expression, and the telling of experience both changes and enlarges what can be told, and opens up experience to reflection. I will argue later that, in the long run, the generative power of stories provides a means to ground even a knowledge of organizational literacy in learners' important life and language experiences. The use of generative stories can work to coalesce the meanings of experience and explore its implications for action, and even make literacy work, incipiently, organizing work.

STORIES AND SOCIAL ORGANIZATION

I have referred above to 'the workings' of stories. Stories, as a distinct form of literacy, produce and carry a distinct social organization. To analyse this social organization, the practices involved in producing stories and the relations created through them, will provide a way to think about both the teaching of narrative literacy and its relationship to other literacies – to see the power and limitations of language experience. Such an analysis will show *how* the things that seem to 'just happen' with stories are produced – how stories are grounded in experience and so are the natural focus of language experience work, and how stories are generative. It will show how narrative literacy practices differ from those of organizational literacy, and thus help build pedagogical practices that can relate one literacy to the other.

In the central practice of the social organization of stories, the teller of stories tells experience. Walter Benjamin (1969: 87) wrote, 'The storyteller takes what he tells from experience – his own or that reported by others. And he in turn makes it the experience of those who are listening to his tale.' The story carries experience into a social relation. In the narrative 'taking' and 'making' of experience that Benjamin describes, narratives tell what people said, did, and felt. Actions are explicitly tied to their agents, those who made what happened happen, and the narrative account of events is thus anchored in the lives of those who lived through them. Furthermore, the teller of a story relates events sequentially, and the hearer understands them, as (or as if) they actually occurred – in time, one thing after another (see, for example, Labov and Waletzsky 1969; Labov 1972; Sacks 1974).

Narratives' reference to experience involves not only *in what order* things happened, but *how* they happen. A reader or hearer who, as we say, 'follows' the actions of the characters, engages in an active process of interpretation. Since the teller of a story can never give an utterly complete account of what happened, the reader, in 'making sense' of the story, must 'fill in' her own sense of how people are and how things work, into what the text gives (D. Smith 1983). She has no choice but to be reminded of her own experience. Thus, to follow a story is to orient both to the experience related, and to one's own experience, as that is used in interpreting what is related. Part of the attraction of stories is that while they allow one to live through things with their characters, at the same time they pull out one's own sense of experience. The reader's experience mingles with that of the characters.

Stories do not merely arise from experience but also are informative about it. The teller selects the story's elements so as to point to its significance, to what it has to say about experience, and in following an unfolding story, a hearer or reader looks for its significance, as a sense-making practice. A story that simply relates a succession of events, without significance, will fall flat, and its teller can be called to account for having no 'point' (Labov and Waletzsky 1969; Labov 1972). The story achieves an 'amplitude' of significance (Benjamin 1969: 89) because it does not attempt to box meaning in, to contain it within words, but points to a meaning that can be seen in the events it reports. Listeners are led to their own experience as it resonates with the significance of the tale they are hearing.

Conversational storytelling is itself socially organized. Speaker and listeners engage with one another at the outset of storytelling, claiming and granting the floor, and at the conclusion, affiliating and resuming other talk. Furthermore, a second story often follows a first, with definite ties in topic, in the manner in which the teller figures in the tale, or in significance (for analyses, see Sacks 1974, 1978).

Because stories are grounded in experience and in ordinary conversational organization, literacy learners readily produce and comprehend much material written in story form. Because readers of a story must use their own experience in following it and seeing its significance, experiences are linked in narrative, and stories are a generative form of literacy. (And because stories are linked through their topics and their significance, so their generative capacity depends on the sharing of experience among those in a circle of storytellers or learners.)[3]

The discourse about language experience asserts the power of the act of writing to transform writers' sense of themselves as literate (see, for example, McBeth 1989). The context of this transformative power of writing is the ordinary relation of those with limited literacy, especially if they are also poor, to a dominant organizational literacy, in which they are silenced. In this relation, their experience, even if written down, does not hold sway. Knowing that writing down one's experience does not count (or may count against one) itself generates illiteracy. Understanding the context of the transformative power of language experience thus requires understanding something of the workings of the dominant literacy.

THE DOMINANT LITERACY

Any literacy is like a currency. It buys into a social organization. Through most everyday printed material, we do not relate directly to one another's experience. Rather we relate to one another, and to objects and events, through organizations. Organizational literacy – in, for example, job applications, legal documents, and union contracts – is concerned with effecting organizational process, not with telling individual experience. It is not about experience but about the ways that experience is managed, ordered, regulated, and controlled.

Levi-Strauss (1973: 18) writes that literacy was initially developed as a tool of domination, that the one phenomenon always linked historically with the appearance of writing is 'the establishment of hierarchical societies.' Writing 'was connected first and foremost with power: it was used for inventories, catalogues, censuses, laws and instructions; in all instances, whether the aim was to keep a check on material possessions or on human beings, it is evidence of the power exercised by some men over other men and over worldly possessions.

In the past six hundred years or so in the West, reading and writing abilities have spread, and the forms of literacy now familiar to us have developed in economic, religious, and political organization (Cipolla 1969; Graff 1981, 1987; Levine 1986). A dominant literacy has often been a means of cultural and political hegemony (Donald 1983; Curtis 1985). In our society, where the dominant literacy is that used in corporations, bureaucracies, media, professions, and academia, an interest in understanding literacy and literacy work leads to an interest in understanding organizational literacy, that is, in 'understanding the nature of power when power is vested in a documentary process' (Smith 1984). In organizational literacy, in bureaucratic, administrative, legal, and professional language (Heath 1979; Campbell and Holland 1982; Redish 1983; White 1983), what counts is how matters can be *written up* (to enter them into an organizational process), not how they can be *written down* (to relate experience or to aid memory). (These common English idioms of verticality in writing express the fundamental divergence of forms of literacy.) Work in the dominant organizations in our society is done essentially, though not exclusively, through texts. Knowledge is organized in textual form. People communicate, it is decided what really happened, and actions are taken, 'on paper.' Even when people engage face-to-face, the significance of what they say lies in what it means 'for the record' (see, for example, de Montigny, in this volume). Organizational literacy enables people dispersed in time and space to develop complementary ideas and to act in concert towards the people or situations that they make account of, administer, interpret, legislate for. People using literacy to do organizational work simultaneously write, conceptualize, and enact organizational processes. They make up a textually mediated social organization (Smith 1984).

Organizational accounts convey more than mere concepts and categories. They often describe particular events, but within organizational frameworks, producing organizational narratives or 'ideological narratives' (Smith 1983a). Psychiatric 'case histories,' newspaper 'stories' and educational 'anecdotal reports' refer to actual events, but intend an organizational and not an experiential understanding. They refer not to experience but to the 'particulars' of events, categorically relevant to their being acted on organizationally. Because organizational literacy is not about personal experience, its users must be separated from the immediate expression of their own circumstances or of the lives of those they write about. (Stories are not a tool of management.) This fracture is essential to organizational reading and writing practices. It is part of 'being literate.'

These literate practices are means of exercising power in our society – power not, ordinarily, available to those who become literacy learners. Learners often hesitate before the written word. Their hesitation, more than a simple lack of skill, is likely to appear when they encounter an unfamiliar form of literacy, and the skills that they do have seem 'out of place.' Such hesitation is commonly described as the 'embarrassment' of people who do not read and write well about admitting it. But to emphasize embarrassment, without locating it in social organization, is to 'blame the victims' (Ryan 1971) for their feelings at moments when they are excluded or subordinated. Learners also often express anger or frustration at organizational language, saying, for example, 'They try to put you down with their big words,' or, 'Why don't they just say what they mean?' That discourses about illiterates so often emphasize their embarrassment, so seldom their frustration or anger, is telling – it reveals that these discourses are part of the dominant literacy rather than of a literacy that stands with those learning to be literate.

People in our society often feel out of place, hesitant, embarrassed, frustrated, or angry, when encountering the printed word, and especially when recognizing that literacy conveys someone else's power. Although these feelings appear in a particularly sharp form in the relations between illiterates and organizations that use literacy in their workings, in our society we all know them, since they derive from a fundamental feature of our social organization.

ORGANIZATIONAL LITERACY PRODUCES ILLITERACY

Organizational literacy presumes certain background knowledge, and certain practices of reading and writing. People who do not have those available, or do not want to use them, are rendered in a sense 'illiterate.' Many who do not use print by habit or daily practice misread organizational texts. This misreading is not being unable to get words off the page, but rather being unable to participate effectively in the social action and relations that are carried in texts and documents – or even to see what that action and those relations are. When literacy learners deal with texts such as newspaper articles, bureaucratic forms, or political pamphlets, they may say nothing, or say, 'I can't read that' (although they produce a fluent oral performance of it), or, 'I can't remember anything I've read.' Learners (as well as teachers) may suffer bewilderment at a reading in which meaning remains opaque, and words seem incalculably to mean more than they say. Let me describe several specific forms of misreading.

Organizational texts routinely presuppose certain organizational background knowledge of their readers. An elementary form of this presupposition occurs when texts delete agents of action. In grammatical forms which are also organizational constructions, they highlight (or 'thematize') organizational processes, obscuring their agents (Kress and Hodge 1979: 15–37; Ohmann 1976). Agentless accounts are produced through such grammatical constructions as nominalization ('*Disturbances* followed last week's *announcement*'), participial modifier ('of the widely *criticized*'), noun string ('*training action plan*'), and agentless passive ('and it *was* hastily *withdrawn*'). An expression like 'Applications must be submitted' similarly severs activity from its agents. When the agents of actions are deleted from texts, readers must 'fill them in,' using a background knowledge of how actions are done and who would do them. These 'gaps' or 'silences' in the text will render 'illiterate' readers who, lacking the presupposed background knowledge, do not recognize the action that the text glosses over.

Competently reading or writing organizational documents requires a knowledge of how they are used in courses of organizational action. Even with the ubiquitous application form, 'novice' users may say, 'Date of application? What does that mean? What do I put there?' – not recognizing the meaning of the item as its projected use in an organizational course of action, perhaps filing-by-date. In a study of people's accounts of their decisions in filling out applications (Holland and Redish 1982), 'expert' users describe what they do with reference to the intentions behind the application and the way it will be read and used. They selectively describe their lives and experiences, paying heed not merely to the questions the application literally asks, but to 'what they're looking for' or 'what will get you points.' 'Novice' users, however, are 'more constrained by the individual items,' and, for example, leave out favourable information about themselves because the form does not ask for it. They tie their inscriptions to experience, not to the ways that they will be viewed in an organizational process. In a similar way, in oral exchanges around the filling out of documents involved in securing personal bank loans, people sometimes are uncertain why bank officials ask the questions they do, and how one seeking a loan can make the best case (Heath 1982). Their difficulty is not reading skills in a rudimentary sense, but practical knowledge about how certain information is organizationally relevant, how it will be used.

Even the simplest newspaper 'stories' routinely anchor bits of information in the organizational processes reported, rather than in the temporally ordered action of the individuals involved. Readers who use narrative reading practices (read actions as individual actions, and read sequences of clauses as sequences of events) will then misread. In one striking form of misreading, literacy students asked to retell the events of a news story may mistakenly recount them in the order that they appear in the text, not realizing that the order of their actual occurrence has been undone in their reporting. Or actions may be read as motivated by individual feelings and desires, rather than by organizational policy.

The significance of such misreadings is *not* that working-class people who have difficulties with organizational documents possess only a language 'restricted' in the range of listeners or readers to whom it is addressed and sensible (Bernstein 1971), or a language that fails to 'abstract.' Abstraction is not a thing in itself, apart from the social organization in which it appears. Many who are little practiced at academic or bureaucratic abstraction create powerful abstraction by metaphor, or discuss abstract problems of love, learning, and so on. In organizations such as unions or churches that serve their own purposes, they are powerfully articulate (cf. Rosen 1972; Heath 1983: 201–11). But certain forms of literate abstraction – arising within unfamiliar organizational frames or scientific conventions, or viewing immediately experienced events from outside, for purposes of accounting or controlling them – can generate what looks like 'illiteracy.'

TELLING STORIES AND TELLING MORE

The splitting of the literacy of experience from the literacy of power is central in both literacy learning and everyday literacy use, in more ways than this essay can elucidate. These rifts are not 'theoretical' objects, but can be observed and conceptualized in the everyday work processes of literacy teachers, and of others who work with people who do not routinely use print. To do so requires taking seriously that practices of literacy are tied up with specific users of literacy and their locations and relations in society.

All of us, literacy learners included, are in a location to use narrative literacy to give accounts of experience and exchange it. Just writing it down gives us the powers of authorship, of reflection on what we have lived through, and of communication with others dispersed in time and space. In teaching work, writing the language of experience is a progressive (empowering) process, in all these ways. Promoting the literacy of experience is also in part a reaction to the exclusion of learners (and others) from the literacy of power. Students who produce material that conveys *their* lives appropriate literacy for themselves, and undercut a sense that literacy only belongs to others. This reaction to exclusion from the literacy of power is valuable, indeed essential.[4] But it can also be a curtailed reaction, treating people's reaction to their domination as the problem to be dealt with, and working with a form of literacy only apparently free from organizational power, in an enclave of 'experience.' And the empowerment of writing experience becomes condescension and disempowerment when literacy workers treat those with limited literacy as merely repositories of personal experience, or act as if they are empowered once they write their stories, and teachers have done what they can do.

The story is the strength of the illiterate and the poor. They know the story. Mostly middle-class literacy workers may have not much to teach about the story, and a lot to learn. However, those who are organizationally competent do know certain practices of reading and writing, and have them to teach, and in teaching them can come to know them more profoundly. This might seem a crucial task for progressive literacy workers, but there has been, I think, a stunting of discussion of extending literacy beyond rudimentary skills and personal expression into organizational literacy. This is in part because of the strength of the available critique of 'functional' literacy as the basis of literacy curriculum – that functional literacy, as usually conceived, silences learners' experiences and stories; and that a description of skill devised for 'managing instruction' cannot be capable of grasping the practical competencies exercised in actual contexts of performance (see, for example, Griffith and Cervero 1977; Kazemak 1985). I would add that the conception of functional literacy gives a flattened portrayal of social relations as merely tasks or demands and fails to grasp the power-carrying character of organizational literacy.

To extend literacy beyond personal expression – without abandoning the gains of anchoring literacy in everyday life – requires more than critique. It requires a studied understanding of the gap that separates narrative from organizational literacy and of the teaching that might move across the gap. I want to discuss programmatically a way of thinking about building on the literacy of experience to suggest how people can develop not a functional literacy that starts outside, but an organizational literacy that starts within their purposes and their stories.

Literacy learners are not generally about to become bureaucrats, teachers, or lawyers, and they do not need the literacy of agents of the dominant organizations. They will, however, deal with bureaucrats, teachers, and lawyers. They will need practices of reading and writing as means of articulating themselves to organizations (cf. Smith 1984) and fitting into organizational frameworks of activity and literacy. Functional literacy, in the sense of being competent to be administered, *is* important.

Furthermore, the capacity to resist being administered is also important. Literacy learners commonly have for years confronted organizations and their literate practices as standing over and against them – on the job, in dealings with government agencies, in education, and in social work and psychiatric interventions. This experience is the basis of a distinct kind of educational work, central to adult literacy. That work involves constructing a knowledge of the practices of organizational literacy, from the position of those on whom those practices are used and who may want to resist them.

A first step beyond simply telling stories must be, paradoxically, to defend their autonomy – to tell and to respect accounts of experience, not in isolation, but facing up to the dominant organizations. Juxtaposing people's own stories with the organizational forms that would redefine them breaks the organizational silencing of experience. Insisting on how we write it down is a defence against being disappeared in how they write it up. So the student's story should be contrasted with the school records, the worker's account with the foreman's, the patient's testimony with the psychiatrist's case history. In this manner, materials for study can be developed in which the difference of voices expresses the opposition between experience and its organizational rendering, and supports people in defining themselves, apart from their organizational definition.

Further, in a narrative literacy process, beginning with individual stories, leading to a collection of linked stories, a theme or frame can be leached out, to articulate what questions that collection poses, to coalesce the meanings of shared experience and explore its implications for action. If the experience reported arises in relation to an organizational process, then a collection of narratives may provide an approach to organizational literacy as learners need to deal with it. Experience itself leads to organization, when organization penetrates into experience.

To embed an approach to organizational knowledge in experience is to display how people come to develop that knowledge for themselves. Dialogue in teaching situations can move forward from the point at which learners' stories end, in restricting encounters with dominant organizations. Materials for study can take the form of the form of stories which 'lead up' to organization, when characters need to deal with organizational documents and texts, and develop for themselves the knowledge required to do so.[5] (Either process may require that teachers alongside learners inquire into the workings of those organizations.)

Collecting stories to display the commonalities of experience can begin a process that goes beyond a literacy of experience and even beyond merely adapting to organizations. Literacy can be a means of empowerment as a constituent of broader social struggles and institutional change. As Gee (1990: 46) notes, the question 'whether literacy can be used as a tool for liberation' is not a question about literacy, 'at least as literacy is traditionally conceived. The question comes down to whether the social groups and institutions that underwrite various types of texts and ways of interpreting them can be changed.'

Beginning with documents commonly encountered, people can begin to inquire together into how society works to give them common experience, to create the circumstances of their lives. Confronting organizational literacy with the literacy of experience may ultimately support demands that organizations serve life rather than merely manage it, and thus support action through popular organizations such as community and aboriginal groups, trade unions, and churches. Of course, this action must take place in a society saturated with organizations and their literacy. So acting must mean, among other things, literate action – producing letters, pamphlets, petitions, newsletters, books, manifestos, that enable people, beginning from their experience, to struggle to create the conditions of their lives. Literacy work in the long run means producing a new literacy that is capable of such action, capable of bringing together literacies of experience and literacies of power in new forms of organization that begin in people's lives and not in a bifurcated management over them. Such a project is of course beyond the grasp of literacy work itself, but literacy work has essential insight, skill, and knowledge to contribute.

NOTES

This article has been adapted, with the permission of the publisher, from an earlier publication, 'The Language of Experience and the Literacy of Power,' in M.C. Taylor and J.A. Draper, eds., 1989, 1991, *Adult Literacy Perspectives*, Toronto: Culture Concepts, 25–40.

1 I want particularly to thank Harold Alden, Evelyn Battell, Sandy Cameron, Linda Forsythe, Nancy Jackson, Christopher Knight, Mary Norton, Carol McEown, Michael Szasz, and Frances Wasserlein.
2 The parallel is not exact. In one case word elements (syllables), and in the other case story elements (event and significance) are separated and recombined.
3 Of course there are differing narrative constructions of 'experience' (see, for example, Scollon and Scollon 1981; Rosen 1986), and students don't tell some stories because they're in school, or because there are mixed genders, races or ages in the room, or because teachers are not prepared to hear (cf. Sola and Bennett 1985; Michaels 1986). I don't focus here on these issues, but on the differences between stories generically, and contrasting forms of literacy.
4 Thus a movement of working-class and community publishing seeks both to demystify print production and to disestablish the category of 'literature' (Morley and Worpole 1982).
5 See for example, Darville (1991), a book for literacy students dealing with consumer and labour contracts.

Bibliography

Abella, R.S. 1984. *Equality in Employment: Royal Commission Report*. Ottawa, Supply and Services

Acker, J. 1987. 'Sex Bias in Job Evaluation: A Comparable Worth Issue,' in C. Bose and G. Spitze, eds., *Ingredients for Women's Employment Policy*. Albany: SUNY Press

– 1989. *Doing Comparable Worth: Gender, Class, and Pay Equity*. Philadelphia: Temple University Press

Adams, R.E. 1975. *Dacum – Approach to Curriculum, Learning, and Evaluation in Occupational Training*. Ottawa: Department of Regional Economic Expansion

Aglietta, M. 1979. *A Theory of Capitalist Regulation: The U.S. Experience*. London: New Left Books

Apple, M.W. 1980. 'Curricular Form and the Logic of Technical Control: Building the Possessive Individual,' in L. Barton et al., eds., *Schooling, Ideology, and the Curriculum*, pp. 11–27. Sussex: Falmer

– 1982. *Education and Power*. London: Routledge and Kegan Paul

– 1986. *Teachers and Texts*. London: Routledge and Kegan Paul

– 1993. *Official Knowledge: Democratic Knowledge in a Conservative Age*. New York: Routledge

– and L. Weiss. 1983. *Ideology and Practice in Schooling*. Philadelphia: Temple University Press

Armstrong, P., and H. Armstrong. 1984. *The Double Ghetto: Canadian Women and Their Segregated Work*, rev. ed. Toronto: McClelland and Stewart

Ashton, P., and R. Webb. 1986. *Making a Difference: Teachers' Sense of Efficacy and Student Achievement*. New York: Longman

Bakhtin, M.M. 1981. *The Dialogic Imagination*. Austin: University of Texas Press

– 1986. *Speech Genres and Other Late Essays*. Austin: University of Texas Press

Ball, S., R. Hull, M. Skelton, and R. Tudor. 1984. 'The Tyranny of the "Devil's

Mill": Time and Task at School,' in S. Delamont, ed., *Readings on Interaction in the Classroom*, pp. 41–57. London: Methuen

Barnsley, J. 1985. *Feminist Action, Institutional Reaction: Responses to Wife Assault*. Vancouver: Women's Research Centre

Barthes, R. 1977. 'The Photographic Message,' in *Image-Music-Text*. Trans. S. Heath. New York: Hill and Wang

– 1981. *Camera Lucida: Reflections on Photography*. Trans. R. Howard. New York: Hill and Wang

Bates, R. 1992. 'Education and Reform: Its Role in the Economic Destruction of Society.' Keynote Address, AARE/NZARE Annual Conference, Deakin University, Geelong, Victoria, Australia

Baudrillard, J. 1988. 'The Evil Demon of Images.' Trans. P. Patton and P. Foss. *Power Institute Publications*, no 3. Sydney, Australia: Power Institute

Beekman, M. 1979. *The Mechanical Baby*. London: Dobson

Benjamin, W. 1969. 'The Storyteller: Reflections on the Work of Nikolai Leskov,' in *Illuminations*, pp. 83–110. New York: Schocken

Berger, P., and T. Luckmann. 1966. *The Social Construction of Reality: A Treatise in the Sociology of Knowledge*. Garden City, NY: Doubleday

Bernstein, B. 1971. 'Class, Codes, and Control,' in vol. 1: *Theoretical Studies Towards a Sociology of Language*. St Albans: Paladin

Bourdieu, P., and J.C. Passeron. 1977. *Reproduction in Education, Society, and Culture*. Beverly Hills: Sage

Boyd, J. 1984. *Understanding the Primary Curriculum*. London: Hutchinson

Braverman, H. 1974. *Labour and Monopoly Capital*. New York: Monthly Review Press

Brim, O. 1959. *Education for Child Rearing*. New York: Russell Sage Foundation

Buchbinder, H., D. Forbes, V. Burstyn, and M. Steedman, eds. 1987. *Who's on Top: The Politics of Heterosexuality*. Toronto: Garamond

Bureau of the Census, United States Department of Commerce. 1984. *Illustrative Statistics on Women in Selected Developing Countries*. Washington, DC: Bureau of the Census

Burnet, J. 1988. *Multiculturalism in Canada*. Ottawa: Secretary of State

Campbell, L.J., and V.M. Holland. 1982. 'Understanding the Language of Public Documents, Because Formulas Don't,' in R.J. DiPietro, ed., *Linguistics and the Professions*. Norwood, NJ: Ablex

Campbell, M.L. 1984. 'Information Systems and Management of Hospital Nursing: A Study in Social Organization of Knowledge.' Unpublished PhD thesis, OISE, University of Toronto

– 1988. 'The Structure of Stress in Nurses' Work,' in S. Bolaria and H. Dickinson, eds., *Sociology of Health Care in Canada*. Toronto: Harcourt Brace Jovanovitch

– 1992. 'Canadian Nurses' Professionalism: A Labour Process Analysis,' *International Journal of Health Services*, 22: 751–65

Canada. 1956. Royal Commission on the Criminal Law Relating to Criminal Sexual Psychopaths. *Report of Private Sessions, Montreal and Toronto*. Papers of the Royal Commission, Public Archives of Canada (Government Document Canada, C9296, M, V.8)

– 1958. *Report of the Royal Commission on the Criminal Law Relating to Criminal Sexual Psychopaths*. (McRuer Commission.) Ottawa: Queen's Printer

– 1965. *Preliminary Report of the Royal Commission on Bilingualism and Biculturalism*. Ottawa: Queen's Printer

– House of Commons. 1982. Standing Committee on Health, Welfare, and Social Affairs. *Report on Violence in the Family: Wife battering*. Ottawa: Queen's Printer

Canadian Consultative Council on Multiculturalism. 1975. *First Annual Report of the Canadian Consultative Council on Multiculturalism*. Ottawa: Author

Cantor, L.M., and I.F. Roberts. 1979. *Further Education Today: A Critical Review*. London: Routledge and Kegan Paul

Carnegie Council in Policy Studies in Higher Education. 1980. *Policy Studies in Higher Education: A Summary of Reports and Recommendations*. San Francisco: Jossey-Bass

Cartledge, S., and J. Ryan, eds. 1983. *Sex and Love*. London: Women's Press

Cassin, M. 1990a. *Women, Work, Jobs, and Value: A Report with Special Reference to Consumers Gas*. Submission to the Ontario Pay-Equity Tribunal, Toronto

– 1990b. 'Women and Work: The Routine Production of Inequality.' Unpublished PhD thesis, OISE, University of Toronto

Chamberlain, P. 1990. 'Homophobia in the Schools, or What We Don't Know Will Hurt Us,' in S.G. O'Malley, R. Rosen, and L. Vogt, eds., *Politics of Education: Essays from Radical Teacher*. Albany: SUNY Press

Chamboredon J.C., and J. Prevot. 1975. 'Changes in the Social Definition of Early Childhood and the New Forms of Symbolic Violence,' *Theory and Society*, 2: 331–50

Chua, B.H. 1979. 'Describing a National Crisis: An Exploration in Textual Analysis,' *Human Studies*, 2: 47–61

Cipolla, C. 1969. *Literacy and Development in the West*. Harmondsworth: Penguin

Clark, L. 1989. *Acceptable Risk: Making Decisions in a Toxic Environment*. Berkeley and Los Angeles: University of California Press

Clark, P., and A. Davis. 1989. 'The Power of Dirt: An Exploration of Secular Defilement in Anglo-Canadian Culture,' *Canadian Review of Society and Anthropology*, 26: 650–73

Clarke, S. 1990. 'Local Autonomy in the Post-Reagan Period.' Paper prepared for the American Political Science Association Annual Meeting

Cockburn, C. 1985. *Machinery of Dominance: Women, Men, and Technical Know-how.* London: Pluto

Coleman J.S., E.Q. Campbell, C.J. Hobson, J. MacPartland, A.M. Mood, F. Weinfeld, and R. York. 1966. *Equality of Educational Opportunity.* Washington, DC: Government Printing Office

Collins, C., ed. 1993. *Competencies: The Competencies Debate in Australian Education and Training.* Canberra: Australian College of Education

Connell, R.W. 1985. *Teachers' Work.* Sydney: Allen and Unwin

– D.J. Ashenden, S. Kessler, and G.W. Dowsett. 1982. *Making the Difference.* Boston: Allen and Unwin

Corrigan, P. 1987. 'In/Forming Schooling,' in D. Livingstone, ed., *Critical Pedagogy and Cultural Power*, pp. 17–40. South Hadley, Mass.: Bergin and Garvey

Curtin, P. 1971. *Imperialism.* New York: Harper and Row

Curtis, B. 1985. 'The Speller Expelled: Disciplining the Common Reader in Canada West,' *Canadian Review of Sociology and Anthropology*, 22: 346–68

Dale, R. 1990. *The TVEI Story: Policy and Preparation for the Workforce.* Milton Keynes: Open University Press

Damisch, H. 1978. 'Five Notes for a Phenomenology of the Photographic Image,' *October*, 5: 70–72

Darville, R. 1991. *Can We Make a Deal?* 2nd ed. rev. (1st ed. 1981). Vancouver: Legal Services Society of British Columbia

David, M. 1980. *The State, the Family, and Education.* London: Routledge and Kegan Paul

Davin, A. 1978. 'Imperialism and Motherhood,' *History Workshop Journal*, 5: 9–65

– 1982. 'Child Labour, the Working Class Family, and Domestic Ideology in Nineteenth-Century Britain,' *Development and Change*, 13: 633–52

D'Emilio, J. 1983. *Sexual Politics, Sexual Communities.* Chicago: University of Chicago Press

– 1992. 'The Homosexual Menace: The Politics of Sexuality in Cold War America,' in J. D'Emilio, ed., *Making Trouble: Essays on Gay History, Politics, and the University*, pp. 57–73. New York: Routledge

de Montigny, G. 1989. 'Accomplishing Professional Reality: An Ethnography of Social Workers' Practice.' Unpublished PhD thesis, OISE, University of Toronto

De Vos, G., and H. Wagatsuma. 1970. 'Status and Role Behaviour in Changing Japan,' in G. Seward and R.C. Williamson, eds., *Sex Roles in Changing Society*, pp. 334–70. New York: Random House

Delamont, S., ed. 1987. *The Primary School Teacher.* London: Falmer

Dirks, N. 1992. *Colonialism and Culture.* Ann Arbor: University of Michigan Press

Donald J. 1983. 'How Illiteracy Became a Problem and Literacy Stopped Being One,' *Journal of Education* (Boston), 165: 35–52

Downey, J., and J. Howell. 1976. *Wife Battering: A Review and Preliminary Enquiry into Local Incidence, Needs, and Resources*. Vancouver: United Way of Greater Vancouver

Dubois, M. 1991. 'The Governance of the Third World: A Foucauldian Perspective on Power Relations in Development,' *Alternatives*, 16: 1–30

Duster, T. 1987. 'Intermediate Steps Between Micro- and Macro- Integration: The Case of Screening for Inherited Disorders,' in K. Knorr-Cetina and A.V. Cicourel, eds., *Advances in Social Theory and Methodology: Toward an Integration of Micro- and Macro-Sociologies*. London: Routledge and Kegan Paul

Edwards, J., and R. Batley. 1978. *The Politics of Positive Discrimination: An Evaluation of the Urban Programme, 1967–77*. London: Tavistock Publications

Edwards, R. 1979. *Contested Terrain: The Transformation of the Workplace in the Twentieth Century*. New York: Basic Books

Egan, J. 1959. '"Toronto Fairy-Go-Round," So the Chief of Police Said to the Royal Commission ...,' *Justice Weekly*, 7 Nov.: 5, 15

Ehrenreich, B., and D. English. 1978. *For Her Own Good: 150 years of the Experts' Advice to Women*. Garden City, NY: Anchor Press

Epstein, J.L. 1987. 'Parent Involvement: What Research Says to Administrators,' *Education and Urban Society*, 19: 119–36

Escobar, A. 1984. 'Discourse and Power in Development: Michel Foucault and the Relevance of His Work to the Third World,' *Alternatives*, 12: 125–52

Fainstein, S. 1989. 'Urban Development and the Transformation of Planning in the United States and Great Britain.' Paper presented at the Symposium on the Public Planning and Processing of Large Scale Development, York University

Field, J. 1991. 'Competency and the Pedagogy of Labour,' *Studies in the Education of Adults*, 23: 41–52

Fine, M. 1988. 'Sexuality, Schooling, and Adolescent Females: The Missing Discourse of Desire,' *Harvard Educational Review*, 58: 29–53

Fleras, A., and J.L. Elliott. 1992. *The Challenge of Diversity: Multiculturalism in Canada*. Toronto: Nelson

Foucault, M. 1970. *The Order of Things: An Archaeology of the Human Sciences*. New York: Vintage

– 1979. *Discipline and Punishment: The Birth of the Prison*. Trans. A. Sheridan. New York: Random House, Vintage

– 1980. *Power/Knowledge: Selected Interviews and Other Writings 1972–1977*. Ed. C. Gordon. New York: Pantheon

Freedman, E. 1987. '"Uncontrolled Desires": The Response to the Sexual Psychopath, 1920–1960,' *Journal of American History*, 74: 83–106

Freire, P. 1972. *Pedagogy of the Oppressed.* New York: Herder and Herder
– 1985. 'The Adult Literacy Process as Cultural Action for Freedom,' in *The Politics of Education*, pp. 43–65. South Hadley, Mass.: Bergin and Garvey
Friend, R. 1993. 'Choices, Not Closets: Heterosexism and Homophobia in Schools,' in L. Weis and M. Fine, eds., *Beyond Silenced Voices: Class, Race, and Gender in United States Schools.* Albany: SUNY Press
Fukutake, T. 1974. *Japanese Society Today.* Tokyo: University of Tokyo Press
Garfinkel, H. 1967a. *Studies in Ethnomethodology.* Englewoood Cliffs, NJ: Prentice-Hall
– 1967b. '"Good" Organizational Reasons for "Bad" Clinic Records,' *Studies in Ethnomethodology*, pp. 186–207. Englewood Cliffs, NJ: Prentice-Hall
Gaskell, J. 1986. 'Conceptions of Skill and the Work of Women: Historical and Political Issues,' in R. Hamilton and M. Barrett, eds., *The Politics of Diversity*, pp. 361–80. Montreal: Book Centre
Gay Teachers Group. 1987. *School's Out: Lesbian and Gay Rights in Education.* London: Gay Teachers' Group
Gee, J.P. 1990. *Social Linguistics and Literacies: Ideology in Discourses.* London: Falmer
Girard, P. 1985. 'Gays, Lesbians, and the Legal Process since 1945.' Unpublished paper
Giroux, H. 1992. *Border Crossings: Cultural Workers and the Politics of Education.* New York: Routledge
Glaser, R., ed. 1962. *Training Research and Education.* 2nd ed. New York: Wiley
Glenn, E., and R. Feldberg. 1983. 'Proletarianizing Clerical Work: Technology and Organizational Control in the Office,' in A. Zimbalist, ed., *Case Studies of the Labour Process.* New York: Monthly Review Press
Gould, C.C. 1978. *Marx's Social Ontology.* Cambridge: MIT Press
Gouldner, A. 1970. *The Coming Crisis of Western Sociology.* New York: Basic Books
Government of Ontario. 1985. *Planning Act, 1983 R.S.O. and Certain Regulations Thereunder*
– 1990. *The Education Act.* Revised Statutes of Ontario, 104(2)
– Information and Privacy Commission. 1990. 'January 1, 1991 Heralds New FOIPOP Act For Ontario,' *Municipal World*, October, 15–18
– Ministry of Education. 1975. *Education in the Primary and Junior Divisions: P1J1.* Toronto: Queen's Printer for Ontario
– Legislature of Ontario. 1982. *Standing Committee on Social Development, First Report on Family Violence: Wife Battering.* Toronto: Queen's Park
– Ministry of Municipal Affairs. 1986. *Subdivision/Condominium Approval Procedures: A Guide for Applicants.* Toronto. Queen's Printer for Ontario

- Ministry of Municipal Affairs. 1989. *Municipal Councillor's Manual*. Toronto: Queen's Printer for Ontario

Government Statisticians' Collective. 1979. 'How Official Statistics Are Produced: Views from the Inside,' in J. Irvine, I. Miles, and J. Evans, eds., *Demystifying Social Statistics*, pp. 130–51. London: Pluto

Grace, A.G. 1948. *Educational Lessons from Wartime Training*. Washington DC: American Council on Education

Graff, H. 1987. *The Labyrinths of Literacy: Reflections on Literacy Past and Present*. London: Falmer

- ed. 1981. *Literacy and Social Development in the West*. Cambridge: Cambridge University Press

Gramsci, A. 1971. *Selections from the Prison Notebooks*. New York: International Publishers

Grant, G., et al. 1979. *On Competence: A Critical Analysis of Competence-Based Reforms in Higher Education*. San Francisco: Jossey-Bass

Griffith, A.I. 1984. 'Ideology, Education, and Single Parent Families: The Normative Ordering of Families Through Schooling.' Unpublished PhD thesis, OISE, University of Toronto

- and D.E. Smith. 1987. 'Constructing Cultural Knowledge: Mothering as Discourse,' in J. Gaskell and A. McLaren, eds., *Women and Education: A Canadian Perspective*. 2nd ed. Calgary: Detselig

- 1986. 'Reporting the Facts: Media Accounts of Single Parent Families,' *Resources for Feminist Research*, 15. 32–43

- 1990. '"What Did You Do in School Today?": Mothering, Schooling, and Social Class,' in G. Miller and J.A. Holstein, eds., *Perspectives on Social Problems: A Research Annual*, vol 2, pp. 3–24. Greenwich, Conn.: JAI Press

Griffith, W. S., and R.M. Cervero. 1977. 'The Adult Performance Level Program: A Serious and Deliberate Examination,' *Adult Education*, 27: 209–24.

Gruber, H.E., and J.J. Vonèche, eds. 1977. *The Essential Piaget*. New York: Basic Books

Hammell, N. 1991. 'Some New Brunswick Nurses' Perceptions of Changes Impacting on Them and Their Nursing Care.' Unpublished Master's thesis, School of Nursing, Dalhousie University

Hansard. 1969. Ottawa: House of Commons

Harbeck, K., ed. 1992. *Coming Out of the Classroom Closet: Gay and Lesbian Students, Teachers, and Curricula*. New York: Harrington Park Press

Harding, S. 1991. *Whose Science? Whose Knowledge? Thinking from Women's Lives*. Ithaca, NY: Cornell University Press

Hartley, D. 1985. *Understanding the Primary School: A Sociological Analysis*. London: Croom Helm

Hartland, N. 1989. 'Texts and Social Organization: An Ethnomethodology of State Documents,' *Journal of Pragmatics,* 13: 395–405

Heath, S.B. 1979. 'The Context of Professional Languages: An Historical Overview,' in J.E. Alatis and G.R. Tucker, eds., *Language in Public Life*, pp. 102–18. Washington, DC: Georgetown University Press

– 1982. 'Protean Shapes in Literacy Events: Ever-Shifting Oral and Literate Traditions,' in D. Tannen, ed., *Spoken and Written Language: Exploring Orality and Literacy*, pp. 91–117. Norwood, NJ: Ablex

– 1983. *Ways with Words: Language, Life, and Work in Communities and Classrooms*. Cambridge: Cambridge University Press

Helterline, M. 1980. 'The Emergence of Modern Motherhood: Motherhood in England 1899–1959,' *International Journal of Women's Studies*, 3: 590–614

Henriques, J., W. Holloway, C. Urwin, C. Venn, and V. Walkerdine, eds. 1984. *Changing the Subject: Psychology, Social Regulation, and Subjectivity*. London: Methuen

Heritage, J. 1984. *Garfinkel and Ethnomethodology*. Cambridge: Polity Press

Heron, A., ed. 1983. *One Teenager in 10: Writings by Gay and Lesbian Youth*. Boston: Alyson Publications

Hilsum, S., and B.S. Cane. 1971. *The Teacher's Day*. Windsor, Berks.: NFER

Hofstadter, D.R. 1980. *Godel, Escher, Bach: An Eternal Golden Braid*. New York: Random House

Holland, M., and J. Redish. 1982. 'Strategies for Understanding Forms – and Other Public Documents,' in D. Tannen, ed., *Text and Talk*, pp. 205–18. Washington, DC: Georgetown University Press

Hyam, R. 1992. *Empire and Sexuality*. Manchester: Manchester University Press

Inden, R. 1990. *Imagining India*. Oxford: Basil Blackwell

Inui, S., and K. Sono. 1977. *Kaigai Chuzaiin no Shijo-Kyoiku*. Tokyo: Nihon-Keizai Shinbun-sha

Ishida, T. 1971. *Japanese Society*. New York: Random House

Jackson, N.S. 1988a. 'Competence as "Good Management Practice": A Study of Curriculum Reform in the Community College.' Unpublished PhD thesis, University of British Columbia

– 1988b. 'Competence, Curriculum, and Control,' *Journal of Educational Thought*, 22: 247–58

– 1990a. 'Wolves in Charge of the Chicken Coop: Competence as Good Management,' in J. Muller, ed., *Education for Work – Education as Work: Canada's Changing Community Colleges*, pp. 113–24. Toronto: Garamond

– 1990b. 'Working Knowledge: Toward a Critical Pedagogy.' Unpublished address, Oslo

Kazemak, F. 1985. 'Functional Literacy Is Not Enough: Adult Literacy as a Developmental Process,' *Journal of Reading*, 28: 332–5

Keeley, J.F. 1990. 'Toward a Foucauldian Analysis of International Regimes,' *International Organization*, 44: 83–105

Khayatt, M.D. 1990. 'Legalized Invisibility: The Effect of Bill 7 on Lesbian Teachers,' *Women's Studies International Forum*, 13: 185–93

– 1992. *Lesbian Teacher: An Invisible Presence*. New York: SUNY Press

Kiernan, M.J. 1990. 'Urban Planning in Canada: A Synopsis and Some Future Directions,' *Plan Canada*, 30: 11–22

King, R. 1978. *All Things Bright and Beautiful?* New York: Wiley

Kinsman, G. 1987. *The Regulation Of Desire*. Montreal: Black Rose Books

– 1989. 'Official Discourse as Sexual Regulation: The Social Organization of the Sexual Policing of Gay Men.' Unpublished PhD thesis, OISE, University of Toronto

– 1991a. '"Homosexuality" Historically Reconsidered Challenges to Heterosexual Hegemony,' *Journal of Historical Sociology*, 4: 91–111

– 1991b. '"Their Silence, Our Deaths": What Can the Social Sciences Offer to AIDS Research?' in *Talking AIDS: Interdisciplinary Perspectives on AIDS*, pp. 39–60. Institute for Social and Economic Research, Memorial University

– 1992a. '"Restoring Confidence in the Criminal Justice System" – The Hughes Commission and Mass Media Coverage: Making Homosexuality a Problem,' in *Violence and Social Control in the Home, Workplace, Community, and Institutions*. pp. 211–69. St John: ISER, Memorial University

– 1992b. 'Managing AIDS Organizing: "Consultation," "Partnership," and the National AIDS Strategy,' in W.K. Carroll, ed., *Organizing Dissent: Contemporary Social Movements in Theory and Practice*, pp. 215–31. Toronto: Garamond

– 1993a. 'The Hughes Commission, Making Homosexuality the Problem Once Again,' *New Maritimes* (Halifax), 11: 17–19

– 1993b. '"Inverts," "Psychopaths," and "Normal" Men: Historical Sociological Perspectives on Gay and Heterosexual Masculinities,' in T. Haddad, ed., *Men and Masculinities: A Critical Anthology*, pp. 3–35. Toronto: Canadian Scholars Press

– 1995. '"Character Weaknesses" and "Fruit Machines": Towards an Analysis of the Anti-homosexual Security Campaign in the Canadian Civil Service.' *Labour / Le Travail*, 35: 133–61

Kliebard, H.M. 1975. 'The Rise of Scientific Curriculum Making and Its Aftermath,' *Curriculum Theory Network*, 5: 27–38

– 1986. *The Struggle for the American Curriculum*. Boston: Routledge and Kegan Paul

Kolb, D., and J. Van Maanen. 1985. 'Where Policy Studies Go Wrong,' *Administration and Society*, 17: 197–216

Krasner, S.D. 1983. 'Structural Causes and Regime Consequences: Regimes as Intervening Variables,' in S.D. Krasner, ed., *International Regimes*. Ithaca, NY: Cornell University Press

Krawczyk, M. 1989. 'Is MIS Investment the Key to Solid Hospital Management?' *Health Care*, June: 10–11

Kress, G., and R. Hodge. 1979. *Language as Ideology*. London: Routledge and Kegan Paul

Krysiak, G. 1987. 'A Very Silent Gay Minority,' *School Counsellor*, March: 304–7

Kuhn, T.S. 1970. *The Structure of Scientific Revolutions*. Chicago: University of Chicago Press

Kuznet. S., et al., eds. 1955. *Economic Growth: Brazil, India, Japan*. Durham: Duke University Press

Labov, W. 1972. 'The Transformation of Experience in Narrative Syntax,' in *Language in the Inner City*, pp. 354–96. Philadelphia: University of Pennsylvania Press

– 1982. 'Speech Actions and Reactions in Personal Narrative,' in D. Tannen, ed., *Analysing Discourse: Text and Talk*, pp. 219–47. Washington, DC: Georgetown University Press

– and J. Weletzsky. 1969. 'Narrative Analysis: Oral Versions of Personal Experience,' in J. Helm, ed., *Essays on the Verbal and Visual Arts*. Seattle: American Ethnological Society

Lareau, A. 1989. *Home Advantage: Social Class and Parental Intervention in Elementary Education*. Philadelphia: Falmer

Latour, B., and S. Woolgar. 1979. *Laboratory Life: The Social Construction of Scientific Facts*. Beverly Hills: Sage

Lazier, K. 1990. 'School Board Gets Low Grades from Gay Students,' *Now*, 6–12 Sept.: 12

Lee, B. 1981. 'Strangers and Sensemaking: An Ethnography of Japanese Housewives.' Unpublished Master's thesis, University of British Columbia

Lieberman, A., and L. Miller. 1984. *Teachers, Their World, and Their Work: Implications for School Improvement*. Alexandria, Virginia: Association for Supervision and Curriculum Development

Levi-Strauss, C. 1973. '"Primitive" and "Civilized" Peoples: A Conversation with Claude Levi-Strauss,' in R. Disch, ed., *The Future of Literacy*, pp. 15–19. Englewood Cliffs, NJ: Prentice-Hall

Levine, H., and A. Estable. 1981. *The Power Politics of Motherhood: A Feminist Critique of Theory and Practice*. Occasional Paper no. 1. Ottawa: Carlton University, Centre for Social Welfare Studies

Levine, K. 1986. *The Social Context of Literacy*. London: Routledge and Kegan Paul

Levine, R.J. 1986. *Ethics and Regulation of Clinical Research.* Baltimore-Munich: Urban and Schwarzenberg

Lewis, F., and M. Batey. 1982. 'Clarifying Autonomy and Accountability in Nursing Service,' *Journal of Nursing Administration,* 12: 10–15

Lightfoot, S.L. 1978. *Worlds Apart.* New York: Basic Books

Little, D., and D. Carnavali. 1976. *Nursing Care Planning.* 2nd ed. Philadelphia: Lippincott

Lortie, D. 1975. *Schoolteacher.* Chicago: University of Chicago Press

Lowe, D.M. 1982. *History of Bourgeois Perception.* Chicago, University of Chicago Press

Lowe, G.S. 1979. 'The Administration Revolution: The Growth of Clerical Occupations and the Development of the Modern Office in Canada, 1911–1931.' Unpublished PhD thesis, University of Toronto

Lukacs, G. 1978. *Marx's Basic Ontological Principles.* Trans. David Fernbach. London: Merlin Press

Lunsford, A.A., H. Moglen, and J. Slevin, eds. 1990. *The Right to Literacy.* New York: Modern Languages Association of America

Lupul, M.R. 1977. 'Some Implications for Canadian Schools of Multiculturalism as State Policy,' *RIKKA,* 4: 3–9

Luxton, M. 1980. *More than a Labour of Love: Three Generations of Women's Work in the Home.* Toronto: Women's Educational Press

Macaulay, T. 1971. 'Minute "On Education for India",' in P. Curtin, *Imperialism.* New York: Harper and Row

MacDonald-Ross, M. 1975. 'Behavioural Objectives: A Critical Review,' in M. Golby et al., eds., *Curriculum Design,* pp. 355–86. New York: Wiley

MacLeod, F., ed. 1979. *Family Violence: The Report of the Task Force on Family Violence.* Vancouver: United Way of the Lower Mainland

MacLeod, L. 1980a. *Wife Battering Is Everywoman's Issue.* Ottawa: Canadian Advisory Council on the Status of Women

– 1980b. *Wife Battering in Canada.* Quebec: Supply and Services

Magnusson, W. 1990. 'The Political Insignificance of the Municipality,' *City Magazine,* 11: 2

Malyon, A. 1981. 'The Homosexual Adolescent: Developmental Issues and Social Bias,' *Child Welfare,* 60: 321–30

Manicom, A. 1988. 'Constituting Class Relations: The Social Organization of Teachers' Work.' Unpublished PhD thesis, OISE, University of Toronto

Mannheim, K. 1936. *Ideology and Utopia.* New York: Harcourt, Brace, and World

Marx, K. 1975. 'Theses on Feuerbach,' in K. Marx and F. Engels *Selected Works.* Moscow: Progress Publishers

– 1977. *Grundrisse.* Trans. Martin Nicolaus. Harmondsworth: Penguin

– and F. Engels. 1970. *The German Ideology.* New York: International Publishers
– 1973. *The German Ideology,* Ed. C.J. Arthur. New York: International Publishers
– 1976. 'The German Ideology,' in K. Marx and F. Engels, *Collected Works,* vol. 5. New York: International Publishers
Maxwell, J. 1969. 'Royal Commissions and Social Change in Canada: 1867–1966.' Unpublished PhD thesis, Cornell University
Maxwell, J.D., and M.P. Maxwell. 1984. 'Royal Commissions: Organizational Sets and the Governing Process of the State. The Trudeau Years.' Paper presented at the annual meetings of the Canadian Sociology and Anthropology Association
Mbilinyi, M. 1984. 'Research Priorities in Women's Studies on Eastern Africa,' *Women's Studies International Forum,* 7: 289–300
McBeth, S. 1989. 'Creating Curriculum: A Learner-Centred Approach,' in M.C. Taylor and J.A. Draper, eds., *Adult Literacy Perspectives,* pp. 145–52. Toronto: Culture Concepts
McConnell-Celi, S., ed. 1993. *Twenty-First Century Challenge: Lesbians and Gays in Education – Bridging the Gap.* New Jersey: Lavender Crystal Press
McCoy, L. 1987. 'Looking at Wedding Pictures: A Study in the Social Organization of Knowledge.' Unpublished Master's thesis, OISE, University of Toronto
McDermott, J.E., ed. 1976. *Indeterminacy in Education.* Berkeley: McCutchan
McKinlay, J.B. 1984. *Issues in the Political Economy of Health Care.* New York: Tavistock
McPherson, G. 1972. *Small Town Teacher.* Cambridge: Harvard University Press
Mechling, J. 1975–6. 'Advice to Historians on Advice to Mothers,' *Journal of Social History,* 2: 46–63
Medical Research Council of Canada. 1987. *Guidelines on Research Involving Human Subjects, 1987.* Ottawa: Medical Research Council of Canada
Meeting, D., G. Saunders, and R. Curcio. 1988. 'Using DRGs and Standard Costs to Control Nursing Labour Costs,' *Healthcare Financial Management,* Sept.: 62–74
Michaels, S. 1986. 'Narrative Presentations: An Oral Preparation for Literacy with First Graders,' in J. Cook-Gumperz, ed., *The Social Construction of Literacy,* pp. 94–116. Cambridge: Cambridge University Press
Mill, James. 1968 [1817]. *The History of British India,* vols. 1 and 2. Notes H.H. Wilson, Introduction J.K. Galbraith. New York: Chelsea House
Mill, John Stuart. 1972. 'On Liberty,' in H.B. Acton, ed., *Utilitarianism, Liberty, and Considerations on Representative Government.* London: J.M. Dent
Milner, S.H., and H. Milner. 1973. *The De-colonization of Quebec.* Toronto: McClelland and Stewart
Mohanty, C.T. 1991. 'Under Western Eyes: Feminist Scholarship and Colonial Discourses,' in C.T. Mohanty, A. Russo, and L. Torres, eds., *Third World Women and the Politics of Feminism,* pp. 51–80. Bloomington: Indiana University Press

Moodley, K. 1983. 'Canadian Multiculturalism as Ideology,' *Ethnic and Racial Studies*, 6: 320–31

Morley, D., and K. Worpole, eds. 1982. *The Republic of Letters: Working Class Writing and Local Publishing*. London: Comedia

Morrison, K. 1987. 'Stabilizing the Text: The Institutionalization of Knowledge in Historical and Philosophic Forms of Argument.' *Canadian Journal of Sociology*, 12: 242–74

Mueller, A. 1987. 'Peasants and Professionals: The Social Organization of Knowledge about "Third World Women."' Unpublished PhD thesis, OISE, University of Toronto

– 1991. 'In and Against Development: Feminists Confront Development on Its own Ground,' *Working Papers on Women in International Development*, no. 219. East Lansing: Michigan State University

Muller, J., ed. 1990. *Education for Work – Educaton as Work: Canada's Changing Community Colleges*. Toronto: Garamond

Neely, R.L., and G. Robinson-Simpson. 1987. 'The Truth About Domestic Violence: A Falsely Framed Issue,' *Social Work*, Nov./Dec.: 485–90

Newson, J., and H. Buchbinder. 1988. *The University Means Business*. Toronto: Garamond

Ng, R. 1988. *The Politics of Community Services: Immigrant Women, Class, and State*. Toronto: Garamond

– 1993. 'Racism, Sexism, and Nation Building in Canada,' in C. McCarthy and W. Crichlow, eds., *Race, Identity, and Representation in Education*. New York: Routledge

– G. Walker, and J. Muller, eds. 1990. *Community Organization and the Canadian State*. Toronto: Garamond

Nias, J. 1988. 'What it Means to "Feel Like a Teacher": The Subjective Reality of Primary School Teaching,' in J. Ozga, ed., *Schoolwork: Approaches to the Labour Process of Teaching*, pp. 195–213. Milton Keynes: Open University Press

– 1989. *Primary Teachers Talking: A Study of Teaching as Work*. London: Routledge

Niranjana, T. 1990. 'Translation, Colonialism, and the Rise of English,' *Economic and Political Weekly*, 25: 773–9

Ohmann, R. 1976. 'Writing, Out in the World,' in *English in America*, pp. 172–205. New York: Oxford University Press

Ontario, Standing Committee on Social Development: 1982. *First Report on Family Violence: Wife Battering*. Toronto: Queen's Park

Palmer, H., ed. 1975. *Immigration and the Rise of Multiculturalism*. Toronto: Copp Clark

Panem, S. 1988. *The AIDS Bureaucracy*. Cambridge: Harvard University Press

Panitch, L., ed. 1977. *The Canadian State: Political Economy and Political Power*. Toronto: University of Toronto Press

Peirce, C.S. 1965. *Collected Papers of Charles Sanders Peirce*, vols. 1 and 2. C. Hartshorne and P. Weiss, eds. Cambridge, Mass.: Belknap Press of Harvard University

Peter, K. 1981. 'The Myth of Multiculturalism and Other Political Fables,' in J. Dahlie and T. Fernando, eds., *Ethnicity, Power, and Politics in Canada*. Toronto: Methuen

Pfohl, S. 1985. 'Toward a Sociological Deconstruction of Social Problems.' *Social Problems*, 32: 228–37

Phillips, J.L. 1969. *The Origins of Intellect: Piaget's Theory*. San Francisco: W.H. Freeman

Pincus, A., and A. Minahan. 1973. *Social Work Practice: Model and Method*. Itasca, Il.: F.E. Peacock

Pletsch, C.E. 1981. 'The Three Worlds, or the Division of Social Scientific Labor, circa 1950–75,' *Comparative Study of Society and History*, 23: 565–90

Pollner, M. 1974. 'Mundane Reasoning,' *Philosophy of the Social Sciences*, 4: 35–54

Powell, R.E. 1987. 'Homosexual Behaviour and the School Counsellor,' *School Counsellor*, Jan.: 202–8

Prairie Research Associates Inc. 1989. *The Gay and Lesbian Youth Services Network Survey of Gay Youth and Professionals Who Work with Youth*. Winnipeg, Man.: Author

Preston, B., and J. Walker. 1993. 'Competency-Based Standards in the Professions and Higher Education: A Holistic Approach,' in C. Collins, ed., *Competencies: The Competencies Debate in Australian Education and Training*. Canberra: Australian College of Education

Radical Teacher, no. 29, 'Teaching Sexuality'

Radical Teacher, no. 24, 'Gay and Lesbian Studies'

Rathzel, N. 1990. 'Germany: One Race, One Nation?' *Race and Class*, 32: 31–48

Reder, S., and K.R. Green. 1983. 'Contrasting Patterns of Literacy in an Alaskan Fishing Village,' *International Journal of the Sociology of Language*, 42: 9–39

Redish, J.C. 1983. 'The Language of the Bureaucracy,' in R.W. Bailey and R.M. Fosheim, eds., *Literacy for Life*, pp. 151–74. New York: Modern Languages Association

Reimer, M. 1987. 'The Social Organization of the Labour Process: A Case Study of the Documentary Management of Clerical Labour in the Public Sector.' Unpublished PhD thesis, OISE, University of Toronto

– 1991–2. 'Women's Invisible Skills and Gender Segregation in the Clerical-Administrative Sector,' *Optimum: The Journal of Public Sector Management*, 22–4: 29–41

Remick, H., and R. Steinberg. 1984. 'Technical Possibilities and Political Realities,' in H. Remick, ed., *Comparable Worth and Wage Discrimination: Technical Possibilities and Political Realities.* Philadelphia: Temple University Press

Rich, A. 1980. 'Compulsory Heterosexuality and Lesbian Existence,' *Signs, Journal of Women in Culture and Society,* 5: 631–60

Richardson, N.H. 1981. 'Insubstantial Pageant: The Rise and Fall of Provincial Planning in Ontario,' *Canadian Public Administration,* 24: 563–85

Richardson, T.R. 1989. *The Century of the Child: The Mental Hygiene Movement and Social Policy in the United States and Canada.* Albany: SUNY Press

Riley, D. 1983. *War in the Nursery: Theories of the Child and Mother.* London: Virago

Rioux, M. 1971. *Quebec in Question.* Toronto: James Lewis and Samuel

Roberts, L.W., and R.A. Clifton. 1990. 'Multiculturalism in Canada: A Sociological Perspective,' in Peter Li, ed., *Race and Ethnic Relations in Canada,* pp. 120–47. Toronto: Oxford University Press

Rofes, E. 1989. 'Opening Up the Classroom Closet: Responding to the Educational Needs of Gay and Lesbian Youth,' *Harvard Educational Review,* 59: 444–53

Rosen, H. 1972. *Language and Class: A Critical Look at the Theories of Basil Bernstein.* Bristol: Falling Wall Press

– 1986. 'The Importance of Story,' *Language Arts,* 63: 226–37

Rosenholtz, S. 1989. *Teachers' Workplace: The Social Organization of Schools.* New York: Longman

Rostow, W.W. 1985. *The Stages of Growth, A Non-Communist Manifesto.* Cambridge: Cambridge University Press

Roweis, S.T. 1988. 'Knowledge-Power and Professional Practice,' in P. Knox, ed., *The Design Professions and the Built Environment.* London: Croom Helm

Roy, C., and H. Andrews. 1986. *Essentials of the Roy Adaptation Model.* Norwalk: Appleton-Century-Crofts

Rubin, L. 1976. *Worlds of Pain: Life in the Working Class Family.* New York: Basic Books

Ryan, W. 1971. *Blaming the Victim.* New York: Pantheon

Sacks, H. 1974. 'An Analysis of the Course of a Joke's Telling in Conversation,' in R. Bauman and J. Scherzer, eds., *Explorations in the Ethnography of Speaking.* Cambridge: Cambridge University Press

– 1978. 'Some Technical Considerations of a Dirty Joke,' in J. Schenkein, ed., *Studies in the Organization of Conversational Interaction,* pp. 249–69. New York: Academic Press

Said, E. 1978. *Orientalism.* New York: Pantheon

– 1981. *Covering Islam.* New York: Pantheon

Sakamoto, U. 1974. *Kaigai Chuzaiin no Yosei Kanri.* Tokyo: Toyo-Keizai Shinpo-sha

Sakamoto, Y. 1976. *Kaigai Kigyo-keiei to Genchi-jin.* Tokyo: Nihon Keizai Shinbun-sha

Salter, L. 1988. *Mandated Science.* Dordrecht/Boston/London: Kluwer

Sancton, A., and B. Montgomery. 1990. 'The Municipal Government's Role in Promoting, Regulating, and Financing Residential Land Development.' Paper prepared for the Conference on the Changing Canadian Metropolis. York University

Sanders, D. 1968a. 'An Exclusive Interview ...,' *ASK Newsletter* (Vancouver) Feb.: 16

– 1968b. 'Homosexuality and the Law: The Mysterious Case of Everett George Klippert,' *Georgia Straight* (Vancouver), 27 Sept. –3 Oct.: 10–11, 17

Sangari, K., and S. Vaid. 1990. *Recasting Women.* New Brunswick, NJ: Rutgers University Press

Schaub, G. 1985. *Professional Techniques for the Wedding Photographer: A Complete Guide to Lighting, Posing, and Taking Photographs that Sell.* New York: Amphoto

Schutz, A. 1973. *Collected Papers.* vol. 1: *The Problem of Social Reality.* The Hague: Martinus Nijhoff

Scollon, R., and S.B.K. Scollon. 1981. *Narrative, Literacy, and Face in Interethnic Communication.* Norwood, NJ: Ablex

Scribner, S., and M. Cole. 1981. 'Unpackaging Literacy,' in M.F. Whiteman, ed., *Writing*, pp. 71–87. Hillsdale, NJ: Lawrence Erlbaum

Schlossman, S.L. 1981. 'Philanthropy and the Gospel of Child Development,' *History of Education Quarterly*, Fall: 275–99

Sen, G., and C. Grown. 1987. *Development, Crises, and Alternative Visions: Third World Women's Perspectives.* New York: Monthly Review Press

Shapiro, M.J. 1988. *The Politics of Representation: Writing Practices in Biography, Photography, and Policy Analysis.* Madison: University of Wisconsin Press

Sharp, R., and A. Green. 1975. *Education and Social Control: A Study in Progressive Primary Education.* London: Routledge and Kegan Paul

Short, E.C. 1984. *Competence – Inquiries into Its Meaning and Acquisition in Educational Settings.* Lanham, Maryland: University Press of America

Sidel, R. 1986. *Women and Children Last: The Plight of Poor Women in Affluent America.* New York: Penguin

Sinnett, W.E. 1975. *The Application of DACUM in Retraining and Post Secondary Curriculum Development.* Toronto: Humber College of Applied Arts and Technology

Siporin, M. 1975. *Introduction to Social Work Practice.* New York: Macmillan

Smith, D., and C. Richardson. 1994. '18: "Thanks for Nothing!"' *Gay Times* (London), March: 6–8

Smith D.E. 1973. 'Women, the Family, and Corporate Capitalism,' in M. Stephenson, ed., *Women in Canada*, pp. 5–35. Toronto: New Press
- 1974a. 'Women's Perspective as a Radical Critique of Sociology,' *Sociological Inquiry*, 44: 1–13
- 1974b. 'The Ideological Practice of Sociology,' *Catalyst*, 8: 39–54
- 1974c. 'The Social Construction of Documentary Reality,' *Sociological Inquiry*, 44: 257–68
- 1975. 'The Statistics on Mental Illness: What They Will Not Tell Us about Women and Mental Illness,' in D.E. Smith and S.J. David, eds., *Women Look at Psychiatry*. Vancouver: Press Gang
- 1977. *Feminism and Marxism: A Place to Begin, A Way to Go*. Vancouver: New Star Books
- 1979. 'Where There Is Oppression There Is Resistance,' *Branching Out*, 6: 10–15
- 1982. 'Women's Inequality and the Family,' in A. Moscovitch and G. Drover, eds., *Inequality: Essays on the Political Economy of Social Welfare*, pp. 156–95. Toronto: University of Toronto Press
- 1983a. 'No-One Commits Suicide: Textual Analysis of Ideological Practices,' *Human Studies*, 6: 309–359
- 1983b. 'Women, Class, and Family,' in R. Milliband and J. Saville, eds., *Socialist Register, 1983: A Survey of Movements and Ideas*, pp. 1–43. London: Merlin
- 1984. 'Textually Mediated Social Organization,' *International Social Science Journal*, 36: 59–75
- 1986. 'Institutional Ethnography: A Feminist Method,' *Resources for Feminist Research*, 15: 6–13
- 1987a. *The Everyday World as Problematic: A Feminist Sociology*. Toronto: University of Toronto Press
- 1987b. 'An Ethnographic Strategy for the Study of Textually-Mediated Relations of Ruling: The Making of a DACUM.' Nexus Project Occasional Paper no. 1, OISE
- 1988. 'The Work of Mothers: A New Look at the Relations of Family, Class, and School Achievement,' in G. Miller and J.A. Holstein, eds., *Perspectives on Social Problems: A Research Annual*, vol 1. Greenwich, Conn.: JAI Press
- 1989. 'Comment,' Symposium on Sandra Harding's 'The Method Question,' *APA Newsletter on Feminism and Philosophy*, 8: 44–6
- 1990a. *The Conceptual Practices of Power: A Feminist Sociology of Knowledge*. Boston: Northeastern University Press
- 1990b. *Texts, Facts, and Femininity: Exploring the Relations of Ruling*. London and New York: Routledge
- 1992. 'Sociology from Women's Experience: A Reaffirmation,' *Sociological Theory*, 10: 89–98

- 1993. 'The Standard North American Family: SNAF as an Ideological Code,' *Journal of Family Issues*, 14: 50–65
- 1994. 'The Relations of Ruling: A Feminist Inquiry.' Unpublished manuscript, OISE, Department of Sociology in Education, Toronto
- and A.I. Griffith. 1990. 'Coordinating the Uncoordinated: Mothering, Schooling, and Social Class,' in G. Miller and J.A. Holstein, eds., *Perspectives on Social Problems: A Research Annual*, vol. 2, pp. 25–44. Greenwich Conn.: JAI Press

Smith, D.E., and G. Smith. 1990. 'Re-Organizing the Jobs Skills Training Relation: From "Human Capital" to "Human Resources,"' in J. Muller, ed., *Education for Work – Education as Work: Canada's Changing Community Colleges*, pp. 171–96. Toronto: Garamond

Smith, G. 1979. 'Occupational Analysis.' Unpublished paper, Ontario Institute for Studies in Education
- 1983. 'In Defence of Privacy,' *Action!*, 3(1)
- 1988. 'Policing the Gay Community: An Inquiry into Textually-Mediated Relations,' *International Journal of Sociology and the Law*, 16: 163–83
- 1989. 'AIDS Treatment Deficits: An Ethnographic Study of the Management of the AIDS Epidemic, the Ontario Case.' Paper presented at 5th International AIDS Conference, Montreal

Snow, C., and C. Ferguson, eds. 1977. *Talking to Children: Language Input and Acquisition Research*. Cambridge: Cambridge University Press

Sola, M., and A.T. Bennett. 1985. 'The Struggle for Voice: Narrative, Literacy and Consciousness in an East Harlem School,' *Journal of Education*, 167: 88–110

Spilker, B. 1984. *Guide to Clinical Studies and Developing Protocols*. New York: Raven

Starr, P. 1982. *The Social Transformation of American Medicine*. New York: Basic Books

Stackhouse, J. 1991. 'Let's Make a Deal,' *Globe and Mail Report on Business*, April: 50–4

Steinberg, R., and L. Haigner. 1987. 'Equitable Compensation: Methodological Criteria for Comparable Worth,' in C. Bose and G. Spitz, eds., *Ingredients for Women's Employment Policy*, pp. 157–82. Albany: SUNY Press

Stone, C., and H.T. Sanders, eds. 1987. *The Politics of Urban Development*. Lawrence: University Press of Kansas

Strange, S. 1983. 'Cave! hic dragones: A Critique of Regime Analysis,' in S.D. Krasner, ed., *International Regimes*, Ithaca, NY: Cornell University Press

Straus, M.A., R. Gelles, and S.K. Steinmetz. 1974. *Behind Closed Doors: Violence in the American Family*. New York: Dodd, Mead

Street, B. 1984. *Literacy in Theory and Practice*. Cambridge: Cambridge University Press

Strong-Boag, V. 1982. 'Intruders in the Nursery: Child Care Professionals Reshape the Years One to Five, 1920–1940,' in J. Parr, ed., *Childhood and Family in Canadian History.* Toronto: McClelland and Stewart

Suchman, L. 1987. *Plans and Situated Actions.* New York: Cambridge University Press

Tagg, J. 1988. *The Burden of Representation: Essays on Photographies and Histories.* Amherst: University of Massachusetts Press

Therborn, G. 1978. *What Does the Ruling Class Do When It Rules?* London: New Left Books

Toffler, A. 1971. *Future Shock.* New York: Bantam

Travers, R.M., ed. 1973. *Second Handbook of Research on Teaching.* Chicago: American Educational Research Association, Rand McNally

Troper, H. 1979. 'An Uncertain Past: Reflections on the History of Multiculturalism,' *TESL Talk*, 103: 7–15

Turner, S.M. 1989. 'Sustainable Development and the Main Business of Land Use Planning,' in *The Guelph Seminars on Sustainable Development.* Guelph: University of Guelph School of Rural Planning and Development

United States Department of Health and Human Services. 1986. *National Institute of Mental Health: Task Force on Youth Suicide.* Oakland, Calif.: National Conference on Prevention and Interventions in Youth Suicide, 11–13 June

Ueda, Y. 1986. 'Japanese Corporate Wives in Canada: Serving the Corporate Order.' Unpublished PhD thesis, OISE, University of Toronto

– 1991. 'Skills Training Strategy and the Development of High Technology Industry in Japan.' Paper presented at the 4th Annual Conference of the Japan Studies Association of Canada, University of Manitoba

United Nations. 1985. *Selected Statistics and Indicators on the Status of Women, 1985.* New York: United Nations

Vogel, E.F. 1963. *Japan's New Middle Class: The Salary Man and His Family in a Tokyo Suburb.* Berkeley: University of California Press

Volosinov, V.I. 1983. *Marxism and the Philosophy of Language.* Trans. L. Matejka and I.R. Titunik. Cambridge: Harvard University Press

Walker, G.A. 1981. 'Doing It the United Way.' Unpublished Manuscript, Toronto, Ontario Institute for Studies in Education

– 1990a. *Family Violence and the Women's Movement: The Conceptual Politics of Struggle.* Toronto: University of Toronto Press

– 1990b. 'The Conceptual Politics of Struggle: Wife Battering, the Women's Movement, and the State,' *Studies in Political Economy*, 33: 63–90

Walker, S., and L. Barton, eds. 1987. *Changing Policies, Changing Teachers.* Milton Keynes: Open University Press

– 1989. *Politics and the Processes of Schooling.* Milton Keynes: Open University Press

Walkerdine, V. 1984. 'Developmental Psychology and the Child Centred Pedagogy: The Insertion of Piaget into Early Education,' in J. Henriques, W. Holloway,

C. Urwin, C. Venn, and V. Walkerdine, eds., *Changing the Subject: Psychology, Social Regulation, and Subjectivity*, pp. 153–202. London: Methuen
- 1988. *The Mastery of Reason: Cognitive Development and the Production of Rationality.* New York: Routledge
- 1990. *Schoolgirl Fictions.* London: Verso
Wallach, J., and G. Metcalf. 1980. 'The Hidden Problem of Re-Entry,' *The Bridge*, 43: 17–18
- 1981. 'Raising Children Overseas,' *The Bridge*, 44: 13–14
Warren, H., and the London Gay Teenager Group. 1984. *Talking about School.* London: London Gay Teenager Group
Weber, M. 1978. *Economy and Society*, vol. 2. G. Roth and C. Wittich, eds. Berkeley: University of California Press
Weeks, J. 1985. *Sexuality and Its Discontents.* London: Routledge and Kegan Paul
Weinstein, G. 1984. 'Literacy and Second Language Acquisition: Issues and Perspectives,' *TESOL Quarterly*, 183: 471–84
Weis, L., and M. Fine, eds. 1993. *Beyond Silenced Voices: Class Race, and Gender in United States Schools.* Albany: SUNY Press
Weiss, N.P. 1978. 'The Mother-Child Dyad Revisited: Perceptions of Mothers and Children in Twentieth-Century Child-Rearing Manuals,' *Journal of Social Issues*, 34: 29–45
Wheeler, S. 1976. 'Problems and Issues in Record Keeping,' in S. Wheeler, ed., *On Record: Files and Dossiers in American Life.* New Brunswick, NJ: Transaction Books
White, J.B. 1983. 'The Invisible Discourse of the Law: Reflections on Legal Literacy and General Education,' in R.W. Bailey and R.M. Fosheim, eds., *Literacy for Life.* New York: Modern Languages Association
White, M.I. 1979. 'The Rites of Return: Re-Entry and Re-Integration of Japanese International Businessmen.' Unpublished paper presented at the 31st Annual Meeting of the Association for Asian Studies
Williams, R. 1983. *Keywords.* London: Flamingo/Fontana
Wilson, E. 1977. *Women and the Welfare State.* London: Tavistock
Wise, A.E. 1979. *Legislated Learning: The Bureaucratization of the American Classroom.* Berkeley: University of California Press
Wittgenstein, L. 1958. *Philosophical Investigations.* New York: Macmillan
Wolfenden Committee. 1957. *Report of the Committee on Homosexual Offences and Prostitution.* London: Her Majesty's Stationary Office
Wood, G. 1985a. 'The Politics of Development Policy Labelling. *Development and Change*, 16: 347–73
- 1985b. 'Targets Strike Back,' *Development and Change*, 16: 451–73
Zimmerman, D. 1974. 'Facts as Practical Accomplishment,' in R. Turner, ed., *Ethnomethodology*, pp. 128–43. Harmondsworth: Penguin

Index

abstraction, ix, 25, 56, 89, 257

academia, 3, 9, 66, 67, 68

access, to the field, 26–9, 68; text as a means of, 76

accomplishment, 36, 39, 45, 57, 85, 104, 120, 122, 144, 173, 183, 185, 191, 192, 201, 206, 225, 226, 227, 246

account, ix, 20, 68, 70, 98, 100, 101, 169, 222, 228, 231, 236, 257; authorized, 237; ideological 31; organizational, 57, 206, 255; professional, 209, 214, 217; speculative, 22; textual, 217, 223

accountability, 177, 194–8, 221, 224–6, 233; administrative, 165; public, 200–3

activation, 36, 82, 100, 184, 186, 188, 246

activism, ix, 3, 6, 12, 18, 22, 26, 160; femist, 66, 70, 74; gay or lesbian, 80, 86, 87, 90, 92, 93

actuality, 100, 169

administrative practices, 7, 36, 43, 46, 101, 146, 157, 158, 159, 165, 195, 199

agent or agency, 53, 56, 84, 174, 252, 256

analysis, 25, 28, 31, 32, 43, 110, 135, 149, 165, 168, 188, 191, 195; critical, 71, 82, 213; textual, 35, 36, 47, 57, 82, 236

bias, 70

bifurcated consciousness, 4

binary (relations), 50, 63, 150

bracketing, 25, 31, 146

bureaucratic practices and relations, 42, 43, 44, 46, 47, 101, 104, 106, 201

capitalist society, 9, 46, 48, 99, 103, 123, 179

causal relations, 66, 102, 142, 223, 229, 230

class, 77, 114, 115, 116, 120, 129, 214, 220, 258; assumptions, 118, 210; difference, 120; and gender, 133, 143; middle, 118, 120, 123, 126, 130, 131, 134, 136, 215, 258; practices 116, 140, 144, 145; relations, 33, 37, 103, 136, 138, 139, 142; working, 119, 120, 261

colonial, empire; 53; rule, 51, 52, 53, 54, 59, 62; text, 52

colonialism, 51, 61, 98

common sense, 36, 46, 47, 188, 211

community, 86; based, 18, 28, 65

competence, 164, 177, 243, 245